The First Male Stars
Men of the Silent Era

by David W. Menefee

THE FIRST MALE STARS: MEN OF THE SILENT ERA
© 2007 DAVID W. MENEFEE

All rights reserved.

No part of this book may be reproduced in any form or by any means, electronic, mechanical, digital, photocopying or recording, except for the inclusion in a review, without permission in writing from the the publisher.

PUBLISHED IN THE USA BY:
**BearManor Media
PO Box 71426
Albany, GA 31708**
www.BearManorMedia.com

LIBRARY OF CONGRESS CATALOGING-IN-PUBLICATION DATA:

Menefee, David W., 1954-
  The first male stars : men of the silent era / by David W. Menefee.
      p. cm.
  Includes bibliographical references and index.
  ISBN 978-1-59393-073-8
  1. Motion picture actors and actresses--United States--Biography. 2. Male actors--United States--Biography. 3. Silent films--United States--History and criticism. I. Title.

PN1998.2.M455 2007
791.4302'8092--dc22
[B]
                                        2007023094

Printed in the United States.

Cover Art by David W. Menefee.

Design and Layout by Valerie Thompson.

Table of Contents

ACKNOWLEDGMENTS		1
FOREWORD		2
PREFACE		6
CHAPTER 1	JOHN BARRYMORE	8
CHAPTER 2	LIONEL BARRYMORE	27
CHAPTER 3	RICHARD BARTHELMESS	50
CHAPTER 4	JOHN BUNNY	73
CHAPTER 5	FRANCIS X. BUSHMAN	91
CHAPTER 6	LON CHANEY	118
CHAPTER 7	JACKIE COOGAN	140
CHAPTER 8	WILLIAM S. HART	152
CHAPTER 9	TOM MIX	174
CHAPTER 10	ANTONIO MORENO	197
CHAPTER 11	JACK PICKFORD	215
CHAPTER 12	WALLACE REID	242
CHAPTER 13	RUDOLPH VALENTINO	269
CHAPTER 14	CRANE WILBUR	296
BIBLIOGRAPHY		311
INDEX		323

My Silent Lover

*I've never heard his low voice murmur love
Or felt his kisses, but our souls unite
Beyond all fleeting sense of time or space,
And float, ethereal, in the starless night.
But, ah! His eyes have spoken when our
Tongues stood dumb with waves of reticence between;
And mine have answered, burning with desire.
My silent lover loves me from the screen!*

Anna Hamilton Wood
(Motion Picture Magazine, *February 1921*)

Acknowledgments

To my mother and father, Eunice and Doyle Menefee, who encouraged me to write this book. And to my faith in Jesus Christ, with whom all things are possible. I want to thank Larry Rayl for his advice and direction. I am grateful to Kate Stanworth at the British Film Institute for her help researching many rare photos and articles. Kristine Krueger, from the Margaret Herrick Library at The Academy of Motion Picture Arts and Sciences Center for Motion Picture Study and National Film Information Service, boosted this manuscript with rare articles researched from their vast files. I am in debt to Randy Jones, who enabled me to create all the digital files of the manuscript and photos. Ronald Raburn was a great help with the photo restorations. Special thanks go to the staff of the Dallas Public Library for their help in researching biographical information. I also thank Kevin Brownlow for painstakingly offering insights from his renowned knowledge of film history. Without his guidance, this book would not have been possible.

Foreword

From the earliest silent films to the blockbusters of today, motion pictures have been the world's foremost entertainment. From the very beginning, film was a medium where personality, technology, dance, theater, and imagination merged to produce unforgettable images. The first male stars gave audiences a larger-than-life depiction of men as heroes, clowns, and lovers.

Fred Ott was the first man to appear before Thomas Edison's motion picture camera. He was an assistant in the Edison laboratories, and he was recruited to record for posterity his well-known sneeze. This short film was shown under the title, *Fred Ott's Sneeze*, in Edison's kinetoscope machines. People peered into a slot, and were delightfully startled at the photographs, which seemed to move in a lifelike manner.

The Edison Company produced a number of films to keep these machines supplied with subjects. A few years later, inventors perfected machinery to project these same films onto screens. An audience of people could then view the subjects larger than life.

Short stories began to be filmed, and in 1903, *The Great Train Robbery* caught the imaginations of early viewers. Small theaters sprang up by the thousands around the world. These early theaters were called nickelodeons, and in just a few years, they all but replaced the thousands of local theaters hosting traveling stage productions. Many of these vagabond actors found themselves out of work, and some posed for the fledgling studios grinding out short films to satisfy the nickelodeon theater's demand for frequent changes of subjects.

The first male stars were (left) the anonymous man riding a horse in a motion picture made in 1870 by Eadweard Muybridge, a San Francisco photographer, attempting to prove that all four feet of a speeding horse completely left the ground while in full gallop. Thomas Edison used a mechanic from his staff, Fred Ott (right), to pose in 1888 for his then-experimental motion picture camera.

In a short time, certain actors began to emerge as popular favorites. John Bunny, a rotund comic, delighted audiences with his comedies made for the Vitagraph Studio. Jack Pickford, the brother of Mary Pickford, played in many early films, and became the first boy prominently featured in the movies. As heroes, Wallace Reid, Crane Wilbur, William S. Hart, Tom Mix, and Rudolph Valentino thrilled hearts. Lon Chaney and Lionel Barrymore found unique niches as character actors, while John Barrymore raised the level of film acting to heights previously known only in the theatre.

As films grew longer in length and more elaborate stories were filmed, producers learned to take their cameras closer to the actors' faces. Audiences grew to intimately know their subtle expressions and personalities. Once their names became known, the actors found themselves ranking as stars comparable to those famous for their work in the theatre. Their newfound fame exceeded that of stage actors.

Unfortunately, it is difficult to view silent films today under appropriate conditions. With the invention of home video, film studios have begun to show an appreciable interest in preserving and packaging silent films to audiences today. Many are seriously flawed because surviving prints are often scarred beyond all standards that would have been acceptable at the time of their original release. Often, the prints are duplicates of copies removed several generations from their original negatives. In spite of these flaws, the personalities of the first male stars shine brilliantly.

This book focuses on fourteen of these men, and their lives, and then delves deeply into one or more films in which either the essence of their appeal was captured, or they astonishingly played a role that struck against their stereotyped image. The behind-the-scenes views of their lives give us an intimate look into the dreams that led them to venture into motion picture work. They were a daring group of men pioneering in a new medium of expression.

Most films made during the first twenty years were produced, exhibited, and then forgotten. No one believed there was a potential commercial market after their initial rentals, and because of this lack of foresight, negatives and prints were all too often destroyed. Many films not destroyed ultimately decomposed as time decayed their nitrate base stock into brown dust.

Fortunately, the first male stars represented in this book have benefited from the sheer quantity of titles in which they appeared. Collectively, they acted in more than 5,000 films. Today, their reputations rest only on those pictures that have survived.

Photographs and advertising layouts have enjoyed a better fate than the actual motion pictures. Each photo and illustration in this book has been digitally restored to remove most of the ravages of time, allowing the reader to enjoy clarity similar to their original condition. Many of these illustrations have been unseen for more than eighty-eight years.

The first male stars were a varied and unusual group of men. They range from the mature and comical John Bunny to the classically profiled John Barrymore. Each actor enjoyed a lonely head start, appearing during the first twenty years of American film in an industry where no one had any previous experience. They broke new ground, and often succeeded in spite of the criticism they faced for appearing in a form of show business initially disdained by those in the so-called Alegitimate theater." In the beginning, it was considered a disgrace to appear in a movie.

While these men were strong and masculine in spirit, their work was fragile and perishable. Women loved them with adoration previously unknown to other celebrities. Before the movies, there was no way to take a man's soul and bring him close up to the face and heart of a woman sitting silently in the dark of a theater. The shadow images of the first male stars inflamed the affections of millions of women around the world.

This volume chronicles some of the men who caught the imagination of a generation with their faces, heroics, and sense of humor. Selecting who to profile was largely a matter of personal choice. There are many other men who deserve to be included. This author's hope is that older readers will enjoy an analysis of one or more of their favorites, and, hopefully, that younger readers will discover for the first time someone who touches their soul in the same way as those first flickering shadows touched the hearts of people so many years ago when they were thrown on hastily hung sheets in the dark, or upon bare, white walls in makeshift storefronts.

Preface

The First Male Stars is the result of several years of research in important archives around the world. In America, The Library of Congress brought information and images from their photo print archives that have been unseen for decades. The Margaret Herrick Library of the Academy of Motion Picture Arts and Sciences shared rare information from their files, illuminating the personal lives and struggles of the first male stars.

In his autobiography, director Cecil B. DeMille often referred to articles published in trade and film magazines to refresh his memory of the events and details of his incredible career. The personal quotes attributed to him, other directors, and stars have barely survived two world wars and the passing of time. Research into copies of *Moving Picture World, Photoplay, Motion Picture Stories,* and other magazines from the years of 1900–1930 provided unique interviews with the first male stars. Not all of these interviews were written from a publicist's imagination. Many were simply reprints of the comments made by the first male stars to a reporter. These insights, lifted from yellowed and often crumbling pages of surviving copies, brought fresh, first-hand accounts of the struggles these men faced as they explored the limits of an untried art. Today, these revealing interviews provide a glimpse into the thoughts and motivations driving these men to pose for the motion picture camera.

Each chapter examines the actor's life and work, and then leads the reader to a revealing look at one signature role that captured the essence of their appeal. This career highlight is closely viewed through the eyes of contemporary reviewers, photos, story synopses, and advertisement copy, providing a close encounter with their work as it was received in their time. When given the choice between one film that has already been dissected to the point where there is nothing new to be gleaned from the effort, and another film that is of equal merit and has not been fully studied, I have chosen the latter. An example would be with John Barrymore and the choice between his most famous film, *Dr. Jekyll and Mr. Hyde*, and a later work, *The Sea Beast*, which gave him an equally stunning opportunity for a transformation from a matinee idol to a grotesque figure of a man. The profile then follows the remainder of each actor's life and career from an overall perspective.

Lionel Barrymore voiced the prevailing attitude of the first male stars when he whispered to Lillian Gish about the vision director D. W. Griffith held for the motion picture. "He really believes we're pioneering in a new art," he said, "a medium that can cross over barriers of language and culture. That's why he drives himself so hard. And you know, Lillian," he added, "I'm beginning to believe he's right."

Chapter 1
John Barrymore

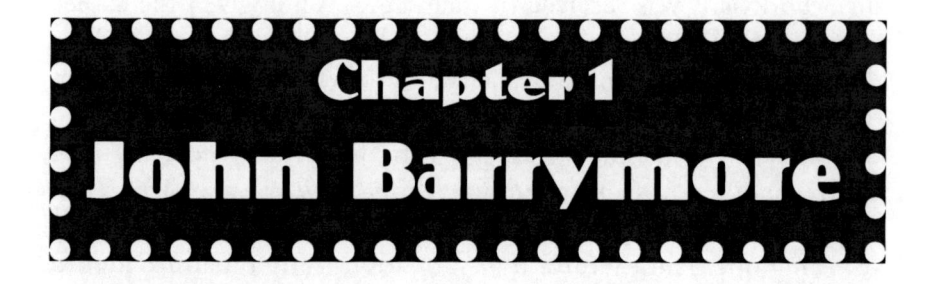

"I don't think he was ever satisfied," remarked Ethel Barrymore about her brother, John, in her autobiography. "I don't think yachts and swimming pools make up for other things."

John's older brother, Lionel, believed his brother was like their father, Maurice. He remembered in his autobiography, "They seem to have possessed precisely the same talent, the same imbalance, the same oddly slanted curiosity, the same ennui with achievement once achieved, the same integrity, and the same capacity for hurting themselves."

John Barrymore was considered by many to be the finest actor of the silent screen, and he was one of the first prominent stage stars to venture into full-length films. He inherited the handsome looks of his father, Maurice Barrymore, and was blessed with a chiseled profile the camera adored. Women loved watching him. He was one of only a few American actors to portray William Shakespeare's *Hamlet* with renown, but in his initial foray into motion pictures, he appeared to nickelodeon audiences as a comedian.

Barrymore brought to motion pictures a jaunty cock of the head, an extremely expressive eyebrow he could raise quizzically, and he knew every possible use of his hands for gracefully expressing thoughts in pantomime. These tools, when coupled with his classic profile, made him an outstanding figure on which early cameras could focus. The camera also revealed the dynamic, haunted force of his personality lying beneath the surface.

John Barrymore was born on February 14, 1882, in Philadelphia, Pennsylvania, the son of the handsome actor, Maurice Barrymore,

A youthful portrait of John Barrymore, ca. 1918, at the beginning of his film career.

and the equally attractive actress, Georgianna Drew. His grandmother, Mrs. John Drew, had established the Arch Street Theater, an extremely respected stock company in Philadelphia. While his parents were out on the road on stage tours, the responsibility fell to his grandmother to provide a strict but loving home.

When he was old enough to go to kindergarten, he and his brother were sent to a little boy's school on Twentieth Street next to a convent. He was a day scholar, and went home to his grandmother in the afternoon. Some years later, he and his brother were sent to Seton Hall, a New Jersey Jesuit school. Summers were spent in various places where his parents rendezvoused between theatrical engagements.

"I went in for theft as a kid," he recalled in an interview with Harry T. Brundidge. "I appropriated my grandmother's jewels and hid them. While detectives were in the house questioning all of us, I looked rather too innocent and, my grandmother, who watched the expression on my face and drew her own conclusions, got rid of the detectives and then used a well-worn slipper on me. Once, before that incident, I had taken money from the other members of the family in small amounts and had hoarded the stolen coins until I had enough to buy a rosary for a symmetrical lady in Philadelphia, many years my senior, with whom I fancied myself in love."

John also recalled being constantly in trouble with school officials at the Notre Dame School in Philadelphia. That institution of learning kicked him out, and he was hastily placed with a Jesuit school in Georgetown that was known for being firm but fair.

"I've never told this story, but on the day of my arrival there, I was then twelve years old, and a priest took me through the school buildings. I paused in the gymnasium to swing on the parallel bars and, as I turned over, there fell from my pockets a razor, a dime novel, and a half pint of whiskey. That mishap gave the priest more information than I could have supplied in eighty confessions. They were very kind to me at Georgetown, and although they eventually expelled me, they did it in a nice way."

He was destined to follow the footsteps of his famous theatrical parents, and when the need for money forced him to go on the stage, he joined McKee Rankin in the role of young Max, the heroine's brother, in a production of *Magda*. He wore a uniform with two rows of brass buttons down the front. It had been made for another actor, one of generous proportions, and since John had failed to try on the outfit prior to the opening night's performance, there was no time to have the wardrobe captain adjust it. The harried outfitter hastily stuffed the outfit with filling, and John was sent on stage in the first act wearing the clumsy costume. As he moved about the stage, the filling began to shift down, and by the end of the act, he sported what appeared to be a potbelly reminiscent of a New York policeman. He sweated, was mortified, and exited the stage thinking he had made theatrical history.

John waited up all night in a warm saloon for the reviews he expected to appear in the morning newspaper. There was only one notice. John remembered in *Confessions of an Actor* the moment he read the review by a critic named Amy Leslie: "The part of Max was essayed by a young actor who calls himself Mr. John Barrymore. He walked on the stage as if he had been all dressed up and forgotten." John later recalled, "The ordinary youngster who goes into the theater is stage-struck, and he has his ambition and illusion to carry him along and brace him up. I didn't even have the desire to succeed as a prop; I didn't want to be an actor. I was there merely because it was supposed that any member of a theater family ought to have something in him that would carry him through a crisis on the stage."

It made little matter because a Denver creditor to whom McKee Rankin owed money had little affection for the tradition of the theater. He rudely attached the scenery and properties in a dispute over an unpaid bill. The box office receipts were so meager that there was no money to redeem the props, and the play quickly closed. John was out of work for the first of many times in his life.

A later attempt for redemption came in the play, *Leah, the Forsaken*. On opening night, John looked through a hole in the curtain, saw several auspicious members of his sister's entourage sitting like a jury in the front row, and panicked.

He frantically applied a thick mask of makeup and a wig so no one would recognize him, and then the moment came for him to enter and say his one line. As the leader of a mob, he was supposed to bellow, "Throw her in the river!" No sooner had he blurted out the one line than a howl of laughter rang out from the front rows. When the scene ended, he removed the makeup, dashed to the nearest Western Union office, and wired a single sentence to his sister, Ethel: "For Christ's sake, send me fifty dollars."

The stern telegraph operator thought the message was profane, and politely refused the telegram. John thought quickly, and then told the doubting clerk the message was not profanity at all. He explained that the manager of the theatrical company was none other than a man named George W. Christ, and it was on his behalf the message was to be sent. The clerk, skeptical but satisfied, relayed the telegram, and his loving sister responded by wiring John the fifty dollars. He fled Chicago and the theater business, hoping never to return.

Once these funds were exhausted, financial necessity forced him to take part in other plays. In time, he became proficient enough to adequately perform roles, but he loved neither the work nor the repeated performances required of a professional actor.

"I am no trouper," John later revealed candidly. "To have that quality that makes for a good trouper is, as I say, of great value, but there are many valuable qualities that bring no particular pleasure to the possessor."

John was an artist, and he loved expressing the grotesque with his sketches. He enrolled at the Art Student's League, intending to pursue his ambition to be a professional artist. His sister, again, rallied to his needs and arranged for him to earn a commission to compose a poster for E. H. Southern's production of the play, *If I Were King*. Daniel Frohman paid him five dollars for the rendition, and it was used for many years to publicize the play.

For John, an artist's life was bleak. He managed to sell a few other sketches of a gruesome nature, and in time, hired himself to the *New York Morning Telegraph* as a staff artist in the advertising department. The *New York Evening Journal* then hired him as an editorial cartoonist, and when an assignment came to illustrate the shooting of Paul Leicester Ford, the novelist who had written *Janice Meredith*, John dashed off a quick sketch. To his chagrin, the cameraman botched the transfer of his original sketch into a halftone image for print, and when the spoiled image published, John was fired. Once again, he reluctantly turned to the theater for a living. It was a disastrous situation for the disappointed artist, an omen of even more calamitous catastrophes to follow.

He left New York for San Francisco in April 1906. One night, after viewing *Carmen* at the Grand Opera House, he had supper and returned home around three o'clock in the morning. Somewhat drunk, he fell into bed, and had only been under the covers at the St. Francis Hotel a few minutes when the first great shock of the infamous earthquake shook the town. The force hurled John from bed and startled him awake. He threw on his evening clothes, the only attire he had, and crawled out into the hall. Bewildered people were wandering through the jumbled hotel halls as John emerged into the fire-choked light of day.

"Everywhere whole sides of houses were gone," John recalled with awe, in *Confessions of an Actor*. "The effect was as if someone had lined the streets with gigantic dolls' houses of the sort that have no fronts. People were hurriedly dressing and, at the same time, trying to gather and throw out what seemed most valuable to them. More prudent people, who could not too readily shake off shyness nor too quickly forget their decorum, were putting up sheets to shield themselves from passers-by."

Wandering dazedly, he passed a friend, Willie Collier, one of the thousands of shocked and surprised victims sitting outside a hotel wearing bedroom slippers and a flowered dressing gown. The square, into which oddly dressed people were thrown with their remaining belongings, presented an uncanny spectacle. He walked up Post Street and found the Bohemian Club open for business as usual. John fortified himself with a glass of brandy, and continued to walk through the strange surroundings in his evening attire. All about him ran people in a chaotic state of undress.

"I find that no one believes anyone else's stories of what he saw during those few days," John recalled. "People have often doubted mine, particularly that I went to help a friend bury a trunk containing some of his choicest possessions in an empty lot, and that afterward, neither he nor I could remember where these things were buried!"

In the melee of confusion, John stumbled upon "Diamond Jim" Brady, who was highly amused to see the actor wandering about in evening dress. After the debacle when the millionaire went back east, he and others circulated ribald stories about John dressing for the earthquake. In later life, John felt certain these stories were the cause of his lifelong reputation for eccentricity. He did little to dispel this reputation, and often added to it with eccentricities even more bizarre.

A second earthquake violently shook what remained of San Francisco, and flames rapidly burned across the entire city. Local authorities began dynamiting to halt the spread of the flames, turning the entire scene into a surreal horror reminiscent of a battlefield during a wartime bombardment.

The United States Army descended on the scene, commandeering all available men to move fallen bricks and help in the salvage operations. John was recruited, and put to work moving debris while he still wore his evening dress. The entire city was in the tight grasp of the militia, and he searched for a way to escape the ravaged city while he worked.

As the city burned, John managed to meet up with members of an acting troupe bound for Australia, a band of actors also landlocked by the calamity. He secured a role with the troupe, and caught passage on the boat that was about to leave and escape the flames engulfing San Francisco. Minutes before they were to depart, he paused long enough to dash off a note to his sister, and then promptly left the continent for the Australia tour. As the boat sailed from the harbor, he watched the smoldering rubble of the wasted city slowly recede into the distance.

Ethel received the letter in New York, and read it to their uncle, John Drew. He considered the contents, and then the wise, older thespian looked strangely quiet.

"What's the matter, Uncle Jack? Don't you believe it?" asked Ethel.

"I believe every word of it," he answered grimly. "It took a convulsion of Nature to make him get up and the United States Army to make him go to work!"

For the next seven years, John applied himself diligently to learning the craft of acting, and for a time, appeared to take the art seriously. He distinguished himself in the plays, *Justice*, *Peter Ibbetson*, and *The Jest*.

With characteristic enthusiasm, he signed to make comedies for Adolph Zukor's Famous Players Film Company in 1914. He had no grandiose ideas about his prowess as an actor, and had no qualms about throwing himself into the slapstick escapades plotted for him in these first films. Comedic opportunities abounded, and John exhibited a comic flair that greatly amused both critics and audiences.

At that time, films were emerging from their primitive beginnings, and one-reel films were becoming a thing of the past. *Queen Elizabeth*, a 1912 French film, starring Sarah Bernhardt, led the way for producers to make longer motion pictures. In addition, Sarah's work in this film suddenly added prestige to the lowly movies, and many stars from the legitimate stage succumbed to the lure of quick money to be gleaned from motion picture work. Always in need of a fresh infusion of cash, John was one of the first stage actors to plunge into the fledgling industry.

"Barrymore did not really want to be an actor," Zukor indicated in *The Public Is Never Wrong*. "His idea of the good life was to paint in his Greenwich Village studio. In the nighttime and the remainder of the days, he liked to romance and to roister."

While in his early thirties, Barrymore was one of the handsomest men in the world of theater, and every producer wanted him. John was unheeding of their desire to keep him out of motion pictures. His brother, Lionel, had spent several years working with D. W. Griffith, and had told him about many interesting aspects of the new industry. John began to listen to offers, and seriously considered the new business of film work.

Zukor approached John in his dressing room, and said, "Jack, I have a screen play for you."

The actor listened in moody silence to Zukor's verbal outline of the story, but the producer left without an answer. Zukor later sent a friend to inquire about John's decision. The actor accepted the offer, and in making his first pictures, *An American Citizen* and *The Man from Mexico*, the star, long reputed for eccentricities and bizarre behavior, was all business. Once on the set, he gave his best and demanded the same from others with whom he worked.

His first comedies were a much-needed success for Famous Players. These films drew heavily on John's preference for athleticism, movement, and comedy. *Are You a Mason, The Dictator,* and *The Incorrigible Dukane* followed closely the congenial appeal of the handsome young star. In films, he found an enormous new audience.

"What I minded about my brothers coming to Hollywood was that I felt it was such a loss for the public," Ethel Barrymore remembered in her autobiography, *Memories*. "Jack and Lionel had both been superb in the theater."

This full-page composite, showing John Barrymore in the motion picture *On the Quiet* appeared in *Motion Picture News* on July 13, 1918.

John later mused, "In the beginning, a great many persons of the theater and out of it looked upon the movies as an inferior art. It isn't. Pictures often go wrong just as stage plays do."

The First World War was already looming on the distant shores of Europe, and money was scarce. Zukor had to practice extreme diplomacy to keep his film factory moving and productions on schedule with the undisciplined actors gravitating from the New York stage into his fledgling film business. John had long become accustomed to late nights and slow days, which often collided with the fast pace schedules of early film work. He was accustomed to working until late at night, unwinding until the early morning hours, and then sleeping until the middle of the following day. It was difficult for him to adjust to the early morning madness required for film work. John was never in a hurry to rise, and when he did he was more likely to forget all responsibilities and settle into a chair to paint. Zukor often had to send emissaries to bring the actor to the set.

Barrymore's inherent laziness brought unintended comic results. Zukor recalled a good deal of trouble between Dick Murphy, a painter who had begun work in films at the same time D. W. Griffith had arrived at the Edison studios, and who was then working on the Zukor film in which John starred. It was called *The Lost Bridegroom*, and John insisted on doing things his way. One scene called for the actor to jump through a stained-glass window. John was determined to personally jump through a *real* stained-glass window, as called for in the story. The realism of the moment was important to him. Dick Murphy had obtained a beautiful, stained-glass window from a church that was being torn down. The script called for the Barrymore character to jump through the stained-glass window to escape an approaching, cuckolded husband. After photographing the real window for establishing shots, a replica was substituted for the leap. Barrymore saw the switch, and refused to go on with the action. He insisted on jumping through the *real* stained-glass window. Zukor strongly objected.

"My desk was almost demolished by his pounding on it," Zukor remembered years later. The producer argued that Barrymore would be hurt, but the actor did not care. When Zukor refused to relent, Barrymore quit the production in protest.

A short while later while Zukor was in his office, he was startled to hear a sudden crash of glass. He leapt from his desk, and came running out to discover the cameras had been running while Barrymore, in complete defiance of Zukor's order, completed his leap through the actual glass window. Shattered glass littered the set, and the actor was in the middle of picking himself up and brushing debris from his body when Zukor noticed a happy expression beaming from his face. He had not a scratch on him. Zukor lost the stained-glass window, but kept his production on schedule, and the star, satisfied and smug, went on with the production.

In 1918, John was obsessed with appearing in a dramatic play, *Redemption*. During this two-year period, the only film he made was *Raffles, the Amateur Cracksman*, an adaptation of a story about a gentleman thief. An anonymous reviewer from the *New York Times* wrote of *Raffles*: "John Barrymore made his screen bow as *Raffles, the Amateur Cracksman*, at the Strand Theatre yesterday afternoon, and the audience seemed to like him in the part as much as both the victims and beneficiaries of the Raffles in the play liked that fascinating individual. Mr. Barrymore was at his motion-picture best in the play, which followed the well-known story with reasonable faithfulness."

Zukor secured another commitment from John for several more films, all the while merging his Famous Players into the newly named Paramount Pictures. *Here Comes the Bride* was quickly followed by another motion picture comedy, *On the Quiet*.

In 1918, the *New York Times* noted John's particular effect on audiences with his superb pantomime in *On the Quiet*: "John Barrymore in *On the Quiet* is back in his amusing manner of farce, and one just sits and enjoys him. His play is nothing—a series of nonsensicalities that give him opportunities for his face and feet and hands, but he misses none of the opportunities, and the spectators laugh, as they are intended to."

While John was making comedies for Paramount, he was also busy in the theater. His later films allowed him to switch from comedy to a more serious vein. *The Test of Honor*, similar in theme and appearance to the play *Justice*, gave full vent to the power of his dramatic abilities. For a time, he appeared to be an actor of double talent. Where he had been previously known on the stage only for his unusual ability with comedy, he now achieved distinction in tragic roles. His serious work was recognized as infinitely greater, but he was remembered with such delight for comedies that some reviewers in 1919 wished it were possible to have both Barrymore types on the stage simultaneously.

An article in a 1919 issue of the *New York Times* explained: "There are two Barrymores growing where but one grew before. The word growing is not misapplied, for John Barrymore seems an even better comedian on the screen than he did on the stage. In addition to being an actor who can speak his lines, he has a remarkable talent for pantomime, which finds full opportunity within the limits of photoplay technique, and he becomes more exact and expressive in each succeeding vehicle."

His work reached a zenith in 1920. While he was performing *Richard III* on Broadway every evening, he was busy during the day filming his best-remembered silent picture, *Dr. Jekyll and Mr. Hyde,* and simultaneously studying for his forthcoming play, *Hamlet.*

John Barrymore on Broadway in *Hamlet*, 1923

For weeks, he repeatedly read the Shakespearean play before making up his mind to do it. Then, he went into the woods near White Sulphur Springs and rehearsed himself in parts of it, playing alone to nothing but the wind and the trees. He prepared his interpretation of *Hamlet* for ten months with Margaret Carrington, the sister of Walter Huston, and one of the finest voice teachers in

New York. His finished performance astounded theatergoers in New York and later in London. The role was his greatest stage success. He gave 101 performances, breaking the previous record set by Edwin Booth, and then, as suddenly as he had decided to take on the challenging role, he ended the New York run.

In her autobiography, Ethel Barrymore remembered his *Hamlet*: "Of course, I saw him in it many times, but the most thrilling performances of all was a dress rehearsal just before opening night. Jack didn't dress for it. He was just in his ordinary street clothes, and I suppose it was the greatest experience I ever had in a theater. He was superb, magnificent, unforgettable, and had in some mysterious way acquired that magical ease, as if he really were Hamlet. It was for me the fulfillment of all I had ever hoped for him and more."

After the *Hamlet* triumph, John seemed to lose interest in the theater. He had done his best work, and having proved his prowess as a serious stage actor, he relaxed into a life of filmmaking that occupied him for the next twenty years. The comparative ease suited him.

Warner Bros. needed the prestige his appearances would bring to their growing film studio, and the Barrymore luster was more than welcomed, it was required. Jack Warner lured the celebrated actor to the west coast with a six-figure amount, the most money he had ever earned.

"An actor is in hard luck because everything he does should be better than the thing he did before," Warner explained before departing for Hollywood. "There is no resting and no going back. I can't get hold of what I want for New York, and I'm not satisfied with giving a second-rate performance." John arrived in Hollywood with his valet and his monkey, Clementine, in tow.

His work for Warner Bros. exploited him as a great lover, but he sought every opportunity to distort his classic profile in parts calling for ugliness. A splendid opportunity came with the role of the tortured Captain Ahab in *The Sea Beast* (1926), a film of Herman Melville's novel, *Moby Dick*. This film, more than any other, captured all the elements of John Barrymore: the intense actor, the man inclined to morbid images, and the passionate lover.

John Barrymore as Captain Ahab in *The Sea Beast* (1926), the motion picture version of Herman Melville's *Moby Dick*.

"The book appeals to me and always has," he reflected in his autobiography. "It has an especial appeal now, for in the last few years, both on the stage and on the screen, I have played so many scented, bepuffed, bewigged and ringletted characters—princes and kings, and the like—that I revel in the rough and almost demoniacal character, such as Captain Ahab becomes in the last half of the picture after his leg has been amputated by Moby Dick, the white whale. What we are going to do for a love interest, I don't quite know. He might fall in love with the whale. I am sure, however, Hollywood will find a way."

Hollywood also found that Dolores Costello, the daughter of film pioneer Maurice Costello, and one of the first child actors to appear in some of the earliest films made, had grown up to become a ravishingly beautiful woman. She was cast in the role of a sensitive, young woman who restored Ahab with her love, a passion Ahab interpreted as pity and self-sacrifice.

John fell in love with Dolores, who was not yet twenty. She had made her screen debut at the age of six, playing in the films her father made for the Vitagraph studio. John courted Dolores during the filming of *The Sea Beast*, and on more than one occasion while cameras turned, he continued kissing her long after the director called, "Cut!"

Mordaunt Hall reviewed *The Sea Beast* in the *New York Times*, calling the film version of the classic story "a triumph." He detailed this opinion: "John Barrymore deserves no little credit for the energy, earnestness and virility he displays in the role of Ahab, the unfortunate man who lost his leg through his jealous brother's treachery."

The reviewer went on to point out:

"Mr. Barrymore's real triumph in this photoplay comes in the second half of the picture, for he has a great opportunity as the grim master of a whaler with a mixed crew of half-mad, yellow, white and black scum. In the introductory chapters his face is classical and pale, his forehead is high and his nose as straight as a die. His hair is wavy. He does not seem to belong to the sea, as there is not the least suspicion of the mark of sun or wind on his cheeks. He looks as if he ought to have elected to be a musician or a painter. In the latter portion of this sea document, however, Mr. Barrymore's make-up is perfect. His hair is wet most of the time, long and unkempt. His eyes are bleary and vicious and he snarls at his men, having only one thought in mind—to find and kill Moby Dick, the great white whale described as heavier than 1,200 men. He insists that nothing will stop him from slaying the monster. The storm, described by Cedilla as the earth and sky meeting, does not deter the obstinate master of the whaler. The mutiny of most of his crew means naught. He must kill the whale that bit off his leg."

In the film, the turbulent seas and the scenes aboard the vessel are particularly well photographed. Long close-ups are frequent, cutting first from one person, and then to another to add emphasis, bringing the viewer into the mind and thoughts of the unfortunate sailors on the vessel.

Another particularly harrowing sequence involves the agonizing use of fire as an antiseptic on the severed leg of Ahab after the whale inflicted its initial attack. This torture, followed by the painful depiction of the man trying for the first time to walk with his peg leg, is rich with cruel details. Viewers watched the ordeal age the man, and witnessed the degrading loss of all conceit concerning his personal appearance.

Dolores Costello appeared in the role of Esther, Ahab's love interest. A strong incident shocked audiences as Ahab, believing Esther is fickle and faithless, decides to burn out the affectionate tattoo on his arm. The camera lingers over the disturbed man as he heats an iron and presses it on his forearm. John contorts his face in hideous close-ups, as Ahab endures the burning pain.

"I'll do it myself, no doubles for my pictures!" John was said to have told the production crew, in an article in *Motion Picture*. He not only worked with his leg strapped back but had buckets of icy water hurled over his slim body in the storm scenes. Where a double could have done this kind of dangerous work, he chose in one scene to personally slide down a rope from the crow's nest to the deck of the vessel. In another scene at night, he dove from the ship into the churning black water, and cut his head badly. He was untrained for a stunt man's work, yet he insisted on doing the dangerous scenes himself.

A reviewer in *Variety* wrote about *The Sea Beast*:

"A finely made picture and with a magnificent performance by John Barrymore. *The Sea Beast* firmly elevates itself above the regular program release while still not reaching the road show class. It's the type of film that lies within these two." The review went on to evaluate, "In *The Sea Beast*, the Warners have a picture they can and do point to with much pride. It's picture making of the best, taking in land and sea, boats and whales. Barrymore's expressions of suffering while having a tourniquet tied to his severed limb, and more so as they applied an antiseptic blazing iron to the raw flesh, are comparable to nothing that has been seen in a moving picture."

Roles in *Tempest* (1928) and *When a Man Loves* (1929),

otherwise straightforward heroes, had sequences inserted giving John opportunities to be thrown in jail and nearly go mad. These sequences harked back to his stellar work on the stage in *Justice* and *Hamlet*, and John relished these opportunities to disfigure his face with torture and agony.

He loved going into physical deformation so much that he had a field day with his role as the famous sleuth in *Sherlock Holmes* (1922). As the world's greatest detective, he submerges his classic profile behind an incredible parade of disguises. Later in another film, *Beau Brummel* (1924), the story features a climax in an asylum in which a faithful old butler visits Brummel, now aged and insane. He believes he is back in his years of splendor, and sets about preparing for a huge feast only to make a toast to his love, and then fall dead with a seizure.

John loved these kinds of strong scenes that were filled with turbulent emotions. His acting was often bravura in the sequences that allowed this style of interpretation, but when the fun moments passed, his serious acting remained. *The Beloved Rogue* (1927) perfectly blended both the comedic abilities and the dramatic attributes for which he was justly famous.

Don Juan (1926) was the Warner Bros.' first venture into synchronized sound. It featured an original orchestra score with sound effects, and was a resounding success, paving the way for all the other sound films that would follow. John made one more silent film in 1929, *Eternal Love*, and then led the way into sound films with a magnificent sequence from the play *Richard III* in *The Show of Shows* (1929), and again in his first full-length talking film, *General Crack* (1930).

From 1930 to 1941, John lent his profound voice and magnificent technique to thirty-three more films, cementing his reputation as one of the finest actors of the screen.

Lillian Gish, in *The Movies Mr. Griffith and Me*, recalled a time when she returned to the theater after many years of work in silent films. She sought out the coaching of Margaret Carrington, the same voice teacher who had trained Barrymore for his initial presentation of William Shakespeare's *Hamlet*. Lillian's sister, Dorothy Gish, told her of having lunch with Barrymore a few days earlier. "He was acting silly," Dorothy recalled, "until she mentioned Margaret Carrington; then he became serious. Everything he had done that was worthwhile, he said, was because of Margaret Carrington. He talked for a half-hour about what a great woman she was. Without her, he claimed, he would have been a fifth-rate actor."

Some critics in his day reviled John for having succumbed to the lure of easy money to be made in Hollywood, but he was frank about the blessing of Hollywood income. In later years, he was denounced for making a mockery of his reputation. Despite the unkind remarks, he stayed in the film capital until the end of his life.

In the early months of 1942, John suffered from the combined effects of cirrhosis of the liver, ulcers, and pneumonia. He spent his last months acting the part of an aging actor and buffoon on the Rudy Vallee radio show, a painful but often hilarious burlesque of his reputation and career.

He died peacefully in May of the same year. John fathered a second generation of film actors that has also bred another generation of young Barrymores who perpetuate the family name and validate their inherited legends.

"I never realized until a few weeks ago what an old punk I am," he mused pensively in a conversation with Harry T. Brundidge. "I was an old man when I was a youth, and as an older man, I have always been a youth. I've never felt older than nineteen years."

In a moment of self-candor, John revealed, "I didn't want to be an actor, I wanted to be a painter. I left the stage to study at art schools, and I only went back to the theater because there is hope—at least money—for the bad actor. The indifferent painter usually starves."

Silent Filmography of
John Barrymore

An American Citizen (1914)
The Man from Mexico (1914)
Are You a Mason? (1915)
The Dictator (1915)
The Incorrigible Dukane (1915)
Nearly a King (1916)
The Lost Bridegroom (1916)
The Red Widow (1916)
Raffles, the Amateur Cracksman (1917)
National Red Cross Pageant (1917)
On the Quiet (1918)
Here Comes the Bride (1919)
The Test of Honor (1919)
Dr. Jekyll and Mr. Hyde (1920)
The Lotus Eater (1921)
Sherlock Holmes (1922)
Beau Brummel (1924)
The Sea Beast (1926)
Don Juan (1926)
When a Man Loves (1927)
The Beloved Rogue (1927)
Tempest (1928)
Eternal Love (1929)

Chapter 2
Lionel Barrymore

"Stand not upon the order of your going, but go at once!" rang the command in young Lionel's ears when his father or mother would announce it was time to go to bed.

If he hurried through a meal, he would often hear the admonition to eat "wisely and slow." Or, when he felt shy and buried his chin in his chest, he would hear, "Look up, Pauline," a line from *The Lady of Lyons*.

Such was life with his parents, Maurice Barrymore and Georgianna Drew, two actors steeped in Shakespeare and other classics. Quotations were often hurled at young Lionel from his parents' memory of their plays when an appropriate situation presented itself.

His family first appeared on the stage in 1752. William Haycraft Lane and his wife, Louisa Rouse, both managed and performed in English theaters. His grandmother, Mrs. John Drew, Sr., his father, mother, and uncles, John Drew and Sidney Drew, as well as all his cousins and aunts, played together on professional theater stages. Lionel was born into this theatrical family on April 12, 1878, in one of the houses owned by his grandmother in Philadelphia.

By the time he was born, his grandmother had become the manager of the Arch Street Theater, quite an achievement for a woman in that time. She owned several houses in Philadelphia, and the one Lionel lived in longest was at 140 North Twelfth Street. The family dubbed that house "The Tomb of the Capulets" because it was directly across the street from a tombstone cutter who displayed an imposing assortment of his marble gravestones in the front yard.

Lionel's family: his uncle, John Drew (upper left), his mother, Georgie Drew Barrymore (upper right), his grandmother, Mrs. John Drew, in costume as Mrs. Malaprop (lower left), and his father, Maurice Barrymore (lower right).

He was first schooled at the St. Aloysius Academy, and in his adolescence, attended Seton Hall, in South Orange, New Jersey. He was in London several times as a child, attending Gilmore School in Warrington Crescent.

One of Lionel's earliest memories was of his father introducing him to a man named Mr. Clemens. When nudged, young Lionel doltishly muttered a modest greeting. Then, his father told him the man was better known as Mark Twain. Lionel had read and savored both *Tom Sawyer* and *Huckleberry Finn*, and he began to recite to the writer the stories.

Lionel recalled years later, "I gave it to him verbatim, mostly whole paragraphs at a time, except for some interpolations of my own, which seemed to improve the tale. My father moved to fetch me a kick under the table and tried to stop me from this impertinence of reciting Mark Twain's own story back to him, but Mr. Clemens laid a hand on his arm and gave me his whole attention. At the end of my recital there were tears in his eyes. He beckoned a waiter and bought me an apple with spice and hot water, omitting, of course, the brandy. I was highly pleased with myself, unaware that I had pulled a pot walloping enormity."

Lionel spent much of his youth touring America by train while his father or mother appeared in plays. His sister, Ethel, remembered one of her earliest impressions of Lionel sprawling flat on his stomach on a train floor, drawing ships and trains with a pencil, as they toured the country with his parents and the famous star, Madame Modjeska. In her company, his dashing father fielded the traditional roles of Romeo, Orlando, and Armand, while his mother played the leading lady to the star. The Barrymore family was on the train with Madame Modjeska, who had her own private car, and the whole Barrymore family traveled together with her. Lionel's bed was usually a hard seat upholstered in red velvet, and his pillow was a rolled garment.

Maurice was more than just an actor. He wrote plays, including *Najezda*, which was produced in San Francisco with Madame Modjeska as the star. Maurice and Modjeska played it later in New York and Baltimore, and then Lionel's father took it to London in 1886. It was suggested to the playwright that the great French actress, Sarah Bernhardt, was the only actress with the scope and power to interpret the play adequately. In a moment of ambition, he sent the play to Sarah.

Bernhardt kept the play for two years, and then she returned it to Maurice without any comment. Shortly after, she appeared as the identical character under the name of Flora Tosca in Sardou's *La Tosca*, and scored one of her many personal triumphs. For years after, Maurice believed the French play was blatantly stolen from his script of *Najezda*, a clear-cut case of plagiarism. Bernhardt dismissed his protests, and nothing was ever done about the theft of his play. Ethel later said, "He never got over it. When he was dying, he still talked about it." Years after, whenever Lionel heard the Puccini opera of *La Tosca*, which was based on the Sardou play, he cringed with venal emotion over the loss his father suffered.

Lionel was bound by the family tradition to take part in a play. He did not want to act; he wanted to paint and draw. The theater was not in his blood. "I was related to the theater by marriage only; it was merely a kind of in-law of mine which I had to live with," he related years later in his autobiography. But the day came when his grandmother forced him to take part in a production of *The Rivals*. The play had an opening scene requiring a short dialogue between several men. Lionel was recruited to fill out the cast to replace an actor. When the horrible afternoon of his debut finally arrived, Lionel felt wretched and frightened. He crept onto the stage feeling apathy and embarrassment. Years later, he recalled muttering his lines like an automaton in need of an oil can. He repeated the scene at the evening performance the same day, believing his one stab at drama was a resounding fiasco. His grandmother was heartbroken over his lamentable performance, and left him a note stating they would delete the opening scene for all future performances. Lionel was overjoyed and relieved to be fired.

After failing to distinguish himself during the next five years, as he reluctantly appeared in a number of plays, Lionel gave up on a theatrical career. He persuaded his family to allow him to enroll at the Art Students League in New York. For the next three years, he painted copiously, but found little success and almost no income. Financial necessity reared its head, and Lionel resorted to a desperate measure: he returned to work on the stage, his only source of potential income.

He found that bearing the name of a Drew or a Barrymore offered little help in obtaining work. Lionel regrettably also found his record of performances carried little value to producers. McKee Rankin, a popular performer in that time, rescued him from oblivion and brought him into his stock company. Lionel was in a number of plays with Rankin, taking any small role not already nailed down by other actors. During this tenure with the widely-known star, he had gradually begun to feel more at ease on stage, and in time, found better parts were offered to him. He made his Broadway debut at the age of twenty-two in a four-act production of *Sag Harbor*. The play ran for seventy-six performances at the Republic Theater.

Georgie Drew Barrymore with her three children, Ethel, Lionel, and John.

His breakthrough role came in the part of Giuseppe the organ grinder in *The Mummy and the Humming Bird*. This was both his first character part and the first even remotely alluring or challenging role. For the first time in his misguided career, Lionel studied the part, and intensely trained for three weeks. The exercise was worth the effort. The play was a turning point in his career, and in this role, he experienced his first success.

The *New York Daily Tribune* reviewed Lionel's performance, reporting, "The one vital character in the play was the organ grinder of young Lionel Barrymore. In his single short scene, he exhibited a burst of genuine passion that was good to feel, for he made you feel it with him. He should in the future prove worthy to carry the family name into the casts of far better plays. . . ."

After his first success, Lionel carried the family tradition into a number of plays. Soon, he met and married sixteen-year-old Doris Rankin, the younger sister of his Aunt Gladys. She encouraged the reluctant actor to again leave the theater and pursue his ambition to be an artist. With money borrowed from his sister, the young couple left America and sailed to Paris. Lionel attended daily art classes for the next four years. He reveled in the Parisian atmosphere of art and history, and though the experience was personally rewarding, his work brought him little income. Finally, he and his wife returned their hopes to their American homeland, and sailed away from Paris.

He returned to America in 1909, and attempted to interest *Collier's* and other magazines with his work. He found little interest, and also found his funds quickly running out. Once again, the need for money forced him to resort to the limited opportunities of the professional stage. He found work in a four-act drama called *The Fires of Fate*, produced by Charles Frohman in Chicago. The play journeyed to New York for twenty-three performances, but without Lionel. He had left the cast to join his cousins in a one-act play in vaudeville.

The Still Voice toured all over the United States in vaudeville, and when it closed, Lionel found himself again without work and without money. He heard friends talking at The Players Club about a new medium called motion pictures, a cheap amusement where an actor could find anonymous work with easy hours and low pay.

Desperate for employment, Lionel went looking for work. With a wife to support, he needed money.

In 1912, motion pictures were considered beneath the dignity of any self-respecting actor, the lowest form of theatrical work, and a shameful resort for those desperate for work. A chance encounter at lunch introduced him to D. W. Griffith, the director of films at the Biograph Company. Lionel offered his services to the director, but found Griffith was not encouraging.

"I am not employing stage stars," stated the director, as he looked the unemployed actor up and down.

"I am not even remotely any such creature," Lionel answered humbly. "I will do anything. I mean absolutely anything. Believe me, I'm hungry. I want a job."

Lillian Gish later stated in *The Movies Mr. Griffith and Me* that she believed Griffith was instrumental in luring Lionel Barrymore to films. Griffith had been creating one or two films each week for the pioneer Biograph Company since 1909. The fast-paced atmosphere of their production schedule required on-the-spot creativity and an ever-changing palette of performers. Actors who were between engagements often wandered in and out of the Biograph Company, seeking quick, anonymous day work and immediate money paid daily in cash. Many penniless players came from the stage to the Biograph Company, worked for a day, and then left with a much-needed infusion of enough cash in their pocket to see them through another week. It was a perilous existence.

Griffith had been on a personal crusade to enlist potentially good players to the Biograph Company, and was secretly gratified when Lionel came to him asking for work. The value of a Barrymore name on his roster of performers appealed to the director, who quietly dreamed of greater achievements in the fledgling industry. For the last four years, Griffith had churned out more than 300 films for the nickelodeon theaters mushrooming by the thousands around the country. They popped up so rapidly that they were replacing many stage theaters in small towns across America. Few actors realized the change heralded the future of the entertainment business. They thought it was a fad.

"All right," Griffith said, "we'll put you on. You be here tomorrow afternoon at two o'clock in a dress suit."

Lionel had to borrow a dress suit to wear to his first day of work at Biograph with Griffith. He joined the players during the week Griffith was making *Friends* with Mary Pickford, a one-reel drama, and he earned ten dollars for the day's work. He found that everyone there was excited that week, not because of his arrival to their studio, but because something new and untried was being developed.

Griffith had his cameraman, Billy Bitzer, try a semi-close-up of the youthful Mary Pickford to be inserted at the very end of the film. When the director and cast seated themselves in the small projection room to watch their finished production, they were startled to see the result of their experiment. Mary plays a girl of questionable reputation entertaining the affections of several men in her room over a saloon. When two of the men pressure the girl to marry, she faces the dilemma of deciding between the two. A subtitle flashes on the screen with the words, "Which shall she choose?" Suddenly, the close-up image of Mary wearing her mother's wedding dress fills the screen, her beautiful eyes showing her struggle, and reflecting her thoughts as she agonizes over which man to marry.

Mary was overwhelmed with the impact of that first close-up, but objective enough to realize its future potential. "I think you'll do more of that, Mr. Griffith," she astutely predicted in a throaty whisper in the dark projection room.

Lionel found his attention riveted on his own image. As the film ended, he leaned forward and incredulously asked Mary, "Am I really that fat? I want you to tell me the truth, little girl," he persisted.

"I'm sorry, Mr. Barrymore, but you are," she replied.

"That does it," he said with conviction. "No more beer for me!"

One day while Griffith worked on a film with his players, Lionel approached Lillian Gish, and the two actors discussed Griffith's vision to lift motion pictures out of the rank often referred to as "flickers" or "galloping tintypes."

Barrymore told Lillian, "He really believes we're pioneering in a new art—a medium that can cross over barriers of language and culture. That's why he drives himself so hard. And you know, Lillian," he added, "I'm beginning to believe he's right."

An early portrait of Lionel Barrymore, ca. 1915.

Griffith had been gradually developing the motion picture from the primitive technique of filming from a fixed position to a complex and artful telling of a story. Griffith's experimentation was often the product of accidental discovery.

One morning, while in the middle of rehearsals for a Biograph film, Lionel accidentally stepped on an insect. Lillian Gish, standing nearby, visibly shuddered. Lionel remarked to the repulsed actress that she did not look as if she could hurt a cockroach. Griffith laughed, and agreed. In a moment, an idea came to him for a story. Lillian recalled his flash of inspiration in her memoir, "He looked around at the actors on the set and settled on Lionel. 'Your grandfather, as played with flowing beard and his usual crustiness by Mr. Barrymore, sees that you have mice in the house, and you, a sweet innocent child, love them. But, unaware of your feelings, Mr. Barrymore has put out poison for them.'"

In this impromptu manner, *The Lady and the Mouse* was improvised to build the interplay between characters, and while working out the scenario with the actors, the hastily-completed story was blocked, rehearsed, and photographed.

Lionel came to Hollywood with Griffith, and worked on films made on a vacant lot at Pico Boulevard and Georgia Street. Canvas dressing rooms were strung around the edges of the lot, and films were made outdoors in the bright California sunshine. They lived in rented rooms or hotels that took an indulgent attitude toward the poor actors.

Lionel remembered playing several parts in Griffith's *Judith of Bethulia*, the first four-reel feature made by the company, and a forerunner for his later masterpiece, *Intolerance*. *Judith* combined multiple stories, and was a noted commercial and creative success. In this film, which was massive in scale for the economically-minded Biograph, Griffith used the most advanced camera techniques of the day to create marvelous moods and exciting action. The sets were the largest ever constructed for his work at Biograph. Lionel appeared in many other films with Griffith, and found happiness with the comparatively easy work in films. He reveled in the freedom the haphazard work schedule afforded him to occasionally paint. He never thought he would remain in film work for long.

Lionel left Griffith and the Biograph in 1914, and freelanced for a year. He appeared in several episodes of Pearl White's phenomenally popular serial, *The Romance of Elaine*. The cast and crew journeyed to Ithaca, Florida, in May 1915, and began working in a new studio erected in the open air of Red Wick Park, an old amusement area at the head of Cayuga Lake. Nine two-reel episodes were planned for production in and around Ithaca with Pearl White and Lionel. Once there, he found he disliked both Ithaca and the series' producers. He withdrew, kept to himself, and read a great deal, prompting the rest of the company to nickname him "The Professor." After making several episodes, Barrymore was replaced in the series by Warner Oland, later famous as Charlie Chan in a series of mysteries made in the 1930s.

Lionel acted opposite Lillian Russell in her only film, *Wildfire*, made long after "The Jersey Lily" had past her prime. A dozen other full-length films made during these years entrenched Lionel to film work. He decided never to appear on the stage again.

The early days of silent filmmaking before the perfection of sound appealed to Lionel. A completely casual air pervaded the Metro studio. They worked informally because they were not inhibited by sound and dialogue scripts. Many of those engaged at that time came from the stage and had known each other for years. Lionel occupied a dressing room in an old frame building with a porch running around it where the actors often sat and talked. Lionel Belmore, Lew Cody, John Gilbert, and Lewis Stone even formed a singing quartet, while Will Rogers kept horses and goats corralled so he could handily exhibit his prowess with a rope. Lon Chaney worked there, and was usually found indoors fussing with make-up and experimenting with devices that would transform his appearance. It was an odd assemblage of actors destined for worldwide fame in just a few years.

In 1917, Lionel directed his sister, Ethel, in *Life's Whirlpool*, a film she made during one of her brief sojourns from the American theater. She later claimed it was one of her best films. Unfortunately, the film appears to have been lost.

Lionel was not a handsome man in the manner of his father or his brother. He found films tended to magnify a side of his own character. During his work at Metro, he discovered that his special appeal lay in portraying the type of man commonly known as a "ne'er-do-well" or "underdog." He made a special study of this sort of character, and they aroused his sympathy. He explained to an interviewer in *The Pictures Magazine* that this type of character "is a much misunderstood man. He is nearly always a fundamentally lovable chap. What I like so much about him is that he is so human. He doesn't put on airs about the amount of money he makes, or the expensive clothes he wears, or the high society he moves in, as so many of the aggressively successful people do. Take him or leave him, he is just himself."

It was not surprising that he found this character type appealing because Lionel was one of the most modest men in the acting profession. He had no delusions about his talent or his family name. He seldom could be induced to air his views on any subject, and when pressed to do so, often made humorous light of a matter.

The subject of an underdog interested him keenly. In the films he made at this time, he had been required to impersonate men who, at least for part of the stories, were misunderstood. In *The Brand of Cowardice, The Quitter, The Upheaval,* and *The Yellow Streak,* he played men who did not find themselves until trying events showed the real stuff of which they were made.

"It is my firm belief," he later mused, "that the underdog can easily, with proper handling, be made over into a useful creature. History is full of such examples, the two most familiar ones probably being Henry V and Edward VII. As princes, both these men were considered irresponsible, giving their lives to thoughtless pleasure. People feared the consequences of the accession of these men to their thrones. But with real responsibilities their true natures asserted themselves. Sham," he went on to explain, "was dropped in favor of the real, and each had such a reign as to excite admiration. No man can be an angel all the time."

Lionel went on to illustrate further, stating, "Surely it is better that he should improve, having learned by experience, than to be a goody-goody in his youth, and deteriorate later. There is something wholesome about a change for the better, something rather tragic about a change for the worse. In most people's opinions, the ne'er-do-well couldn't change much for the worse, and he generally does change for the better."

Lionel spoke about the core nature of the type of man he would play during the rest of his film career. "Somehow the ne'er-do-well doesn't seem to take much interest in money. Other things interest him so much more. The ne'er-do-well is a drifter, lacking concentration, perhaps."

Lionel believed he found the key to his niche in motion pictures lay in portraying the type of a man who originally has sufficiently strong impulses, but balked, either by an accident, necessity, or undue influence. His type of character often was denied the opportunity to become what he most desired. "I know a man who was anxious to go on the stage," he said. "His family objected violently, and he drifted from one thing to another without really succeeding at anything. Finally his father died and his mother withdrew her objection. The man, though rather late in life, attained his heart's desire and became eminently successful.

"The ne'er-do-well has in him something even more fascinating than achievement, and this is possibility. He is a lovable person whose potentialities are great—and it is the duty of the rest of us to understand him, and help him to come into his own."

While Lionel was working out the type of character he would portray through most of his films, his brother was preparing a stunning, new play with a role he felt would be perfect for his brother. John invited Lionel to appear on Broadway with him in *Peter Ibbetson.* The play took several years to become a reality. During this time Lionel had taken work with the Metro film company, and he was reluctant to return to stage work again. His aversion to the stage was intense, but his brother prevailed upon him to join him in the production. Encouraged by Constance Collier's direction, Lionel reluctantly agreed to take part in the play. He was thrilled to find the experience worth his while: the opening was a smash hit, one of the few he ever experienced on the stage.

Peter Ibbetson ran for two years, including a lengthy tour that followed the New York production. Then, Lionel enjoyed another stage success with his brother after returning to New York. The play was called *The Jest,* and it proved to be a tour-de-force for both brothers.

His contract with Metro expired in 1917, and Lionel did not engage with that company again. After *The Jest* closed, he was encouraged by his first taste of renown, and he then considered an unusual role in a play called *The Copperhead.*

Gus Thomas had written this play about a forty-five-year-old man named Milt Shanks who is suspected of being a spy during the Civil War. In the story, Shanks is rumored to have given information to the Confederates that causes both the death of his son and those of some of his friends. Many years later, when Milt is a septuagenarian, and the happiness of his granddaughter is at stake, a letter from Abraham Lincoln is unearthed. This dramatic incident reveals that he was not the traitor everyone believed.

The Copperhead offered Lionel a chance to play a richly varied character role, an underdog, the very type of man he portrayed best. Most strikingly, the role offered him the opportunity to visibly age at widely different stages of the bucolic patriot's life. Lionel recognized the profound break the role gave him to exercise his talent for character acting, and was excited to learn the producers had found no one willing to take on the challenging part. Lionel had been a lifelong admirer of both General U. S. Grant and Colonel John Singleton Mosby, the Confederate cavalry raider. He had read the autobiography of General Grant, and was an authority on the man's life and the Civil War era. He lobbied for the role and won it.

For audiences barely removed by one generation from the Civil War, *The Copperhead* struck a powerfully responsive chord. It was an immediate hit. The opening night was a triumph for Lionel, and he earned fifteen curtain calls. *The Copperhead* became Lionel's most successful stage role. Paramount bought the right to recreate the play in motion pictures, and Lionel was brought with it to recreate his sterling performance. Once again, he abandoned the theater to return to film work.

A farmland in Elmhurst, Long Island, was located for the studio to reconstruct the Millville, Illinois setting for *The Copperhead*. Sets for the exteriors showing the home, courthouse, church, and other buildings were constructed unlike most movie sets. They were built with all four sides intact, all carefully weather-stained to create the illusion of authenticity. The film was shot in sequence, and as Lionel's character and the story aged across many decades, the sets were also aged along with them. Exteriors took on the degradation suffered during the length of the war. When released, the film of *The Copperhead* was another triumph for Lionel, a peak in his career in motion pictures.

The motion picture version of *The Copperhead* was fashioned from the original story by Frederick Landis, not the play penned by

Lionel Barrymore, as Milt Shanks in *The Copperhead*, aged forty-five years during the story. He is shown (left) as young Milt Shanks in the 1918 Broadway play version, and (right) as old Milt Shanks in the 1920 Paramount film version.

Augustus Thomas. It was adapted and directed for the screen by Charles Maigne, who brought to the film much of the simple humanness and dramatic strength that distinguished the stage play. In this new version, he embodied the role of the rock-hard character, Milt Shanks, who enrages his fellow small-town patriots by voicing sympathies with the South during the Civil War. The town hates him, and in turn, hates his granddaughter, played in the film by Anne Cornwall, until he reveals to the astonished inhabitants of their village that Abraham Lincoln had appointed him to infiltrate the Copperheads, Southern conspirators in the North, during the war. He had been sworn to lifelong secrecy, and reveals his true nature only to save the reputation of his granddaughter.

The *New York Times* thought the film succeeded on several levels. "It is the character of Milt Shanks that makes it important. And it is Lionel Barrymore who makes Milt Shanks important . . . for the time of his presence on the stage or screen, he is convincing. He is not questioned until later, and even then, so unforgettable is Mr. Barrymore's performance, the average person is likely to cling to its reality despite all logical objections."

The review went on to illustrate the plausible performances of Doris Rankin, Lionel's real-life wife, and others in the cast. The newspaper also gave unqualified approval to the adaptation and direction, and especially the appearance and atmosphere of the Civil War town built on Long Island.

By comparison, the film critic from *Variety* was harsh in his description of the conversion of the film from a stage play into a motion picture. "Its fault is largely a matter of not losing out because the eloquence of the human voice is missing to add to the intenseness of the drama, but primarily because its bigger moments have been allowed to flop in a slipshod fashion. In the cutting process it seems that in an effort to strengthen its continuity value again, it has become more discordant than perhaps when it was first assembled. The result of this means that the director asks so much to be taken for granted without even offering a vestige of reason." The *Variety* reviewer gave one example to show how the film's direction offset the emotional impact needed in the picture: the moment when Barrymore's character is informed that his wife had died. In the following interval, after having been refused admittance to view the body of his son who had died earlier, *Variety* noticed that "An opportunity calling for pathos or for some expression measuring up to an anticipated climax passes off without effect. Such scenes are worthy of rehearsing innumerable times to secure the needed climatic values, and when they are allowed to pass as listlessly as they do then there is little left to hold the spectator enthralled."

The *Variety* review praised the film in its handling of the death scene of the "Copperhead," played by Lionel. "It is this moment that makes *The Copperhead* worthwhile for all its obvious shortcomings when brought to comparison with other feature pictures dealing in a similar subject and possessing more interest."

After his success with *The Copperhead*, Lionel signed with First National Pictures for a series of four pictures. For *The Master Mind* and *The Devil's Garden*, First National billed him as "America's Foremost Actor" in their advertising. These films, and his next two, *The Great Adventure*, and *Jim, the Penman*, gave him the same kind of underdog character parts he had so completely found to his favor, and reaffirmed his aversion to starring in traditional leading man roles. He would follow this direction for the rest of his career.

Jim, the Penman had the record of having been produced more times on the stage than any other English play, and each time it repeated its original triumph. For the American film version, the plot was preserved intact, as well as the names of the characters. The locale was transferred from England to America, and the characters given places in American life corresponding to those in the original play. For examples, the English village became a town on Long Island, and action in London was shifted to New York. It was one of the most elaborate productions in which Lionel had appeared.

The release of this melodrama completed the series of pictures, and represented Lionel's versatility to a remarkable degree. In the space of six working months, he made the four full-length films. The contrast between these First National roles was noteworthy. *The Mastermind* was a study of the psychological effect of circumstance upon a man wealthy and brainy enough to attempt to control his own destiny; *The Devil's Garden* dwelt with the reactions of a man fettered by his own condition in life; *The Great Adventure* was a delicious comedy; *Jim, the Penman* was a melodrama.

After completing his First National contract, Lionel dared to venture back to the stage in a compelling, new production of Shakespeare's *Macbeth*. Having seen his other family members play Shakespeare successfully so many times, Lionel attempted an ambitious production of Shakespeare's tale of murder and revenge. It was designed with brilliance, and promised to be the best work anyone in the Barrymore clan had ever attempted. The expensive production was made under the direction of Arthur Hopkins, and the scenery designed by Robert Edmond Jones, both of whom had added much to the revival of *Richard III* with his brother, John, the previous year. The scenic settings were extremely modern and weirdly fantastic. Unfortunately, it failed with such a resounding thud that the disappointment shook Lionel's faith in his own ability. Neither audiences nor critics would accept it, and it was sadly withdrawn after only twenty-eight performances. "Failure of any kind of an artist who has the egotism to thrust himself before the people and dare the consequences is bleak enough," Lionel lamented, "but when you are an actor and have been snubbed you feel like the only sick goldfish in the aquarium." This failure stunned him to his roots, and he vowed to never work in the theater again. The *Macbeth* accident chastened him, and was the prime reason he finally deserted the theater. He finished his stage career by fulfilling four productions for which he had already made commitments, appearing in rapid succession in *Laugh, Clown, Laugh* for David Belasco, *The Piker* for A. H. Woods, *Taps* for the Shuberts, and *Man or Devil*. The early 1920s saw the end of his work on the New York stage and the beginning of twenty-six years he would spend working exclusively in motion pictures.

In 1921, Lionel did more work in films, playing a man undone by passion in *The Claw,* a thief undone by love in *Boomerang Bill,* and Boston Blackie, a reformed crook undone by his past, in *A Face in the Fog*.

The end of his career on the stage also brought an end to his marriage to Doris. An interlocutory decree of divorce was granted to the couple on December 2, 1922. On June 6, 1923, Lionel sailed for Havre on his way to Rome to work with Bert Lytell in the Goldwyn film, *The Eternal City*. With him was Irene Fenwick, an actress who was one of Broadway's most engaging stars in light comedies. They were married in Rome on the afternoon of June 14, 1923.

Lionel resorted to exclusive film work by default. "I had no more notion of making a serious and permanent alliance with motion pictures than I had of becoming a tattooed man in a county carnival," he recalled in his autobiography. He *preferred* pictures, having found the comparatively easy work to his liking, and he *disliked* the stage and the humiliation abject failure brought. A chance encounter brought him a contract to appear in *The Girl Who Wouldn't Work* with Marguerite de la Motte, and with that, he ended his stage career entirely. He went to work on a picture for MGM, and there he remained for the next twenty-six years.

Sound was blended with motion pictures in a number of Edison films in the early years of the 20th century. As early as 1908, *The Merry Widow* had been presented at the Bijou Dream in New York. Music and three vocal numbers were featured throughout this sixteen-minute film. Another film, exhibiting Max Reinhardt's pantomime of *The Miracle,* paired sound with film as early as February 1913. These and many other experimental sound films had one thing in common: absolutely perfect synchronization was not possible at each and every screening. Perfection was achieved at some exhibitions, but it was with great effort, and theaters could not guarantee precision every time they ran these films with synchronized sound. This flaw prevented sound films from taking hold of the industry.

In 1927, the perfection of sound and film was finally achieved, and it frightened those in Hollywood as nothing had alarmed them before. A complete revolution in acting, production technique, photography, and writing took place over the span of about twelve months. Actors who had no stage training received the changes with sheer terror. Those unfortunate men and women who had heavy, ethnic accents, or had untrained voices found that they faced either a complete change in the type of roles they were given, or they were doomed to be cast aside. Many prominent stars found their careers skidding to a halt.

"Why, relax from your bad dreams, gentlemen," Lionel recalled telling the MGM executives. "As an old and experienced hand to whom nobody has paid any attention these many years, let me explain. Sound won't make quite as much difference as you fearfully expect. Action will remain the chief ingredient of these cultural dramas of ours. The main difference will be that the titles will from now on be uttered—hopefully in something approximating English—instead of printed."

Lionel was one of the few actors in silent films with a wealth of experience on the stage. MGM made him a director during the difficult transformation of films from silence to sound. His first picture was a short called *Confession,* and starred Robert Ames. *The Rogue Song,* one of the first talking pictures in color, brought Lionel behind the cameras directing Lawrence Tibbett and Catherine Dale Owen.

He led Ruth Chatterton through her paces with the time-proven tearjerker, *Madame X,* and directed three other films for the MGM studio. While filming *Madame X,* a scene featured the actress moving across the expanse of a wide set and talking with each step. Lionel could find no way to record the sound of her voice during the movement. In a moment of inspiration, he recalled a fishing pole belonging to one of his assistants. The burdensome microphone was quickly attached to the end of the fishing pole and precariously dangled just out of the camera range over the head of Miss Chatterton as she moved across the set. In this makeshift manner, the "boom" microphone was first used. Lionel later claimed the inspiration was his one contribution to the art of filmmaking.

Between *Free and Easy* (1930) and *Lone Star* (1952), Lionel lent his face, voice, and character to seventy-five more films. Then in 1937, tragedy struck in the form of an accident that would reshape his character and body for the rest of his life. He was working on *Saratoga*, the film then in progress with Jean Harlow. She died of uremia during the making of the film, and the picture was painstakingly salvaged. The film story was rewritten to juggle the photographed scenes into some sort of tale that made sense. While taking part in the film's reconstruction, Lionel tripped over a cable strung along the floor and fell on his left hip. While sidelined during months of painful hospitalization, the accident prevented him from playing the coveted role of Dr. Meade in *Gone With the Wind*. Inflammatory rheumatism had recurred repeatedly during these last years, and when he emerged from the hospital following the hip accident, he was in a wheelchair. He immediately reported to Frank Capra for the role of Grandpa Vanderhof in *You Can't Take It With You*, and won the admiration of many for continuing to work despite the debilitating handicap. From that time on, every role in which he appeared was carefully constructed to allow him to appear as a man in a wheelchair.

His autobiography was published in 1951 after a successful serialization in *The Saturday Evening Post*. He played himself in his last picture, appearing with his sister, Ethel, in *Main Street to Broadway*, offering sage advice to a young theater aspirant.

Lionel died on November 15, 1954, on a Monday night. "I like to think that he and Jack are together—and that they will be glad to see me," Ethel wistfully hoped.

In 1950, Lionel humbly remarked about himself, "How fortunate, I say, for the sheep that can munch in unison and adjust to the world. How painful for the artists, the musicians, and the actors who fail to keep time."

SILENT FILMOGRAPHY OF
LIONEL BARRYMORE

FRIENDS (1912)
SO NEAR, YET SO FAR (1912)
THE CHIEF'S BLANKET (1912)
THE ONE SHE LOVED (1912)
GOLD AND GLITTER (1912)
MY BABY (1912)
THE INFORMER (1912)
BRUTALITY (1912)
THE NEW YORK HAT (1912)
THE BURGLAR'S DILEMMA (1912)
A CRY FOR HELP (1912)
THE GOD WITHIN (1912)
THREE FRIENDS (1913)
THE TELEPHONE GIRL AND THE LADY (1913)
AN ADVENTURE IN THE AUTUMN WOODS (1913)
OIL AND WATER (1913)
NEAR TO EARTH (1913)
FARE (1913)
THE SHERIFF'S BABY (1913)
THE PERFIDY OF MARY (1913)
A MISUNDERSTOOD BOY (1913)
THE LADY AND THE MOUSE (1913)
THE WANDERER (1913)
HOUSE OF DARKNESS (1913)
THE YAQUI CUR (1913)
JUST GOLD (1913)
THE POWER OF THE PRESS (1913)
A TIMELY INTERCEPTION (1913)
THE WELL (1913)
DEATH'S MARATHON (1913)
THE SWITCH TOWER (1913)
A GIRL'S STRATEGEM (1913)
CLASSMATES (1913)
HOUSE OF DISCORD (1913)
THE MASSACRE (1914)

Strongheart (1914)
Men and Women (1914)
Judith of Bethulia (1914)
Brute Force (1914)
The Woman in Black (1914)
The Span of Life (1914)
The Seats of the Mighty (1914)
Wildfire (1915)
A Modern Magdalen (1915)
The Curious Conduct of Judge Legarde (1915)
The Romance of Elaine (1915)
The Flaming Sword (1915)
Dora Thorne (1915)
A Yellow Streak (1915)
Dorian's Divorce (1916)
The Quitter (1916)
The Upheaval (1916)
The Brand of Cowardice (1916)
The End of the Tour (1917)
His Father's Son (1917)
The Millionaire's Double (1917)
Life's Whirlpool (1917)
The Copperhead (1920)
The Mastermind (1920)
The Devil's Garden (1920)
The Great Adventure (1921)
Jim the Penman (1921)
Boomerang Bill (1922)
The Face in the Fog (1922)
Enemies of Women (1923)
Unseeing Eyes (1923)
The Eternal City (1923)
Decameron Nights (1923)
America (1924)
Meddling Women (1924)
I am the Man (1924)
The Iron Man (1925)

Fifty-Fifty (1925)
The Girl Who Wouldn't Work (1925)
Children of the Whirlwind (1925)
The Splendid Road (1925)
The Wrongdoers (1925)
The Barrier (1926)
Brooding Eyes (1926)
Paris at Midnight (1926)
The Lucky Lady (1926)
The Temptress (1926)
The Bells (1926)
Wife Tamers (1926)
The Show (1927)
Women Love Diamonds (1927)
Body and Soul (1927)
The Thirteenth Hour (1927)
Drums of Love (1928)
Sadie Thompson (1928)
The Lion and the Mouse (1928)
Road House (1928)
River Woman (1928)
Alias Jimmy Valentine (1928)
West of Zanzibar (1928)

Chapter 3
Richard Barthelmess

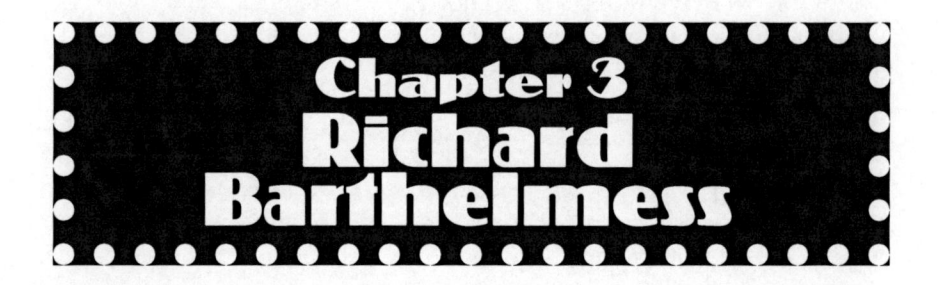

Richard Barthelmess was one of the best loved of the first male stars to appear in films after World War I. A pleasant leading man and producer, Richard later helped found the Academy of Motion Picture Arts and Sciences to bring recognition to the achievements of the finest professionals in the industry. He won a special Academy Award for *The Patent Leather Kid* (1927), and was individually nominated for his work in *The Noose* (1928).

Richard was equally admired by both men and women for his handsome, dark looks, and exuded an all-American personality that was greatly appreciated in his time. Women loved his open, expressive face, and his smoldering, soulful eyes. An unusual facial characteristic was his slightly crooked mouth, which slanted at the lower corner when he smiled.

On May 9, 1895, Richard Semler Bartelemys was born in New York City, the son of actress Caroline Harris. His father, Alfred Bartelemys, was an importer by trade. He died when Richard was barely a year old.

That year, Alfred's young widow turned to the stage as a means of livelihood, and performed using the name Catherine Harris in her theater work. She did so well that she was soon featured favorably in stock and road show companies. She played with Sidney Drew in *Billy*, with Mme. Petrova in *Panthea*, and with Thomas Ross in *The Only Son*.

Between school years, Richard enjoyed taking part in local plays in summer stock with his mother, often playing small roles in her stage productions when there was need of a child. He grew up with this knowledge of the theater as part of his background.

This painting of Richard Barthelmess appeared on the cover of *Motion Picture Magazine* in the issue published November 1922.

While Richard attended Trinity College in Connecticut, he revised his birth name to "Barthelmess." As a student, his mother encouraged him to appear in the university stage productions.

"My mother was on the stage," he later recalled in *Motion Picture Magazine.* "My father died before I was a year old, and while both my mother and I felt college was the thing, I often used to do something in the way of dramatics during my vacations."

Richard played the peg-legged boy in *Mrs. Wiggs of the Cabbage Patch* with a stock company in Canada. The following summer, he stage-managed in stock, and found work as an extra in a serial starring Billie Burke. He also appeared as an extra in the famous film *Romeo and Juliet,* with Francis X. Bushman and Beverly Bayne.

Richard was suspended from Trinity College for six months after taking part in a fight with another boy. He took a knockout blow, and aroused the anger of the professors for giving in to the use of his fists. Dumped out on the streets, he had to fend for himself for the very first time. Finding work as a teenager was not easy.

He haunted the Philadelphia theater circuit looking for work in that winter of February 1914. A desperate need for money motivated him. He trudged through man-high drifts of snow and wind blizzards, a stranger in town, knowing no one and having almost no money. He found lodging at a seedy hotel near the train station, a room that was stained, narrow, overrun with insects, and gloomy. He took a trolley out to Columbia Avenue where the Emily Smiley Players put on two shows a week at a little theater in Wildwood, New Jersey, and Philadelphia. There, he found work as a callboy, stage manager, curtain ringer, sceneshifter, and property boy. He even got to play a part in *The Girl of the Golden West*. It was marvelous training for an eighteen-year-old, but the twenty dollars a week he earned barely paid for a minimum existence. He took the experience on the chin, thinking it was the punishment he deserved, and resolving to make the best of the grim situation.

"You couldn't call it a life," Richard remembered in a 1925 *Movie Weekly* interview. "I couldn't buy clothes with this sum, not suits or coats, or anything of that sort. Now and then, I bought a new pair of shoes or replaced a storm-battered and dust-crusted hat with a new one—that was all. When I could, after I had eaten and paid for my room, I would tuck away a dollar or two against the time when my six months of penance should be done and I could turn my face toward Trinity College again."

Richard finished his experience with the Emily Smiley Players and returned to New York without a clue what to do. He connected with an old friend who got him a job in Ottawa, Canada for

$25 dollars a week. The gig ended, and he went back to college, made his peace with the professors, and bore down for more serious study. He was forced to take the freshman course over again.

During the summer of 1914, World War I escalated. While Richard was on vacation from Trinity College, he worked as a stage manager in summer stock. In the summer of 1915, he decided to parlay his experience in dramatics with the Hartford Film Corporation, a newly formed organization that had high hopes of turning the wilds of Connecticut into another Hollywood. The film company came to a nearby village on location to film a two-reel, slapstick comedy. Richard was impressed with their work, and participated as an extra. As often happened with independent companies, the corporation went bankrupt within a few weeks, and he spent the rest of the summer working for the Travelers Insurance Company. His original purpose remained focused on entering business when he left college. The summer of 1915 had not been a very profitable one, but it was an exciting experience, and it planted the idea of film work firmly in his mind. He dismissed thoughts of a business career, and while in his junior year, left Trinity College to seek the financial security offered by a career as an actor in motion pictures. "When I saw my friends earning $7 to $8 a week in banks, I decided I better go after it," he said later.

During his 1916 vacation, Alla Nazimova was preparing to make her motion picture debut. Remembering the youth she studied while taking English lessons, Nazimova thought the young man perfect to play her son, Arno, in her debut film, *War Brides*.

"While plans for *War Brides* were going on, I was getting terribly discouraged. I had spent weeks making the usual rounds of the Fort Lee and New York studios," Richard recalled, "and had about made up my mind that there was no room for me in motion picture work. I suddenly decided to sign up for a naval training cruise to tide me over the summer. I had always loved the sea, and this seemed like an opportunity to do something before going back to Trinity College for my senior year. On the evening when I was to depart on the cruise, fate smiled ironically and decided to alter my life. A telephone call came from Nazimova asking me to see her at the hotel.

"I was not yet twenty-one when this turning point in my life occurred, but had the call come the next day, I would have been away on the cruise and probably become a second-rate business man at the end of my college days," Richard later remembered. "A small part was going begging in the film, and after screwing up my courage to a sticking point, I diffidently ventured to ask for it." Richard later confessed he had always harbored an inferiority complex, and applying for the job required stepping outside of his inherent shyness. It was to prove a fateful step. Richard sought a recommendation from Alla Nazimova to Lewis J. Selznick for the small role of her son in a film to be made from her sensational vaudeville play, *War Brides* and Richard left college to eagerly take part in the film for $7.50 a day.

War Brides, the play by Marion Craig Wentworth, had a theme of tremendous proportions, and required intense emotional acting. When *War Brides,* in screen form, had its initial showing at the Broadway Theater in New York, it was presented to a packed house. The audience was brimming with enthusiasm, and the gala occasion accorded much applause. Notables of all sorts were present, including many screen and stage stars. The lobby was banked with blowers, and the director, Herbert Brenon, was called upon for a speech. He delivered one gracefully, including specific thanks to everyone concerned. A charming musical accompaniment enhanced the effect of the film presentation, and the resulting film gripped and held the spectators. It was thought to be a masterful production, and according to one reviewer who attended, "clutches the heartstrings and holds them taut until the moment when they shall be released with a snap that is almost excruciating."

Nazimova gave herself over to superb abandon in the role, one that required high emotional powers, and masterfully expressed the story in the simple form of silent movie pantomime. The film was constructed with swift flashes of rapid action, contained very little of actual war, and featured many intimate scenes of home life. It was supported by well-chosen subtitles, superb action, and excellent photography. The film was calculated to stir the emotions to a pitch, which would have a pronounced psychological effect upon the individual viewer, and in turn, affect the outcome of World War I with its pacifist message. Richard rode the film's success to overnight recognition. Both audiences and film producers took notice.

On completion of his role in *War Brides,* director Herbert Brenon was greatly impressed with Richard's work. When Brenon left Selznick to produce films on his own, he brought Richard to his new company with a one-year contract at $50 a week. Richard dismissed all further thoughts of a business career, and left Trinity College to seek a career as an actor in motion pictures. It was financial security that motivated him, not a desire for further fame.

The motion picture version of *War Brides* proved to be a sensation, and brought much renown to all who participated in it. Richard was concerned about leaving college, but felt he could not deny himself the golden opportunity for work in the film industry.

"Later on I got a chance to go to California," he later recalled. "On the journey out I thought things over and decided to stick to pictures. I knew they meant more or less travel—travel for which I hankered, and which I would probably never get in any other way. They meant a great deal of time outdoors. I have a soft spot for the sunshine. I don't think I'd like an office job. And motion pictures meant good money."

First, Marguerite Clark asked him to play opposite her in *Snow White* (1916), and then he appeared in *The Eternal Sin,* his first film for Brenon's independent company, cast as a young man who did not know his mother was the infamous Lucretia Borgia.

Dorothy Gish was at that time starring in an extremely popular series of comedy films for Artcraft. When she saw him in *War Brides,* she said, "I want him for my pictures." Lillian Gish remembered in her autobiography: "Dorothy had an instinct for picking potential stars. Her co-star in many of her films was Richard Barthelmess, who had the most beautiful face of any man whoever went before a camera." His appearance suggested both gentleness and masculine strength, attributes that made him an appealing and virile hero immediately popular with audiences everywhere.

Dorothy Gish had to wait a while before she could get him. He was quickly seized by many female stars in the business: Olga Petrova, Gladys Hulette, Theda Bara, Madge Kennedy, Winifred Allen and Ann Pennington. Even George M. Cohan, the celebrated

Broadway star and writer/singer of "(I'm a) Yankee Doodle Dandy," nabbed Richard for one of his few films, *Hit the Trail Holiday* (1919).

Dorothy Gish finally got him in *The Hope Chest* and *Boots* in 1919. Shortly after, D.W. Griffith saw in Richard the ideal, all-American hero he needed for several upcoming films, and signed Richard to a contract to appear in *The Girl Who Stayed at Home, Broken Blossoms,* and *Way Down East.*

The greatness of *Broken Blossoms* was almost as fragile as its sensitive title. It was a film very easily shattered by insensitive audiences, an exquisite romance with a tragic ending. Griffith's film eloquently asked for understanding between different races and different religious beliefs. It provided a marked contrast with the gigantic spectacles and melodramatic romances for which Griffith had previously been renowned. Richard played a young Chinese who came to London's Limehouse section, hoping to bring with him the peace of Eastern religious beliefs. His only joy in the crushing poverty of his life was in the silent adoration he felt for a winsome street waif, superlatively played by Lillian Gish. Richard's performance of this ethnic character won plaudits around the world. With Griffith, he achieved prominence.

Another struggling actor, later known as Rudolph Valentino, auditioned for the role of a Spanish bandit in Griffith's next film, *Scarlet Days* (1919). Griffith thought Rudolph was too foreign-looking, and he lost the role to Richard. With an added moustache and a Latin costume complete with a sombrero, Richard fit the role well.

The *New York Times* said of his work in *Scarlet Days,* "Clearest and most compelling among the characters is Alvarez, a Spanish bandit and adventurer, impersonated by Richard Barthelmess. Mr. Barthelmess is rising rapidly. As the Chinese hero of *Broken Blossoms,* he set a new standard for himself, and in *Scarlet Days,* he shows that he did not just once go beyond his reach. He makes Alvarez the bright center of the story. At all times he is the romantic Spaniard, and never more exactly and completely than when, defending himself against attack, he dodges and darts about, shoots this way and that, in an evident ecstasy of joy, a throbbing delight that comes from pure love of excitement. It is anti-climatic when he recovers from his wound and goes away with the girl who loves him."

Griffith followed *Scarlet Days* with three films in a row featuring Richard as the leading man: *The Idol Dancer, The Love Flower* and finally, *Way Down East* (1920). These films made him a star of the first magnitude, and in the last film, he almost died.

Way Down East was one of the great blockbusters of all time, shown to this day in festivals, and still popular in video sales and rentals. It was a difficult film to produce. Many scenes in the thrilling climax took place outdoors in freezing temperatures and falling snow. "We lost several members of our crew from pneumonia as the result of the exposure," explained Lillian Gish in her memoirs. "Though he worked with his back to the wind whenever possible, Mr. Griffith's face froze."

The famous chase at the climax of *Way Down East* shows Richard risking his life, as he jumps over ice floes to rescue the nearly frozen and unconscious Lillian Gish while she drifts down a river toward a waterfall.

"The scene of Anna's rescue from the falls was all too realistically re-created," acknowledged Lillian Gish. "Mr. Griffith was directing Dick from a bridge over the river, but the noise of the falls drowned out his directions. Dick, a slight young man, was hampered by the heavy raccoon coat and spiked boots he had to wear. As I headed toward the falls on my slab of ice, Mr. Griffith shouted to Dick that he was moving too slowly, but Dick couldn't hear him. The people on the banks were also yelling frantically. As Dick ran toward me he became excited, leaped and landed on a piece of ice that was too small. He sank into the water, climbed back out, finally lifted me in his arms as I was about to go over, and ran like mad to the shore."

He rescues Lillian at the very moment the ice floe teeters over the edge of the waterfall. The still-shocking realism of this scene is unprecedented in the annals of film history. The two stars used no stuntmen or doubles for the life-threatening scene. The exciting climax remains one of the most suspenseful moments in a dramatic motion picture. To this day, breathless audiences sit on the edges of their seats while Richard stands on the ice floe about to plunge over the waterfall. The moment never fails to bring audiences to their feet cheering.

Richard Barthelmess, ca. 1920, at the time of the production of the film *The Patent Leather Kid*.

Years later, at a screening of *Way Down East* at Richard's home, he and Lillian reminisced about the ice floe scene. "I wonder why we went through with it. We could have been killed. There isn't enough money in the world to pay me to do it today," he told Lillian. "But we weren't doing it for money," Lillian reminded him.

A pert, beautiful young actress and Ziegfeld girl, Mary Hay, was in the cast of *Way Down East*. She and Richard fell in love and married on June 18, 1920. Immediately after, the newlywed couple went on the road promoting *Way Down East*.

Richard left Griffith, and formed Inspiration Pictures to make *Tol'able David* (1921), and gave one of his best performances as a boy who saves the U.S. mail from outlaws. "David was a role which I tried not only to characterize, but also to idealize," he explained to Adele Fletcher in *Motion Picture Magazine*. "A mountain boy would not have been as I played David. His hands would have been gritty. His hair would have been uncombed. His teeth would have been yellow. I studied David and thought David for weeks. And when I finally came to play David, I gave him a dash of poetry. I think they liked him better that way."

Writer Adele Fletcher said what so many others have thought about Richard: "And since then when we have remembered Dick, we have, at the same time, remembered the nicest boy in our hometown. That is the atmosphere he gives you some way or another. And it is easy to like him. He is young and sane and normal. He is good to look at, too, with his firmly set mouth, his deep brown eyes and his warm brown skin—with his feet standing firmly on the ground—and his eyes finding the stars."

He became one of Hollywood's biggest stars with his work with Inspiration Pictures, appearing in eleven more films that were always popular, though not of the caliber of the Griffith films. Inspiration Pictures rolled off slick, polished productions that never disappointed his fans.

The pressure of fame was the greatest disadvantage in his life. His marriage to Mary Hay ended because of the strain of maintaining two film careers under one roof. They divorced in 1926.

A new contract with First National to make three films a year at a reported $375,000 a year gave Richard one of his greatest personal successes. In *The Patent Leather Kid* (1927), he turned in one of his best performances in a stirring war story about a cocky, second-rate prizefighter with a flair for patent leather in everything from his shoes to his hair. As Curley Boyle, a conceited, young boxer to whom the flag of his country means less than the towel his trainer waves in his face, Richard plays a young man unwillingly drafted into the army. Curley is a demon battler in fist combat, but proves to be a coward afraid to put on a uniform after his induction. He later redeems himself while in a heated battle. The story sweeps from a Broadway honky-tonk through the frenzy of the fight game, climaxing with the living hell-on-earth of World War I.

The Rupert Hughes novel was hailed as a masterpiece of visualization at its very first reading. For its translation to the screen, a motion picture had seldom been conceived under more auspicious circumstances. To those responsible for the production, Richard seemed like an ideal choice for the part of Curley Boyle. To translate the story from print to screen, some characters were altered, and some were shifted. Owing to Richard's prominence as a star, the focus of the story had to center more on the character of Curley Boyle than it did on other characters that were more elaborated upon in the lengthier, original novel.

The character of Curley Boyle was the main theme of the story, and the war scenes served as merely the background. The hero in this film is pictured with natural traits, a man who can stand up against the best of fighters and bring them down for the count. His weaknesses are brought out when he becomes a doughboy. He is shown as a shaking spectacle, while his stuttering trainer, Puffy, who would never have dared to put on gloves in the boxing ring, proves to be a man of steel under fire. Curley makes good in the end, spurred on to take battlefield chances after Puffy's death. He reveals his true nature in a shell hole, and when he plunges ahead to bomb a church belfry, he is inspired by hatred for the enemy who killed his friend.

The stupendous undertaking of filming the war scenes was done at Camp Lewis, Washington, with the full aid and cooperation of the War Department. Advice from Col. Robert Alexander, in command of Camp Lewis, assisted in the technical accuracy of the war scenes.

An odd difficulty presented itself during the pre-production efforts: no one could locate an actual copy of a draft card issued when conscription became the law in the war. The card was to be used in a close-up. The producers found very few men had kept their official war summons, and a long search followed for an actual copy of a draft card before one was found and used in the film.

So much detail occupied the shooting of these war scenes that Richard A. Rowland, General Manager of First National Pictures, personally made several trips to the distant location to assist Al Rockett, Production Manager, and director Alfred Santell in their work.

An advertising poster showing Richard Barthelmess in *The Patent Leather Kid* (1920).

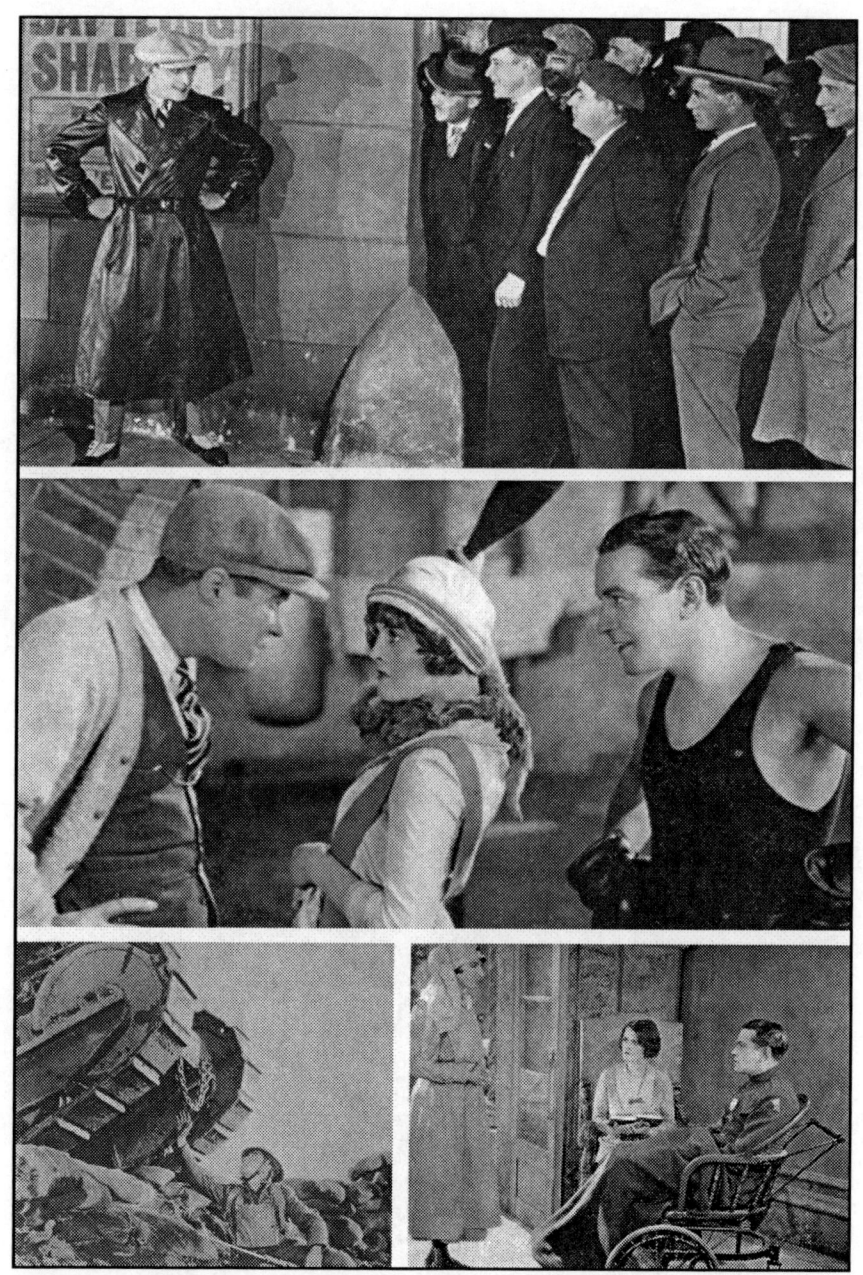

Four scenes from *The Patent Leather Kid* (1927): (top) Richard Barthelmess as Curley, greeting hangers-on after a fight. (middle) Molly O'Day and Richard discuss a fight with his manager. (lower left) Richard as Curley in the battle. (lower right) Richard as Curley about to be decorated for bravery.

A love story of sorts is woven throughout the picture. Molly O'Day, the young actress picked from 2,000 applicants for the part of the Golden Dancer who loved Curley, found her career peaked as a result of this part. 3,000 U.S. regulars, 600 civilians posing as German soldiers, and $5 million worth of U.S. army guns, tanks, and equipment were used in the war scenes.

Cameras, perched sixty feet in the air, covered the expanse of the battlegrounds for the production, which was shot by twelve cameramen. 175,000 feet of wiring connected the planted mines for the explosions. One particular shot of a procession leading up to the battlefield extended over a distance of five miles.

To provide realism, more than fifty tanks charged in the grand advance over German trenches and shell-torn territory. Coupled with artillery barrages and airplane attacks, the heightened effect was a sensational recreation of the war.

Mordaunt Hall reviewed *The Patent Leather Kid* in the *New York Times,* on August 16, 1927: "Under the direction of Alfred A. Santell, who has already made his mark in the motion picture world, Richard Barthelmess, in a film called *The Patent Leather Kid,* excels any performance he has hitherto given. There is not a single flaw in his acting throughout this long feature." The reviewer also noted some telling effects accomplished with sound in the presentation of the picture while at the Globe Theater in New York, including the use of phonograph voices synchronized during the prize fight scenes and piped through the loud speakers into the auditorium.

A review of the film in *Variety*, August 17, 1927, said, "For Barthelmess, perfect, even if Barthelmess is made to play what at times is a repulsive role, that of a slacker during wartime, and admittedly so. Barthelmess is such a big portion of this long film, in action and work, that he must come before the picture itself ... probably the reddest red-fire finish any picture ever has had. The Patent Leather one, in battle and performing a valiant act for which he was decorated, after all of his professed cowardice, is under the care of his sweetie." The review went on to note the amplifiers employed broadcasting sound from disc recordings to supplant ringside noises during the film's big fight scenes.

Richard did not win the Best Actor Academy Award for *The*

Patent Leather Kid, but he won a Special Award for his work in that film.

In *The Noose*, Richard gave a superb performance in a heart-gripping melodrama as the son of a bootlegger, who in a moment of anger, while in charge of one of the trucks running booze, slays Montagu Love, the leader of the bootleg ring. Richard is shown in graphic detail, as he walks the death march to his execution. The theme of capital punishment rang true with audiences, and the Academy of Motion Picture Arts and Sciences recognized his work in the film as one of the outstanding portrayals by an actor in 1928. He was nominated for Best Actor in *The Noose*, but lost to Emil Jannings.

In *Wheel of Chance* (1928), Richard appears in a tense drama of a man prosecuting his twin brother for murder, believing his brother was killed in childhood. He plays the dual roles with distinction—the black-headed, polished lawyer, and his red-haired, uncouth gangster brother.

His pleasing voice translated well into sound films, beginning with *Weary River* (1929). Richard plays a singer of a popular song of the same name as the film. In his sound picture debut, he accounted for a very effective performance, but the role created an unexpected furor.

Ads for *Weary River* proclaimed the quality of his singing voice, heard by cinema audiences for the first time in this film. Richard could not sing well enough to put across the title song, and Warner Bros. inserted another performer's voice for the song vocals. The studio credited Richard with the vocalization and did not realize the reaction the public would have to his apparent singing. When people clamored for more musical vocals from the actor, they were shocked to learn that it was not him actually singing. The uproar reverberated throughout Hollywood. He was compelled to truthfully come out in the press explaining the process of dubbing and quell the demands for more of his singing.

To Samuel Mook, a writer for *Picture Play,* Richard explained: "I have been severely criticized for permitting Johnny Murray to double for me in singing 'Weary River.' It was impossible to omit the singing and still have a picture. Unfortunately, I cannot sing. Had I attempted to, it would have completely destroyed the illusion of the film, because no one would have believed that a person who sings as I do could have built the reputation for himself that the convict did. Far from trying to trade on Murray's talents, his doubling for me was the best thing in the world for him, because it was the means of his getting a contract with the studio."

Richard went on to explain, "The fans understand that many of the high dives and parachute leaps they see in pictures are performed by doubles. They know that pictures of people balancing on the edge of buildings supposedly high in the air are really filmed about three or four feet from the ground. They never mind any of those things because they add to the illusion, so why should they object because I had a voice double for the same purpose?"

"As to the advertising 'Hear Richard Barthelmess sing and talk,' the sales department was responsible for that," Richard claimed. "I had nothing to do with it. The only thing I could do was the thing I did do as soon as I discovered it, and that was, first, to tell the press that I had not done the singing and, second, to make them cut it out of the advertising."

The use of sound in a film was a new technique in this early effort from 1929. Writers and directors had not yet worked out a smooth blend to the new medium. Mordaunt Hall, from the *New York Times*, said in his January 25, 1929 review: "Richard Barthelmess was heard as well as seen last night from the screen of the Central Theater in a First National Vitaphone picture called *Weary River*. The chief attribute of this banal jailbird tale is that it has some interesting prison sequences, and perhaps there are those who may enthuse over Mr. Barthelmess' rendition of a song, also known as 'Weary River.' He does sing it quite well, but it would take a far better singer and a much better song to atone for the lack of imagination and suspense in this photoplay, which is one of those that slip from silence to sound every now and again."

The Dawn Patrol (1930) and *Cabin in the Cotton* (1932) were two other outstanding efforts by Richard in sound films. He had been a star for nearly two decades by the early 1930s. He had been on the screen since 1916, and was one of the few old-time favorites who survived the upheavals in the industry without losing one iota of his popularity.

When asked what it meant to be a star, *Hollywood Magazine* reporter, Jan Vantol, prodded Richard to venture his opinion.

"Just what does it mean to be a star?" Richard asked after pondering her question for several moments. "That question takes a good deal of territory, doesn't it? It is not an easy one to answer off hand. It means certain things to me, yet perhaps, it means something entirely different to the whiskered gentleman who is eating his lunch over there on the other side of the room," Richard said, pointing to John Barrymore in character makeup and relaxing on the set of his film, *Svengali*.

"Let's put it this way," rephrased the interviewer, "in your individual case what is the one outstanding advantage of being a star?"

Richard smiled and answered, "To my way of thinking the one all-important offering of stardom is security—financial security, I mean. There are other advantages, of course, but they all pale into insignificance when compared with that one vital consideration."

Richard added, "I think that the saddest feature of Hollywood life is the host of old-timer stars who have lost their place on the screen and now have absolutely nothing to show for their huge earnings. There are many of them in just that situation. And they might just as well have retired with sufficient income to insure them lives of comfort and ease. I've always regarded my profession as a business and risked being called frugal in order to save my money. I was twenty-one years old when I started in pictures, but even then I had set my heart on winning financial security. I realized that I could earn more money as a motion picture actor than I could in any other line of work. I couldn't see the use of earning it if I did not invest it properly."

"Most stars prefer to talk about the satisfaction of giving an artistic performance and rather minimize the financial consideration," noted the interviewer.

"With the possible exception of a few individuals, that is just a lot of hooey," Richard stated bluntly. "You may depend upon it—almost every actor in Hollywood gives a great deal more thought to his weekly pay check than he does about his art. Naturally we want to be good actors, but the fundamental reason for our desire to excel is, after all, a financial one."

Richard was not without aspirations for his artistic achievements. He had a surprising, long-standing desire to play the role of Rip Van Winkle, a desire he never fulfilled.

The loss of personal privacy was another irritant Richard could not escape. "The moment that I am recognized as Richard Barthelmess, the screen star, I am overwhelmed by the curiosity of the crowd, which apparently regards me with the same interest that would be accorded a dancing mouse or any other strange animal."

Richard enjoyed being in the spotlight. Instead of resenting the presence of reporters when arriving at a hotel, he was always delighted by their attention, and flattered rather than annoyed by the recognition of the crowd. But he often steeled himself for the usual comments people would fling when first seeing him. The five-foot-ten, 152-pound actor lamented, "It is extremely annoying to hear flappers say, 'I didn't know he was short—I thought he was taller!' Or, 'Look, there's that crooked smile! He really has it!' Or 'That's really his shiny black hair. I thought maybe he made it up that way for pictures!'"

The Last Flight (1931) was one of the most unusual pictures he ever made. It was a story of four aviators' lives *after* the war. "It is a down-to-earth, human tale done with utter simplicity," Richard remarked while filming. "It will be either a great attraction or a dismal flop!"

In 1934, Richard met and married Jessica Stewart Sargent of Los Angeles, and adopted her son by her first marriage. This matrimony was different from his first love, Mary Hay. Richard resolved to refrain from intimacy with any woman involved in acting. He wanted more than anything a stable home life and a woman who prized wifely duties more than a professional career. He valued the security of insurance, sound investments, real estate and paid bills. "Which all indicates that I should never in the world have married a cute little girl who was a dancer and not, by any stretch of anything but a love-fevered imagination, a potential housewife and mother," he later agonized in an interview with Gladys Hall. "And then I met Jessica. We met on shipboard, bound for Europe. We were both married at the time, or rather, we were not yet divorced, either of us. There could be no question of marriage between us and as a matter of fact the last thing either of us wanted at the time was marriage with anyone. We were on that trip for freedom and a good time and to forget things that had hurt. Naturally, we turned to the person or persons with whom we could have the most fun. We turned to each other." In "Jessie," Richard found the woman of his dreams.

After nearly twenty years as a top star in Hollywood, Richard said to Gladys Hall in *Modern Screen*, "I have said good-bye to youth. I am no longer young and I know it. I have stood at the crossroads. I've looked behind me and I've seen, down that long bright road the figures of *Tol'able David*, of the boys who were in *Broken Blossoms* and *Way Down East* and others, retreating into the past. I've waved good-bye to *Tol'able David*. I know that he is gone forever."

"I knew," he confessed, "several months ago that I stood at the crossroads. My pictures were terrible. *I* was terrible. I was miscast and ridiculous. People were laughing at me, not weeping with me. The reviews matched the pictures. I was dying—and I knew it."

The crossroads of which Richard spoke pointed in four directions and he had to choose. One fork pointed to retirement, a retreat from his career into complete seclusion, scrapbooks full of memories, and the love of his family. The second fork led to retiring from the acting business and evolving into the new roles of producer and director. In light of the falling picture grosses during the Depression, that road was scary and unwise. The third fork led to signing with some other studio to act in stories he would not like and no empowerment to do anything about them. And finally, the road that led to freelancing. Richard chose the way of a freelance actor. He had enough money saved to take care of his life for the remaining years, and vowed to go forward with only those projects that interested him.

Four Hours to Kill! (1935) brought him to Paramount to play a murderer. This new film intrigued audiences with the story of a murderer doomed to hang. While handcuffed to a detective, the two have four hours to kill before the train departs to take him to his hanging. They attend a theater show where he sees the wife of Noel Madison, the man who testified against him. He brushes closely to the manager in the lobby of the theater and deftly takes the manager's gun. After he calls Madison to tell him his wife needs him at the theater, he quietly waits in a phone booth to shoot Madison on arrival at the theater. Madison arrives, Barthelmess is discovered, and shot.

Four Hours to Kill! presented a new Richard Barthelmess in a thrilling murder mystery, an excellent vehicle chocked-full with five subplots and an antihero character.

During the next ten years, Richard appeared in his last five films. He returned to the stage in 1936 to appear in *The Postman Always Rings Twice.* He made a striking debut as a California vagrant who takes a job in a gas station because he took a fancy to the peculiar beauty of the wife of the station owner.

Brooks Atkinson of the *New York Times* thought the new play was as good as the novel by James M. Cain on which it was based. "It turned up callously at the Lyceum last evening with Richard Barthelmess as the snide killer and Mary Phillips as the killeress," he wrote. "Nearly everything that the stage can do for such an impetuous exercise in crime, Mr. Cain and his theater associates have done with considerable technical skill, and many of the twelve scenes sputter with garish excitement."

Regarding Richard, Atkinson also pointed out, "As the reckless lover of a gas station strumpet, Mr. Barthelmess does a blameless job in his first starring appearance on Broadway. He is pleasantly forthright, although he lacks the rasp and bite that are needed to make Frank Chambers a credible adventurer. He is up against some excellent actors in his stage debut . . . "

In 1936, he received an honorary degree from Trinity College in Hartford, the university he attended but from which he left to appear as an actor in films.

During this time, good roles were few. He launched a "comeback" with a strong role in Howard Hawks' *Only Angels Have Wings* (1939), as a disgraced flyer redeeming himself during a time of crisis. He played supporting roles in a few more good films, *The Man Who Talked Too Much* (1940), *The Spoilers* (1942), and *The Mayor of 44th Street* (1942).

When World War II began, Richard aborted his film career and joined the navy as a Lieutenant Commander. After the war ended, he retired to his country home on Long Island, comfortable as a wealthy man, and harboring no wish to return to the screen. After starring in eighty-one motion pictures, fifty-seven of which were silent, Richard moved into his autumn years living in satisfied retirement.

He amassed substantial real estate holdings, and in 1955 sold a fifty-acre beachfront estate, The Dunes in South Hampton, to Henry Ford II. He said he had only one regret after he stopped acting: selling his production company in the 1920s to accept a lucrative contract with the First National Film Corporation. Richard was justly proud of the films he personally produced during those years.

In 1958, he developed throat cancer and underwent several operations. He eventually lost his voice, and died of cancer on Sunday, August 18, 1963, at his summer home at 800 Park Avenue in New York City. He was sixty-eight years old. With him at the time of his death was his wife, Jessie. His adopted son, Stewart, then living in Paris, and his daughter, Mrs. Mary Hay Bradley, survived him.

For more than twenty-five years, the boyish matinee idol of the silent film era brought great sighs from women in movie houses throughout the country. He was the clean-cut American hero; not strikingly handsome, but good-looking, masculine, unassuming, and modest. His shy, crooked smile and sleek black hair brought him an average of 6,000 fan letters a month at the height of his career.

Doris Kenyon, the silent movie star, wrote this poem about Richard that perfectly captured the essence of his personality:

> *"Muted strings on a violin;*
> *Eros dressed in overalls;*
> *Scent of new-mown hay under a summer shower;*
> *Ideals and ideas woven into a May basket;*
> *A country lane carpeted with apple blossom petals;*
> *Tobacco jar and slippers by a fireplace;*
> *And pictures in a campfire."*

SILENT FILMOGRAPHY OF
RICHARD BARTHELMESS

GLORIA'S ROMANCE (1916)
WAR BRIDES (1916)
SNOW WHITE (1916)
JUST A SONG AT TWILIGHT (1916)
THE MORAL CODE (1917)
THE ETERNAL SIN (1917)
THE VALENTINE GIRL (1917)
THE SOUL OF A MAGDALEN (1917)
THE STREETS OF ILLUSION (1917)
CAMILLE (1917)
BAB'S DIARY (1917)
BAB'S BURGLAR (1917)
NEARLY MARRIED (1917)
FOR VALOUR (1917)
THE SEVEN SWANS (1917)
SUNSHINE NAN (1917)
RICH MAN, POOR MAN (1918)
HIT-THE TRAIL HOLLIDAY (1918)
WILD PRIMROSE (1918)
THE HOPE CHEST (1919)
BOOTS (1919)
THE GIRL WHO STAYED AT HOME (1919)
THREE MEN AND A GIRL (1919)
PEPPY POLLY (1919)
BROKEN BLOSSOMS (1919)
I'LL GET HIM YET (1919)
SCARLET DAYS (1919)
THE IDOL DANCER (1920)
THE LOVE FLOWER (1920)
WAY DOWN EAST (1920)
EXPERIENCE (1921)
TOL'ABLE DAVID (1921)
THE SEVENTH DAY (1922)
SONNY (1922)
THE BOND BOY (1922)

Fury (1923)
The Bright Shawl (1923)
The Fighting Blade (1923)
Twenty-One (1923)
The Enchanted Cottage (1924)
Classmates (1924)
New Toys (1925)
Soul-Fire (1925)
Shore Leave (1925)
The Beautiful City (1925)
Just Suppose
Ranson's Folly
The Amateur Gentleman (1926)
The White Black Sheep (1926)
The Patent Leather Kid (1927)
The Drop Kick (1927)
The Noose (1928)
The Little Shepherd of Kingdom Come (1928)
Wheel of Chance (1928)
Out of the Ruins (1928)
Scarlet Seas (1928)

Chapter 4
John Bunny

John Bunny was the first hugely popular motion picture comedian. Although he was advanced in years at the time he began work in the fledgling film business, he delighted early nickelodeon audiences with many films, and created a type of funny man still in vogue today.

Bunny was born on September 21, 1863 in New York City. Some sources have claimed that he was born in Britain, but this may have been confused with his father, George Bunny. The last of several generations of captains in the British Navy, George immigrated to America from Cornwall, England. Bunny's mother came from County Claire, Ireland.

He is recorded as having attended St. James High School in Brooklyn. In his early twenties, Bunny worked in a market selling shoestrings and potatoes. This tedious and unromantic work paled quickly for the young man. He ran away with a minstrel show, joining the ranks of the thousands of rambling players roaming America in touring stage productions.

In 1890, he married Clara Scallen, and three years later, a son, George Bunny, Jr., was born. From 1897–1898, Bunny was the manager of the Grand Opera House in Salt Lake City. From 1898–1905, he was the stage manager for William Brady Productions.

For the next three years, he appeared in various stage shows as a variety artist, circus clown, light opera performer, and Shakespearean actor. Bunny found acting opportunities scarce because of his rotund size. For a while, he played as a tambourine man in obscure minstrel shows. His early stage career was varied, but one role that

John Bunny, ca. 1912, the cinema's first comic star, as he appeared at Vitagraph.

added a proud laurel to his credit list was the part of "Hi Holler" in the original New York stage production of *Way Down East*.

In 1905, he joined Lew Fields in the New York production of *Old Dutch*. In this play, a little child actress by the name of Helen Hayes made her stage debut.

In her autobiography, *On Reflection*, Helen thought back to her first work at the age of eight on the American stage with Bunny in *Old Dutch*. She remembered everyone in the cast was kind to her, except Bunny. She recalled how the overweight actor "gluttonized, snorted, and slept when he wasn't on stage." Helen said, "He always had to be awakened from one of his deep, noisy, ogre-like slumbers when it was his cue. There were times when the stage manager would pretend he had forgotten, so that I could rush to the rescue by poking the grouchy giant awake, backing away in terror but saving the day."

In the first decade of the 20th century, thousands of theatrical road shows of varying degrees of quality crisscrossed America. The rising popularity of motion pictures in the years of 1905–1912 brought a gradual but swift end to this stage tradition. Many actors found work increasingly difficult to obtain. Those in the legitimate theatre looked at films with contempt. It was considered work only for those in need of quick, anonymous cash.

Bunny found himself all too frequently unemployed and in need of quick cash. In the summer of 1910, he finished an engagement with Annie Russell in *A Midsummer Night's Dream,* and decided to risk the contempt of those in the legitimate theater and try work in the movies.

Francis Agnew, in her book *Motion Picture Acting,* asked him how he began his work on the screen. Bunny recalled, "That's a long story. About three or four years ago, I was one of the foremost comedians on the stage. I have played good parts with the Shuberts, Charles Frohman's productions, and all the biggest managers. However, I awoke to the fact that the stage game was not what it had been and that the movies were the coming thing. So I decided I would rather be behind the guns than in front of them. I wanted to be with the 'shooters' rather than with the 'shot,' so I canceled my thirty weeks' contract with the Shuberts, threw aside all the years of experience and success I had, and decided to begin all over again."

He began working in motion pictures comparatively late in life. At the age of forty-six, Bunny could tell from the films he had seen that facial expression was perhaps the most important part of early film acting. It was an art within itself. The scenes and action alone did not tell the minute details of a story. Eyes were really the focus of the personality of the player in films. With the aid of other facial features, they could express almost all the emotions and passions felt by a human soul. Bunny had long found that the use of his flexible face was an asset guaranteed to excite the interest of audiences.

He came to the Vitagraph studios on East 15th Street and Locust Avenue in Brooklyn, New York, inquiring about work. Albert Smith, President of Vitagraph, recalled in his memoirs, *Two Reels and a Crank,* "When he came to Vitagraph, we were unimpressed, though his warmth and friendliness shown through from the very first. His face was extraordinarily expressive despite small features almost lost in a head big and round as a billiard ball. He was short, dumpy, thick-chested, a sort of firm-bodied Sydney Greenstreet."

Bunny fearlessly told Albert Smith he would work in pictures without pay to prove his ability. Smith gave him a chance, and paid him the standard $5 day wage. *Dr. Cupid* was Bunny's first picture, and it presented him as a stern father opposing his daughter's prospective marriage. Smith was impressed with his mimic ability. "When he sniffed a piece of Gorgonzola cheese," Smith reminisced, "there was no doubt whatever that his nose was seriously offended; when he viewed an eligible young lady, he was moved with emotions so extravagantly honorable that they seemed almost too grievous to be borne."

Bunny had more success on the stage than most of the early film stars, having appeared with Maude Adams, and having played Bottom in Annie Russell's production of *A Midsummer Night's Dream*. Smith was astonished to learn that Bunny had an extensive theatrical background, and feared he would be unable to afford to employ the pliable Bunny. He wondered what kind of offer could be made that would not offend the actor.

"Do I get the job?" asked Bunny, after the screening of his first performance in the picture. His eyes twinkled and teased, but his voice betrayed a serious overtone.

"There is a place for you here," Smith answered, "but we're facing a problem of price."

"Well, make me an offer," Bunny pressed.

"I'm afraid it would be useless," Smith replied.

Smith finally blurted out the amount of $40 a week. Before he could finish the sentence, Bunny interrupted with a hearty laugh, and said, "I'll take it!"

In an era when the average beginner for a minor part received from $2.50 to $10.00 each day he played in motion pictures, Vitagraph's beginning offer to Bunny was generous.

Bunny later remembered, "And that was my beginning with the Vitagraph, the only company for which I've ever worked or ever will. It is owned by the biggest-hearted men in the world, generous, thoughtful and always ready to help a fellow when he's down . . . before I had finished my first picture they asked me to play in the next and I agreed, saying nothing till I had finished the first. Then I asked them what they could do for me in stock. I must admit that I did not receive a very enthusiastic reception."

Bunny lamented the passing of time and the loss of much of the nation's live theaters during the early years of the 20th century. He said, "The pictures as an industry and a profession are really yet in their infancy. Not half their possibilities have been realized. They offer a field for the ambitious, which is not simply for this day and generation, but for the infinite future. They have wrought a strongly perceptible change in the status of the dramatic stage."

When Francis Agnew asked for his opinion of the legitimate stage stars who were beginning to appear in motion pictures, Bunny shrugged his shoulders, rolled his remarkably expressive eyes, and in a most imitable manner, illustrated his replied: "Yes, a few years ago they turned up their haughty noses at people in the movies, and now they are thinking of going into the pictures. Some of them think a long while when they seek the work, for it is very often found that the best of actors and actresses on the stage fail in the pictures. They do not understand how to 'put it over' by action, as they have grown dependent on the effect of the voice."

Some of the rules of the fledgling motion picture art known to those with some experience were:

1. Don't look at the camera when acting in pictures. It detracts from every vestige of natural work.

2. Don't overact. Be natural in all your portrayals, actually living for the moment the role in which you are placed.

3. Express ideas and emotions with thoughts indicated through your eyes and posture, rather than with gestures and spoken words.

Bunny illustrated to Francis Agnew this new style of acting, noting, "Just recently, one of the stars of the dramatic stage gave a really splendid portrayal of his most famous role before the camera, but when the film was screened, though his expressions and actions were excellent, it was easy to see that he was not an experienced motion picture player. He had not been taught the many little tricks of the work, which would have made the picture perfect. Therein lies the difference between acting in the pictures and on the stage."

To the hopeful aspirants of future film work, Bunny added, "The talented amateur has as good a chance as the experienced professional, and very often better. He is more apt to be natural, not 'stagy,' employing simplicity in his actions rather than wild meaningless gestures, and more quick and willing to learn than some of our so-called present-day stars."

After the initial success of Bunny films flooded the Vitagraph studio with sales, the comedian insured his face for $100,000, a shocking amount for the time, because it exceeded the entire value of the studio. Within four years, Bunny was earning $1,000 a week, and his name and face were known all over the world.

Vitagraph was also deluged with letters and photographs in the wake of Bunny's popularity, all from similarly portly men trying to break into pictures. In desperation, the studio posted a sign in front of their property and ran advertisements containing the declaration: "Fat men need not apply."

So great was the rush to gain admittance into motion picture work, Vitagraph had difficulty controlling the lines outside their location each morning. Margaret Talmadge, the mother of Norma and Constance Talmadge, remembered in her autobiography the day she first took Norma to apply for work at the Vitagraph studio. "When we reached the studio, it seemed to us as though

Clara Kimball Young and John Bunny in a Vitagraph film ca. 1911.

everyone else in Brooklyn was doing just what we were doing—or trying to do."

"They are all ahead of us," Norma remarked despairingly to her mother.

Mrs. Talmadge showed a letter of introduction to the official in charge and, after scrutinizing her daughter from the tip of her head to the immaculately shined toe of her boot, he announced, "You'll do. Good eyes—good teeth. Please sit down and fill out this blank."

The word "legitimate" in theatrical parlance is the term used to denote the ordinary speaking stage, or dramatic and musical branches of the profession, as contrasted with the variety or vaudeville stage, or the new branch called "moving pictures." In the first decade of motion pictures, it was still considered undignified for an actor to work in films unless he was starving, and despite his later comments to Francis Agnew, Bunny often referred to his work in motion pictures as a "hobby."

Helen Hayes, who had already appeared on the New York stage for several seasons while working as a child actress, had barely settled into the routine of the theater when Fred Thompson, her director from the Columbia Players in Washington, approached her mother about bringing Helen to Vitagraph. He urged her to let Helen play in one of the films he was then directing, *Jean and the Calico Doll*.

Helen's mother quietly led her out to the Vitagraph. Both Helen and her mother were startled when they literally bumped into Bunny on their arrival. "We were stunned and then amused," Helen recollected.

"I won't tell on you," Mr. Bunny blustered, "if you won't tell on me!"

Helen's mother kept a pack with Bunny. Neither mentioned to any of their associates they were working in motion pictures. It was considered a disgrace. Mrs. Hayes even went to the extreme of trying to disguise young Helen by curling her hair for the first time and changing her mouth with makeup to keep her from being recognized in the film. "But when my first picture in support of a collie dog named Jean was shown, there I was, unmistakably me, but me looking very odd indeed. The silver screen was hardly the place to hide."

Helen remembered making pictures at the Vitagraph was a lark and a vagabond-like existence. The producers piled the cast and crew into a long line of automobiles, and drove until they spotted an estate that had the visual appeal needed for the film in production. They would jump from the cars with their tripods, cameras, and props, and hurriedly play a scene on the lawn of the estate before someone from the residence would spy them and send them packing. "We always ran faster than the owners or their servants, who sometimes came out to chase us off their property," Helen reminisced.

Bunny's popularity was immense, and peaked when Vitagraph sent him to London to make a series of films based on Dickens' *The Pickwick Papers*. The London public loved the rotund actor in the role of Mr. Pickwick. The populace besieged him wherever he went. Special details of bobbies were required to handle the enormous crowds.

Bunny earned an additional $1,000 a week for personal appearances. For the usually anonymous motion picture actor, such personal appearances broke the monotony of regular picture work, and gave the player that which was lacking in the studio—applause. It was not always conceit which incited players to long for this indication of public appreciation; more often it was a yearning for encouragement and a desire to know that their efforts to make good were not in vain.

While in London, a competitor of Vitagraph offered Bunny a huge increase over his present salary. The actor cabled Albert Smith and told of the exciting offer. Smith countered with a triple increase of his present two hundred dollars per week. Bunny accepted, and returned to work happy.

It was not every city or town that had the privilege of seeing and hearing the players personally in this way. In towns where a stock company was located to make motion pictures, it was not so difficult for the manager of a local theater to make such arrangements with the prominent players, but other cities not possessing the desired locations and scenery for films could not enjoy this privilege. For those who could, producers often took advantage of the large crowds attending a film screening by supplying one or more of the actors. They gauged the film's appeal, and the stars found first-hand what people thought of their work.

After working all day in the studio for their next offering, Bunny and Clara Kimball Young were tucked away in a motorcar and whisked all around New York City and neighboring communities to appear in person before an audience that jammed theaters to capacity.

"It sounds easy," said Miss Young in an interview with *Motion Picture Stories,* "when you read on the billboard 'Miss Young will appear at 9:30 tonight,' but no one realizes that I have to appear at three or four theaters in an evening. I never know what I am going to say to them, either. I rush onto the stage, breathless, usually after having been shot from Brooklyn to Newark in twenty minutes or so, and say anything that comes into my head."

Bunny exploited his 300-pound weight in many of the plots of these early comedy films. As a comedian, his characterization in the *Pickwick Papers* series won great admiration from the Vitagraph producers, but his American followers would have no part of the change. They preferred the Bunny they had come to know: the comic actor feigning terror, panic, or mock despair.

Like Fatty Arbuckle and other later film comedians, Bunny was funny when disguised as a woman. In *Bunny's Dilemma,* he became a maid to avoid meeting a woman visitor, and then found himself attracted to her with ensuing comic flirting and other nonsense.

The popularity of John Bunny can be attributed to the succulent fun of the music hall and the circus, not the dry wit of sophisticated comedies. He was jolly, boisterous, and broad in his acting, and because of this style, he connected strongly with early nickelodeon audiences.

In a 1913 interview in *Motion Picture Acting,* he prophetically mused, "I believe the time is coming when motion picture machines will be a part of the equipment of every school and college in the country, and many branches of learning now so objectionable to children will be made interesting by the use of motion pictures. My principal worry is the fact that I can't hope to live long enough to do all the work that I've mapped out for myself. I have planned fifty years of activity in the motion picture business, which I fear I will not live to carry out entirely. I want to see Latin and Greek mythology taught in every school and college in the United States by the use of films. It can and will be done and will be one of the biggest gifts to mankind the world has ever known."

Regarding the motion picture industry as a profession, Bunny reflected to Francis Agnew, "There's nothing like it. No other work gives an actor or would-be actor the same advantages. In the pictures, a player gets fifty-two weeks in the year. Where is the theatrical manager who can offer that? Not even vaudeville stars can get such bookings. At best, thirty weeks is about all an actor can expect on the stage. He may get summer stock work, but even so it is of uncertain duration. Stage work is a gamble. Even when you have been engaged for a production, rehearsed from three to six weeks without pay, and no doubt bought your own costumes for the piece, you have no guarantee that it will be a success. If the public does not set its stamp of approval, your job is all over perhaps after but one performance, and you can only repeat the procedure by trying again with someone else, charging the other to your loss account, with a credit notation probably on the page marked 'experience.'"

John Bunny, Jimmy Morrison, and Mabel Normand in the Vitagraph film, *Troublesome Secretaries* (1911).

Bunny went on to describe his experience with filmmaking: "It is so much different in the pictures. There you get a weekly salary, no long tedious rehearsals, and an occasional off-day as the result of inclement weather, lack of parts for your type of player, or other reasons, and still draw your salary if on a contract basis."

"In many cases—as, for instance. your humble servant—there is an occasional open week when the film company will give a player permission to appear in vaudeville. I have made such appearances—at Hammerstein's, and other theaters, and also in the larger cities of both East and West. I do a special, typically a moving picture act that is a novelty, goes big, and I enjoy it, too. It brings a little loose change as well as an intimate acquaintance with an audience, which you do not get when on the screen, of course. This shows you what an inducement it is to me."

Bunny spoke frankly about the type of people finding success in motion pictures: "Yes, there are many in the business who had no professional experience whatever before going into pictures. I know of at least six or more now at the Vitagraph who began their theatrical careers in the pictures and are now enjoying incomes of $2,000 to $5,000 a year—that is about $40 to $100 weekly . . . the qualifications are essentially talent and the ability to be natural rather than to act."

The Vitagraph Company opened their own motion picture theater in New York: The Vitagraph. On the occasion of the grand opening, their latest production was screened, and the audience was treated to a live stage act starring Bunny and Clara Kimball Young. The two leading Vitagraph stars and other studio players performed a one-act pantomime similar to the type of comedy the studio often filmed.

Bunny never lost his love of the live stage, and he longed for the excitement of an audience. In 1913, he left films to go on the road with a musical comedy company, *Bunny in Funnyland,* but after only two weeks, the company was penniless. Bunny personally kept the show funded for eight more weeks until he became sick, depressed, and exhausted. According to an article in *Variety, Bunny in Funnyland* was so poor that it was no wonder he lost money with it. "At a nickel a throw to see the screen star in his silent antics, perhaps the billing is appropriate, but at a dollar per copy to see him at the Bronx Opera House cavorting around with a mediocre company of mixed talent, presenting a brand of entertainment that forcibly suggests memories of a one-night stand tabloid, it's a bit pathetic," the review lamented. The show was described as "a sort of amateur carnival" with a screening of an old Bunny film in the middle of the various acts. The climax of the vaudeville specialty was a finale in which the entire troupe participated. Bunny impersonated Theodore Roosevelt before a huge American flag that was unfurled to the melody of the national anthem. The spectacle earned only polite applause from the weary audience.

"After the intermission, one of the enjoyable periods," quipped the *Variety* reviewer, "Bunny returned in a comedy sketch wherein the public was given a glimpse of life within the walls of a film factory." The sketch earned scatted laughs from the benign audience. Next, Bunny obliged with a song, in which he ". . . proved why he was never professionally found until the camera invaded the amusement field," wrote the *Variety* reviewer. Other acts lamentably followed, including The Piccolo Midgets, and other assorted odd acts.

Bunny in Funnyland struggled to find appreciative audiences in that March of 1913. After considerable losses, the musical review mercifully closed in Philadelphia.

He returned to Vitagraph, and was welcomed by Albert Smith as the Prodigal Son. "All that is over now, John," Smith said to Bunny. "A picture will be ready for you Monday morning."

Bunny never saw Monday arrive. He died on April 26, 1915 of Bright's Disease.

Long before Charlie Chaplin and the other Keystone comics brought hilarity to the early film audiences, John Bunny was the cinema's first great comedian. He appeared in more than 200 one-reel and two-reel comedies in his brief, five-year film career. Tragically for audiences today, most of his films have been lost. Norma Talmadge recalled in a *Saturday Evening Post* interview the neglect the studios gave to their own productions. She said Vitagraph burned many of its negatives for lack of storage space. Bunny's popularity was as enormous as his pants, and his success paved the way for all the other comedians who followed him.

Silent Filmography of
John Bunny

Cohen's Dream (1909)
Cohen at Coney Island (1909)
Davy Jones and Captain Bragg (1910)
Captain Barnacle's Chaperone (1910)
Jack Fat and Jim Slim at Coney Island (1910)
He Who Laughs Last (1910)
In Neighboring Kingdoms (1910)
Doctor Cupid (1911)
Davy Jones in the South Seas (1911)
Queen for a Day (1911)
The New Stenographer (1911)
A Tale of Two Cities (1911)
Captain Barnacle's Courtship (1911)
Davy Jones; or, His Wife's Husband (1911)
A Widow Visits Springtown (1911)
An Unexpected Review (1911)
Little Nemo (1911)
The Wooing of Winifred (1911)
The Leading Lady (1911)
Troublesome Secretaries (1911)
Soldiers Three; or, When Scotch Soldier
    Laddies Went in Swimming (1911)
Teaching McFadden to Waltz (1911)
Two Overcoats (1911)
The Latent Spark (1911)
The Woes of a Wealthy Widow (1911)
The Subduing of Mrs. Nag (1911)
The Return of 'Widow' Pogson's Husband (1911)
Treasure Trove (1911)
The Clown's Best Performance (1911)
The One Hundred Dollar Bill (1911)
Intrepid Davy (1911)
In the Arctic Night (1911)
Captain Barnacle's Baby (1911)
My Old Dutch (1911)

The Wrong Patient (1911)
Her Crowning Glory (1911)
The Tired, Absent-Minded Man (1911)
His Sister's Children (1911)
Her Hero (1911)
Ups and Downs (1911)
The Missing Will (1911)
Selecting His Heiress (1911)
Kitty and the Cowboys (1911)
Madge of the Mountains (1911)
The Gossip (1911)
The Politician's Dream (1911)
A Slight Mistake (1911)
The Ventriloquist's Trunk (1911)
Vanity Fair (1911)
The Old Doll (1911)
In the Clutches of a Vapor Bath (1911)
Windsor McCay, the Famous Cartoonist of the New York Herald and His Moving Comics (1911)
Captain Jenks' Dilemma (1912)
Chumps (1912)
Captain Barnacle's Messmates (1912)
The First Violin (1912)
Umbrellas to Mend (1912)
Bunny and the Twins (1912)
A Cure for Pokeritis (1912)
Stenographers Wanted (1912)
Irene's Infatuation (1912)
The First Woman Jury in America (1912)
Mr. Bolter's Infatuation (1912)
The Suit of Armor (1912)
His Mother-in-Law (1912)
The Unknown Violinist (1912)
Burnt Cork (1912)
At Scrogginses' Corner (1912)
Captain Jenks' Diplomacy (1912)
Working for Hubby (1912)

How He Papered the Room (1912)
Red Ink Tragedy (1912)
Thou Shalt Not Covet (1912)
Leap Year Proposals (1912)
Diamond Cut Diamond (1912)
An Eventful Elopement (1912)
Who's to Win? (1912)
Pandora's Box (1912)
Chased by Bloodhounds (1912)
Pseudo Sulton (1912)
The Troublesome Stepdaughters (1912)
Her Old Sweetheart (1912)
A Persistent Lover (1912)
Martha's Rebellion (1912)
The Awakening of Jones (1912)
Suing Susan (1912)
Bunny and the Dogs (1912)
The Bogus Napoleon (1912)
The Lovesick Maidens of Cuddleton (1912)
Two Cinders (1912)
Bunny's Suicide (1912)
Bachelor Buttons (1912)
Bunny All at Sea (1912)
An Expensive Shine (1912)
Bunny at the Derby (1912)
Michael McShane, Matchmaker (1912)
Cork and Vicinity (1912)
Doctor Bridget (1912)
Who Stole Bunny's Umbrella? (1912)
Ida's Christmas (1912)
Freckles (1912)
The Browns Have Visitors (1912)
Mr. Bolter's Niece (1913)
Three Black Bags (1913)
Ma's Apron Strings (1913)
And His Wife Came Back (1913)
The Pickwick Papers (1913)
Bunny Blarneyed; or, The Blarney Stone (1913)

When the Press Speaks (1913)
John Tobin's Sweetheart (1913)
The Adventure of the Shooting Party (1913)
The Autocrat of Flapjack Junction (1913)
The Wonderful Statue (1913)
Which Way Did He Go? (1913)
Those Troublesome Tresses (1913)
There's Music in the Hair (1913)
Stenographer Troubles (1913)
The Schemers (1913)
The Pirates (1913)
The Pickpocket (1913)
One Good Joke Deserves Another (1913)
A Millinery Bomb (1913)
Love's Quarantine (1913)
The Locket (1913)
Hubby's Toothache (1913)
Hubby Buys a Baby (1913)
His Honor, the Mayor (1913)
He Answered an Ad (1913)
The Golf Game and the Bonnet (1913)
The Girl at the Lunch Counter (1913)
A Gentleman of Fashion (1913)
The Fortune (1913)
The Feudists (1913)
Cupid's Hired Man (1913)
Bunny's Dilemma (1913)
Bunny's Birthday Surprise (1913)
Bunny as a Reporter (1913)
Bunny and the Bunny Hug (1913)
The Brown's Study Astrology (1913)
Love's Old Dream (1914)
Polishing Up (1914)
Bunny's Birthday (1914)
Love, Luck and Gasoline (1914)
A Train of Incidents (1914)
Pigs Is Pigs (1914)
The Honeymooners (1914)

Bunny's Little Brother (1914)
The Vases of Hymen (1914)
Tangled Tagoists (1914)
Such a Hunter (1914)
Private Bunny (1914)
The Old Maid's Baby (1914)
The Old Firehouse and the New Fire Chief (1914)
Mr. Bunny in Disguise (1914)
The Locked House (1914)
Hearts and Diamonds (1914)
Father's Flirtation (1914)
A Change in Baggage Checks (1914)
Bunny's Swell Affair (1914)
Bunny's Scheme (1914)
Bunny's Mistake (1914)
Bunny Buys a Hat for His Bride (1914)
Bunny Buys a Harem (1914)
Bunny Backslides (1914)
The Jarrs Visit Arcadia (1915)

Chapter 5
Francis X. Bushman

Years before the women of America sighed over film idols like John Barrymore and Richard Barthelmess, Francis X. Bushman was a star adored by women from the darkness of early nickelodeons before he ever made a motion picture. Having been a leading man on Broadway and a renowned sculptor's model, Francis was known as the "handsomest man in the world." His story is a remarkable circle of life, climbing the road of motion picture fame to the pinnacle, followed by the near loss of his film career, and a later resurgence establishing him as a silent movie icon.

His life began on January 10, 1883. His mother, Mary Josephine Bushman, and his father, John Henry Bushman, lived in Baltimore, Maryland at the time their son Francis Xavier was born. He was one of their twelve children.

Young Francis attended eight years of school and studied at Ammendale College in Baltimore. His father wished for him to enter the medical profession, but Francis discovered his love of the theater overshadowed the tedium of schooling.

In 1902, at the age of eighteen, he married Josephine Flauduene. The young couple had five children in nine years. His wife worked as a seamstress while he struggled to find work in the theater. With five children to feed, jobs were an urgent necessity for Francis. In 1907, he took a variety of roles with the George Fawcett stock company and experienced his first taste of the theater. He loved exhibiting himself before the public, and would remain engaged in this endeavor for the rest of his life.

The film business had been taking the country by storm as early as 1903, when G. M. Anderson played several roles in the motion

The famous profile of Francis X. Bushman, ca. 1918.

picture, *The Great Train Robbery*, for the Edison Company. The film's success was a phenomenon, and led to Anderson assuming the role of "Bronco Billy" in dozens of films for the competing Vitagraph Company. These early films were shown in nickelodeons springing up in storefronts all over the world. These little film theaters all but brought an end to the neighborhood live theaters in most American cities at the same time Francis was trying to find work.

While Francis made his initial foray into the world of the theater, new motion picture companies were springing up to meet the demands of exhibitors. William N. Selig formed the Selig Company, and in 1907, when "Bronco Billy" Anderson left Vitagraph, he met Selig's partners, George Klein and George K. Spoor. Together, they formed a new company with a name derived from their initials, S and A. The Essanay Film Manufacturing Company was founded from this association.

Struggling actors often found additional money posing for artists and photographers. The Maryland Institute and the Charcoal Club in Baltimore offered fifty cents an hour to Francis to model for their artists. His finely-honed physique suited their needs, and Francis found work with other noted sculptors, including Isadore Konti and Alonzo Kimball. His likeness was chiseled in stone and forged in bronze in many illustrious statues during the years of 1905 through 1908, while he took small roles in various East Coast stage productions.

Francis first appeared on Broadway in *The Queen of the Moulin Rouge* at the Circle Theater in New York on December 7, 1908. The play was a big success, and ran for 160 performances. He also took a leading role at the Belasco Theater in the Shuberts' production, *Going Some*. Once this play closed, he was again searching for work.

He found modeling jobs with photographers who sent his images into motion picture theaters by way of song slides. Early nickelodeon operators projected lantern slides onto their film screens to entertain their audiences while they changed reels. Some of these slides featured lyrics to popular songs of the day, and were illustrated by models posing in scenes reflecting the theme of the song. Francis found he could earn some extra money posing anonymously for these lantern slides.

As he modeled for sculptors and photographers, Francis learned to angle his chiseled profile appropriately and strike poses that showed his six-foot physique and wavy brown hair attractively. Photographs of him in scanty costumes adorned the cabinets of his growing legion of women fans. While playing *The Bishops Carriage* on the stage in Philadelphia, Francis attracted the attention of Richard Foster Baker from the pioneering Essanay film company, and made his first film for them in 1911. *His Friend's Wife* was released on June 3, 1911. Francis played an artist discarding his wife. The jilted woman marries his best friend, and when the artist and former wife meet again in a dramatic scene, the artist suddenly dies of a heart ailment.

"We averaged a picture a week. This is inconceivable today," Francis later reflected in several interviews. "They didn't even turn off the studio lights between pictures. I would just change my costume and go right into a new role . . . ." With the burgeoning film industry came a tidal wave of movie magazines feeding photos and interviews to the anxious fans that were curious about their favorite stars. Other memorabilia included postcards, commemorative spoons, posters, and postage stamps. The likenesses of Francis appeared in all of these, and in a short time, his popularity reached stellar heights.

He was a favorite romantic idol of women in these early films. Essanay paired him with Dorothy Phillips for a number of his pictures made during 1911 and 1912. Then, a woman who would change the course of his life crossed his path.

Pearl Beverly Bayne, a pretty schoolgirl, went on a tour of the Essanay Film Company with one of her friends. She took along some photographs to show to the head director, Henry McRae Webster. He liked her youthful, innocent face so much that he asked the girl to return a few days later and take part in a ballroom scene for a film being produced that week. They later invited her to return the following week, and then offered her a contract to work. Within a few months, Essanay teamed Beverly with Francis in *A Good Catch*. The 1912 film began Francis' obsession with Beverly. He found he could work easily with her, and often asked the company to put her in roles opposite him. In time, their casual and professional relationship took on another dimension.

Essanay fully realized what an asset it had with Francis. His sturdy physique and classic profile were frequently put to good use in adventures and costume melodramas. He wore a wide variety of dashing costumes, looked equally well in a top hat and tails, and cut a fine figure in many society dramas.

Gloria Swanson, another of Essanay's big stars at that time, recalled in her autobiography, *Swanson on Swanson*. "Mr. Bushman wore a large violet amethyst ring on his finger and he had a spotlight inside his lavender car that illuminated his famous profile when he drove after dark. Everybody at Essanay knew he was married and had five children, but to the public that was a deep dark secret. Studios felt that if word got out that stars were married and had children like ordinary people, it might destroy their image as romantic lovers." Gloria recalled the Essanay rule that male performers were not supposed to come anywhere near the women's dressing rooms, but "Francis seemed to easily find his way into Beverly Bayne's room. Whenever we heard whispering in Miss Bayne's dressing room, we always knew Mr. Bushman was breaking the rules. We would climb on our dressing tables and try to hear what was going on," Gloria later recalled.

After 135 films for Essanay, many paired with the radiant Beverly Bayne, he left to pursue greater heights. When the new Metro Company formed in 1915, Francis was one of the first stars put under contract. One stipulation in Francis' contract was that his marriage would be kept secret. The public was not to be told that their heartthrob was unavailable. When her contract with Essanay expired, Beverly followed Francis to Metro and accepted their offer of a generous contract.

Romeo and Juliet (1915) was perhaps their best film, said to be a richly textured, faithful adaptation of William Shakespeare's famous tale of the two lovers of Verona. The two stars had become firmly entrenched in the minds of moviegoers as a love team.

A five-reel comedy-drama, *Pennington's Choice,* was released in November 1915, the first Metro film pairing the passionate lovers. They made a large number of films together for the next several years, and enjoyed the public's adoration. Then, disaster struck.

Beverly Bayne and Francis X. Bushman were in love, and they unwisely sought to make real what was being shown on the screen. Their love turned lethal when Bushman divorced his wife and married Beverly Bayne on July 31, 1918.

The ensuing scandal shocked wartime audiences and tore through the media with a vengeance, wrecking both their careers. Not only was the public surprised to finally learn of Francis' marriage of

Sheet music for "One Wonderful Night" by Uriel Davis was composed as a promotional tie-in with the Francis X. Bushman and Beverly Bayne film, *One Wonderful Night* (1914).

many years, but when they learned he had divorced Josephine to marry Beverly, they were indignant. In an unexpected backlash, the public viewed their marriage as moral delinquency, and many theaters quickly banned their films. Metro responded by declining to renew either star's contract. Their final film, *God's Outlaw*, was re-edited with comedy titles and converted into a lampoon of their tainted romance. It pounded the death nail into both of their film careers.

The struggling Vitagraph studio often employed actors who could not find work elsewhere, and they paid Beverly and Francis to star in *Daring Hearts,* a 1919 film that earned generally dismal reviews and was quickly rejected by theaters.

Francis enjoyed many extravagant eccentricities: $100 tips to waiters; a lavender limousine; lavender cigarettes specially made with his name imprinted on the side; eighteen secretaries to answer his fan mail; a 280-acre estate outside Baltimore stocked with Great Danes and race horses. His pride in these trappings of fame and fortune would be short-lived.

In 1920, a film ironically titled *Smiling All the Way* again teamed Beverly and Francis in decidedly smaller roles than they had previously played. They were no longer the stars, and were forced to take what work they could find. There were fewer smiles in his personal life as well. Francis maintained an apartment with Beverly while still listing a permanent address in Baltimore with his wife, but as expenses mounted, he was compelled to sell his possessions to raise funds to pay off the hounding creditors. His extravagant lifestyle, and the expense of financing two separate lives, mounted, and Francis resorted to a return to the stage, appearing in a play called *The Master Thief* in late 1919. His fame and notoriety packed theaters with curiosity seekers, and the play toured the country well into the following year.

Beverly and Francis then toured in *Poor Rich Man* throughout 1921 in vaudeville on the Orpheum circuit. The couple enjoyed meeting their old fans with great enthusiasm wherever they appeared. For a time, it appeared they would survive the loss of their once-renowned film careers.

Francis produced a new film in 1923, aptly titled *Modern Marriage*. He and Beverly accompanied the film on a tedious exhibition schedule, interrupted in the middle of the screening so that they could cajole audiences with anecdotes and witticisms. They proceeded with the remaining half of the picture by offering a live narration to accompany the film.

Happiness failed to go together with Beverly and Francis during these stormy years. Their self-touted, mutual adoration began to wane, even after a son was born to the couple. Beverly kept a pensive calm over the loss of her film career, though she had been through an emotional, downward spiral. She had painfully acquired a measure of wisdom out of the debacle, despite the disappointing reception to *Modern Marriage*. Both Beverly and Francis had received some offers to appear alone, but as a couple, motion picture producers no longer wanted them. Their glory days were over.

In March 1924, MGM announced that Francis was to play the villain, Messala, in their new production of *Ben-Hur*. Beverly realized she would have to break with her onscreen teaming with Francis or face unemployment in motion pictures. She began to search for solo roles.

In the same year, she signed with Warner Bros. for a film ironically titled *Her Marriage Vow*. Monte Blue, not Francis, would be her co-star in this production. The studio put her into two more films the same year, *The Tenth Woman* and *The Age of Innocence*. In January 1925, she announced their separation, and on April 17 she cited the often-used cause of desertion, and quietly filed for a divorce. One of Hollywood's greatest romances and onscreen love teams ended without excitement. Beverly left the film capital, and she stayed away for the next seven years, appearing in vaudeville, taking care of her child, and tending to the needs of her ailing mother.

Francis began preparations for the role of a lifetime. The original *Ben-Hur* novel by General Lew Wallace had broken all publishing records, apart from the Bible, and it was the first fictional manuscript blessed by the Pope. For religious reasons, the author steadfastly refused all offers for the sale of his work for dramatizations. During its first nine years in print, two men doggedly persisted in their efforts to obtain the stage rights. Mark Klaw and Abraham Erlanger finally got the General to relent, and opened a production on Broadway in November 1899. It was staged on an immense scale for nearly a year, complete with a simulated chariot race performed by horses galloping on treadmills. In this stage production, years before he ventured into motion pictures, William S. Hart played the role of Messala, the central villain in the story.

After General Wallace died, his son controlled the literary property, and he was against any screen presentation of his father's work. Every major company had bid for the motion picture rights. Abraham Erlanger formed the Classical Cinematograph Corporation solely for the purpose of acquiring the screen rights for exploitation. Once accomplished, he posted the story for sale at the increased price of one million dollars.

In 1922, the Goldwyn Company purchased the motion picture rights from Erlanger with an unprecedented arrangement involving a percentage of profit rather than money up front. Goldwyn settled into the challenge of adapting the massive tome into silent motion pictures, and entrusted the task to the proven talents of the accomplished screenwriter, June Mathis. Her first decree was to insist that the film be made on location in Italy. Her second battle was the casting of the central character. Contenders lined up for the coveted role, and after many screen tests, no one involved in the production could agree on a choice.

Goldwyn had a roster of handsome males already under contract, and dutifully tested Ben Lyon, Allan Forrest, William Desmond, Ramon Novarro, Edmund Lowe, Robert Frazer, John Bowers, and Antonio Moreno. Other actors at other studios also auditioned. The search was taking them so long to arrive at a final decision that some Hollywood insiders began jokingly betting the ultimate choice would end up being Jackie Coogan, a popular child star of the day, who would grow to young manhood by the time the film would begin production.

The only casting they did agree on was that of Francis in the role of Messala, the villain of the story. The actor had never played anything but a hero, and he feared taking the role of a villain. He sought out William S. Hart, who had played Messala in the original Broadway production, for advice. Hart told Francis the role of the villain was the best part in the show, and encouraged him to take the part and run with it.

Francis took Hart's advice, and soon sailed to Rome to begin filming *Ben-Hur,* a film that for him would be a remarkable "comeback," and for MGM, a heroic fiasco that would evolve into a brilliant victory.

Francis X. Bushman in his comeback role as Messala in *Ben-Hur* (1925).

When he arrived in Rome, he was surprised to learn that the production was far from ready to begin. Francis took the opportunity to take his sister on a tour of Europe. The pre-production efforts took so long, he was able to visit twenty-five countries before he was required to return to the location in Rome and begin his work.

The producers finally decided on George Walsh for the title role of Ben-Hur. He arrived in Rome and was shocked to find that he was kept in the background and virtually ignored. He learned he would not be needed for any actual filming for some time, and then settled into a long wait.

Walsh found everyone's attention was scrambling around the construction of the boats for the huge sea battle scene and the enormous Circus Maximus set where the climactic chariot race was to take place. Director Charles Brabin had his time consumed dealing with the frustration of working with the Italian labor force that spoke no English.

Weeks of inactivity passed without a foot of film shot. Finally, after many difficult delays attempting to float vessels that met with the exacting requirements of the Italian government, the production began with the filming of the sea battle. Ben-Hur was to languish in chains as a slave in the galleys. The epic sea fight was staged on the shores of Anzio, with reels of film taken from many angles. After the expensive effort, production heads screened the footage taken by Brabin and found it fraught with unprofessional details, including awful makeup and terrible wigs.

After being off the screen for nearly two years while waiting for his work to commence, George Walsh had not yet appeared in any film shot for *Ben-Hur,* although a number of production stills showed him in full costume. As the producers began to reorganize the runaway production, Walsh was abruptly replaced with Ramon Novarro, a promising new star that Louis B. Mayer was trying to build up as a box office attraction. Francis was retained as Messala, as were most of the actors hired for secondary characters.

Further changes erupted when director Charles Brabin was fired. He promptly filed suit for $583,000 in damages, claiming he had been denied the needed equipment to properly do the job and forced to work in conditions of chaos and futility.

Complications also took place back in Hollywood. Louis B. Mayer's company was merging with the Goldwyn and the Metro companies. Once accomplished, control of the *Ben-Hur* project was transferred to Mayer and Irving Thalberg.

Fred Niblo replaced Charles Brabin as director. New ships were built to replace the cheesy ones photographed in the original staging of the sea battle. On the day filming began, extras were cautioned to leap into the water in an organized manner and await dinghies standing by to pick them up. According to director Niblo, "We had about 2,800 men in the sea scrap and as many as 300 galley slaves on one of the vessels." Twenty-eight cameras were positioned on the vessels, on the decks of the dozens small vessels floating further out at sea, mounted on sixty-foot towers on the shore, and others on the decks of the large boats.

At the director's signal, the battle began. The pirate ship sailed through the water on its course to ram into the side of the Roman ship filled with galley slaves. At the moment of impact, the Italian extras panicked. To make matters worse, the carefully timed flames were suddenly blown by unexpected winds to ferocious levels, and quickly spread through the entire ship. The extras forgot their safety instructions, and madly scrambled over the side into the water. Those wearing armor sank helplessly into the waves. Their screams could be heard all the way to the beach at Anzio. The director ordered the cameras to keep rolling.

"I heard their cries for help," Francis later recalled. "I said to Niblo, 'My God, Fred, they're drowning, I tell you!'"

"'I can't help it,' he yelled back. 'Those ships cost me $40,000 apiece!'"

By nightfall, there were three extras unaccounted for. According to Kevin Brownlow in his book, *The Parade's Gone By*, other cast members differed as to the casualty rate. The Italian authorities investigated the spreading rumors about the loss of human lives, and threatened to arrest the director. Fred Niblo was spirited away to Rome and narrowly avoided their wrath while the investigation officially took place.

Later, additional scenes were shot under tense circumstances. The construction of the Coliseum set had stretched from a seven-week schedule into a seven-month ordeal. By that time the autumn

(Top) George Walsh, the original actor playing the title role in *Ben-Hur* (1925), facing Francis X. Bushman as Messala. (Bottom) Ramon Novarro, the actor playing Ben-Hur in the final film, facing Francis X. Bushman as Messala.

season had arrived, lighting conditions changed, and it became impossible to avoid the long shadows cast by the low angle of the sun. Some moments of the great chariot race were staged in spite of this obstacle, with many injuries to both horses and men. After all the time and expense, most of the footage obtained was unusable. Irving Thalberg finally called a halt to the production after a fire swept through a property warehouse.

Though far from complete, the film had already arranged bookings back in America. Sid Grauman contracted for a one-year booking at his Egyptian Theater in Los Angeles, and the Knickerbocker Theater had leased a two-year showing in New York. MGM had spent more than $3 million on the project and exposed about a million feet of film before writing off much of the Italian experience. They determined to complete the production in Los Angeles. They concluded the only course of action was to cut their losses, scrap all the footage, restage the sea battle, and start over again under strict controls. They shut down production, and moved the entire cast back to California. Cedric Gibbons and A. Arnold Gillespie designed a new Circus Maximus set, and it was built on a lot in Culver City. After four months, the great chariot race was again set to take place on home ground.

Ramon Novarro and Francis X. Bushman in the chariot race from *Ben-Hur* (1925).

Thousands of people filled the Circus Maximus, including many of Hollywood's biggest directors and stars. They took seats as extras, eager to see and participate in the most spectacular scene of this epoch-making motion picture. Some 10,000 extras were on hand in costumes, beards, and wigs by 9:00 o'clock that morning when they took their positions in the vast amphitheater. Adolph Seidel, chief costumer of the MGM studio, organized an army of costumers, wig and hair experts, and armor specialists to prepare the legions of performers. Batteries of cameras were mounted and ready.

The Culver City police force was on hand to help guard the scene, the City of Los Angeles sent a reserve force, and the U.S. Army came to the aid with a hundred soldiers. Troop B of the 11th Cavalry lent fifty-four men with their horses and equipment under the command of Captain Adamson and Lieutenant Sand to ride into the arena as Roman Imperial Guard members during one of the first sections filmed. After this was done, these men quickly changed costumes, and reappeared as buglers.

Forty-two cameramen were concealed in positions to capture the event from every effective angle possible. Dozens of assistant directors were hired to control sections of the huge crowd on cues. Forty-eight horses were waiting to charge around the track in a race with twelve chariots driven by Francis X. Bushman, Ramon Novarro, and various stunt drivers. The director demanded a no-punches-pulled race, and offered a money incentive to insure a hell-for-leather effort.

In the stands, many people were rushing to and from their seats to the betting corner. Hundreds of wagers were recorded, even though they knew that story had the race stacked in favor of Ben-Hur.

Director Niblo mounted a 100-foot tower and stood beside his chief assistant and head cameraman to shout orders through his megaphone. The chief assistant relayed these orders over a loudspeaker system to each of the dozens of assistants in the various sections of the arena. William Wyler, later to direct the sound version of *Ben-Hur* several decades later, was one of these assistant directors.

At the sound of the starting signal, an astonishing display took place. The twelve chariots began racing around the track while the crowd reacted with intense excitement. One horse lost his shoe in the tumult, sending the projectile hurling past a camera and narrowly missing spectators. A second race brought a sensational pile up toppling six chariots and twenty-four horses that was captured on film. Later, director Niblo vehemently asserted the crash and pile up were not prearranged. He told reporters, "And some people will think that this scene is cruel to the animals. To blot out that idea, let me say that every horse and every man who figured in this accident was employed fifteen minutes later."

Francis gave his own account to reporters some years later, "I know for a fact five horses were killed in that one crash alone." Francis raced past the cameras more than forty times while straddling his rocking chariot, lashing a whip, and gripping the reins with all his strength.

At the end of the day, according to the director in an interview with the *New York Times*, MGM had shot more than 53,000 feet of negative, part of the million feet of film used for the whole film. Niblo said one reason was that the producers had decided to have four negatives instead of the usual two.

When the footage was later screened, Louis B. Mayer was outraged at what he saw. He accused Francis of scene stealing. He tore into the actor for upstaging his protégé, Ramon Novarro, and ordered him to stop attracting so much attention to himself. The fact that when Francis was on the screen his mere presence made other actors pale by comparison seemed not to matter to Mayer, who wanted only to promote Novarro.

Filming continued long after the crowds left. For weeks afterward, the crew bore in for the many close details of the race—lashing whips, flaring manes, flexing muscles, racing wheels, and the reaction shots of Ramon Novarro and Francis X. Bushman.

The final edit of the chariot race used only 750 feet of the tens of thousands of feet of film amassed. The sequence was one of the most awe-inspiring ever filmed. It was well worth the long wait.

Ben-Hur opened on December 30, 1925. The *New York Times* reviewed the film on January 6, 1925:

> "There will be no further reason for a future production of *Ben-Hur* for the screen, unless there is some tremendous change in the art of visualization of the dramatic that is as yet unrealized.

Then and only then, providing that there is some tremendous advancement in the art of direction and photography, will another *Ben-Hur* be necessary. As the industry today stands, so does *Ben-Hur* stand; the greatest accomplishment on the screen for not only the screen itself, but for all motion picturedom.

"The word 'epic' has been applied to pictures time and again, but at the time that it was utilized there was no *Ben-Hur*, therefore you can scrap all the 'epics' that have been shown prior to the arrival of *Ben-Hur* and start a new book. This is the 'epic' of motion picture achievement to date and don't let anybody tell you otherwise.

"It isn't a picture! It's the Bible! And as does all literature as to fundamental plot come from the Bible, so does this picture above all pictures come from the same source.

"*Ben-Hur* is a picture that rises above spectacle, even though it is spectacle. When produced as a play the great Chariot Race scene was relied on to carry the play. On the screen it isn't the Chariot Race or the great battle scenes between the fleet of Rome and the pirate galleys of Golthar, which after all are the most tremendous scenes of this ilk that have ever been portrayed, that carry the great thrills. It is the tremendous heart throbs that one experiences leading to those scenes that make them great. *Ben-Hur* will go down the ages of the picture industry to mark an epoch in its progress, an event that swung the tidal wave of humanity to the screen, and the miracle picture that will convert the most skeptical. Francis X. Bushman does a comeback in the role of the heavy (Messala) that makes him stand alone. Don't let 'Bushy' ever go back to the heroic stuff. He can land in that, but if he will stick to heavies there is no doubt but with this background he will be the heavy of all times. *Ben-Hur's* force is its religion and it's a tremendous force. This MGM picture could well have been called 'The Birth of Religion' in a subtitle had its sponsors a desire to bring forth that side, which they have not. But it will speak for itself. *Ben-Hur* is the greatest single thing for religion, for the theater, for the church, for the stage and screen, and for the masses, high and low, ever uttered."

In another article, the *New York Times* said, "It is probably the most comprehensive and important spectacular subject that has ever been filmed. One of the unforgettable incidents in this production is the thrilling chariot race, in which one perceives the teams of horses crashing together and for a fraction of a second piled up in the arena, a mass struggling to get apart. The vehicles are smashed and the wheels either go spinning or are broken in twain; there are glimpses of the horses riding pell-mell for the audience, disappearing in the darkness of the theater. Then one also sees the long shots down on the arena in which the people look like flies and the chariots with their mighty teams of four horses look like nutshells being pulled by mice. This film version of General Lew Wallace's story shows the advance in picture artistry and also in production technique. It causes one to think that nothing much is beyond the ken of the cameraman."

Francis' troubles with Louis B. Mayer were not over. Mayer turned red-faced with anger one night when he attempted to come backstage where Francis was appearing in a Los Angeles play, *Midsummer Masquerade*. A new butler Francis had recently employed turned him away. Mayer flew into one of his tyrannical rages over the unintentional snub, and shortly after, Francis found himself "blacklisted" by all film studios. "I was there receiving people and Louie at that time was one of my dearest friends," Francis remembered. "Later, he told me, amid obscenities, that I would never work in Hollywood again. People today can't believe that a man could be that powerful, but he was. For the next twenty-five years, I worked only on the stage or radio." Ironically, it was Francis who helped launch Mayer in the movie business. "He was a distributor in Boston and he wanted to produce movies," Francis later recollected. "He came to me begging, saying that if I would agree to star in his first movie, the banks would give him a loan. I did, and Mayer started on the road to becoming the most powerful tycoon in Hollywood."

Despite Mayer's ban on hiring Francis, Universal put him into a series of pictures beginning in 1926. First National Pictures cast him in *The Lady in Ermine* (1927), and even MGM hired him to play George Washington in a two-reel film about the making of the American flag. *The Flag* was released on September 14, 1927.

Disaster again struck Francis when he lost most of his $6 million fortune in the 1929 stock market crash. He was forced to file a bankruptcy petition showing he was more than $100,000 in debt.

He continued to work into the 1930s in a number of films, including his talkie debut in *The Call of the Circus*. After five more sound films, Francis played in a fifteen-episode serial, *Dick Tracy*, as Anderson, the Chief of Police. MGM again hired him for a small role in *Thoroughbreds Don't Cry* (1937) with Judy Garland and Mickey Rooney. Francis had several other lesser film roles during the 1940s and 1950s.

Later in life, innumerable roles on radio, and dozens of parts in television and low-budget films kept him before the public. In 1960, he played in Fred Gebhardt's drive-in film, *12 to the Moon*. The film made money, and Francis enjoyed delivering a stalwart performance as the Secretary General of the International Space Order, in the story about an ill-fated voyage to the moon.

In 1961, in a shabby building at Producers Studio, Francis took a starring role in a science-fiction picture, *The Phantom Planet*. The seventy-six-year-old actor played Sesom, which is Moses spelled backwards. Another role in a film targeted for the teenage market followed: *The Ghost in the Invisible Bikini* (1966).

In 1966, Francis was engaged as a official greeter by Caesars Palace for the first three days of festivities celebrating the formal opening of the $25-million-dollar Las Vegas Palace luxury hotel.

At an age when most people were put out to pasture, Francis found a whole new career available to him in teenage movies. This new start came after Darryl F. Zanuck broke the barrier imposed by Louis B. Mayer that prevented him from working in films. The then eighty-two-year-old actor completed work in *Bikini Party in a Haunted House* for American-International. "In my next picture I will costar with Fabian. It's a great life. Bring on the girls with the bikinis!" he told James Bacon from Associated Press. When asked to what he owed his still-handsome appearance, Francis answered, "Excess."

Francis X. Bushman and his son, Francis X., Jr., in 1927, as they were both working on separate films at Universal Studios.

As a silver-haired, great-grandfather, Francis never let age slow him down. For a brief time, he operated a café, and later owned a Chicago liquor store. He kept busy with a round of personal appearances judging cooking shows, presenting an award on the Academy Awards show, attending film premiers, making personal appearances at movie theater openings, and appearing in roles on television. He had reestablished himself as the courtly master-of-ceremonies of a late-night movie show on a local television station. He had appeared as a villain in the *Batman* television series, and had completed an assignment on the television series, *Voyage to the Bottom of the Sea*. Francis planned to return to films in his first Western, *Huntsville*, to be made at Paramount.

Recalling his earlier success, Francis thought back and said years later, "Once in pictures I was on the Main Line. I raced always with abandon. There were thrills, hills, curves, and ecstasy. It was glorious."

Looking back on his career decline, Francis remarked with a sense of humor, "I was unknown and on a side road, picking my way through villages and hamlets, a genuine Via Dolorosa. Once a man like myself begins to slip there are kicks, bludgeons, blows. I have no regrets. People look on me as a legend. It's pretty nice to be a legend and alive."

Commenting on the changing styles of screen acting, Francis had no apologies for the visual style with which he worked. "Nowadays, people say without changing expressions, 'Hello, dear, Mother's dead.' In the old days we gave it lots of feeling, breast-beating, and arm-waving." He was highly amused when watching a rerun on television of one of his earliest films. "When my face flashed on the screen, I laughed so hard I cried. I said, 'Look at that. I'm putting all of my emotions in my jaw!'"

One Sunday morning in August 1966, Francis suffered a fall in his Pacific Palisades home, injuring his shoulder and hip as he stepped from the bathtub. A few days later, he slipped in the kitchen while making a cup of coffee, struck his head on a cupboard, and lost consciousness. His wife summoned police, but officers arrived to find him dead. An ambulance crew was summoned, and he was pronounced dead at the scene. A coroner's autopsy indicated, ". . . his death was due to a rupture of the heart." He was eighty-three years old.

When newspaper headlines around the world mourned his passing in 1966, many young people asked, "Who was Francis X. Bushman?" Charlton Heston, then-president of the Screen Actors Guild, and who had played the title role in the sound remake of *Ben-Hur*, said, "His passing marks the fall of one of the landmarks of Hollywood history. He represented all that was best in the tradition of Hollywood as well as one of his own profession."

Silent Filmography of
Francis X. Bushman

His Friend's Wife (1911)
The Rosary (1911)
God's Inn by the Sea (1911)
Her Dad the Constable (1911)
The New Manager (1911)
The Gordian Knot (1911)
Fate's Funny Frolic (1911)
The Dark Romance of a Tobacco Tin (1911)
The Burglarized Burglar (1911)
Live, Love and Believe (1911)
Saved from the Torrents (1911)
Lost Years (1911)
A False Suspicion (1911)
Bill Bumper's Bargain (1911)
He Fought for the U.S.A. (1911)
The Madman (1911)
The Goodfellow's Christmas Eve (1911)
The Mail Order Wife (1912)
The Count and the Cowboys (1912)
Alias Billy Sargent (1912)
The Melody of Love (1912)
Tracked Down (1912)
The Little Black Box (1912)
Out of the Depths (1912)
At the End of the Trail (1912)
The Laurel Wreath of Fame (1912)
Lonesome Robert (1912)
The Rivals (1912)
Napatia, the Greek Singer (1912)
Out of the Night (1912)
The Eye That Never Sleeps (1912)
A Good Catch (1912)
The Mis-Sent Letter (1912)
The Passing Shadow (1912)
The Return of William Marr (1912)

Billy and the Butler (1912)
The Butterfly Net (1912)
White Roses (1912)
Signal Lights (1912)
The Understudy (1912)
Her Hour of Triumph (1912)
The New Church Organ (1912)
The Old Wedding Dress (1912)
An Adamless Eden (1912)
The Magic Wand (1912)
The Hermit of Lonely Gulch (1912)
Twilight (1912)
The Fall of Montezuma (1912)
Neptune's Daughter (1912)
The Voice of Conscience (1912)
The End of the Feud (1912)
The Warning Hand (1912)
Chains (1912)
When Wealth Torments (1912)
House of Pride (1912)
The Penitent (1912)
The Iron Heel (1912)
The Virtue of Rags (1912)
When Soul Meets Soul (1912)
Daydream of a Photoplay Artist (1912)
The Romance of the Dells (1912)
The Trade Gun Bullet (1912)
The Farmer's Daughter (1913)
The Thirteenth Man (1913)
The Discovery (1913)
A Mistaken Accusation (1913)
The Pathway of Years (1913)
Spy's Defeat (1913)
Let No Man Put Asunder (1913)
A Brother's Loyalty (1913)
The Power of Conscience (1913)
The Whip Hand (1913)
Sunlight (1913)

The Right of Way (1913)
For Old Time's Sake (1913)
Tony Antoine the Fiddler (1913)
The Way Perilous (1913)
The Toll of the Marshes (1913)
The Woman Scorned (1913)
The Little Substitute (1913)
The Stigma (1913)
Hearts and Flowers (1914)
The Hour and the Man (1914)
Through the Storm (1914)
The Girl at the Curtain (1914)
Dawn and Twilight (1914)
The Other Girl (1914)
Shadows (1914)
The Three Scratch Clue (1914)
In the Moon's Ray (1914)
A Man for A'That (1914)
The Spirit of the Madonna (1914)
The Mystery of Room 643 (1914)
Ashes of Hope (1914)
Mongrel and Master (1914)
The Voice in the Wilderness (1914)
Blood Will Tell (1914)
The Elder Brother (1914)
The Countess (1914)
Finger Prints (1914)
Trinkets of Tragedy (1914)
A Night with a Million (1914)
His Stolen Fortune (1914)
Night Hawks (1914)
One Wonderful Night (1914)
The Motor Buccaneers (1914)
Ambushed (1914)
The Masked Wrestler (1914)
Under Royal Patronage (1914)
Sparks of Fate (1914)
The Plum Tree (1914)

A Splendid Dishonor (1914)
In the Glare of the Lights (1914)
The Other Man (1914)
The Private Officer (1914)
An Unplanned Elopement (1914)
The Prince Party (1914)
Scars of Possession (1914)
Every Inch a King (1914)
The Fable of the Bush League Lover Who Failed to Qualify (1914)
The Battle of Love (1914)
Any Woman's Choice (1914)
The Shanty at Trembling Hill (1914)
The Gallantry of Jimmie Rodgers (1915)
The Ambition of the Baron (1915)
Thirteen Down (1915)
The Accounting (1915)
Stars and Their Courses Change (1915)
The Great Silence (1915)
The Return of Richard Neal (1915)
Thirty (1915)
Graustark (1915)
The Slim Princess (1915)
Providence and Mrs. Urmy (1915)
The Second in Command (1915)
The Silent Voice (1915)
Pennington's Choice (1915)
The Man Without a Conscience (1915)
Pigeon Island (1915)
Richard Carvell (1915)
To the End of the World (1915)
The Yellow Dove (1915)
Man and His Soul (1916)
The Wall Between (1916)
A Million a Minute (1916)
A Virginia Romance (1916)
In the Diplomatic Service (1916)
Romeo and Juliet (1916)

Boots and Saddles (1916)
The Bribe (1916)
The Red Mouse (1916)
The Great Secret (1917)
National Association's All-Star Picture (1917)
Their Compact (1917)
The Adopted Son (1917)
The Voice of Conscience (1917)
Red, White and Blue Blood (1917)
Voice of One (1917)
Under Suspicion (1918)
The Brass Check (1918)
With Neatness and Dispatch (1918)
Cyclone Higgins, D.D. (1918)
Social Quicksands (1918)
A Pair of Cupids (1918)
The Poor Rich Man (1918)
Gay and Festive Claverhouse (1918)
God's Outlaw (1919)
Daring Hearts (1919)
Smiling All the Way (1920)
Modern Marriage (1923)
The Masked Bride (1925)
Ben-Hur (1925)
The Marriage Clause (1926)
The Lady in Ermine (1927)
The Thirteenth Juror (1927)
The Flag (1927)
The Grip of the Yukon (1928)
Say It with Sables (1928)
Midnight Life (1928)
The Charge of the Gauchos (1928)

Chapter 6
Lon Chaney

The amazing career of the mystery man of the screen cannot be sketched in simple lines. As a motion picture star, he followed none of the rules. He was not handsome or young; he shunned publicity; he did not answer fan mail; he was aloof and inarticulate. Against the general Hollywood crowd, he was as an individual like a cliff against the sky, and as distinctive as black thunder looming over a harvest field.

To pull the mask off Lon Chaney is to reveal an actor many regarded as having the greatest pantomime skills in silent films. In 1927, he liked to say, "There is no Lon Chaney. There is only the character I am creating."

Lon was born in Colorado Springs, Colorado, on April Fools Day, 1883, the son of deaf and dumb parents. When most people talked happily about their childhoods, Lon merely recounted, "I had to work hard, but I had time enough to play football."

From his maternal grandmother, Emma Kennedy, Lon inherited his greatest gift: stamina that defeats failure. Life tried to break Emma Kennedy. She was a healthy and brilliant woman struggling to raise two daughters and a son. Each of those children was born without the faculty to speak or hear. This misfortune of fate would have been enough to fell most women, but not Emma. From her embracement of the circumstances that fettered her own life, she founded the Deaf and Blind Institute of Colorado, becoming a symbol of protection and love for a host of other similarly afflicted people, and she shepherded all of them to maturity.

Emma's oldest daughter married Hugh Harbert, a kind man who aided in the work at the institute. He served as editor of the paper

A portrait of Lon Chaney, ca. 1918.

they put out for years, the *Colorado Deaf and Blind Index*. Her youngest daughter married a kindly man, mute as she was. Lon was the second child born to the couple. Their eldest son, John, preceded Lon, and two other children, George and Caroline, followed. All four children were perfectly normal, healthy youths.

Lon's stern lines of character were carved by the difficult, young life he endured. By the age of ten, his mother suffered the worst blow that could have fallen upon her. She was stricken with inflammatory rheumatism and was locked powerless in its grip. Her hands, which had prepared the family meals and conserved their income, were also her ears and tongue. For three years, she was to be unable to use them.

His parents' afflictions separated the Chaney children from others boys and girls. Lon knew the cruel honesty so carelessly flung by playing children. The aloofness he came to enjoy as a man began while he was still in grade school.

While his brother had a job, Lon took the responsibility of coming home from school to care for his mother. He was her nurse, her confidant, and her jester. He communicated with her by way of pantomime, developing the very gestures that the public later enjoyed seeing on the screen. His skillful hand use was the byproduct of the tenderness he learned while taking care of his mother. He learned to talk to her so that she could comprehend his every word. He learned to read her innermost thoughts, though she could not communicate them to him by sign or sound. From her, Lon gained a complete knowledge of expression without words, expression with subtle facial change. Also from her, he learned tenderness, sensitiveness, and understanding.

Lon dropped out of school, and for months, he swept, cooked, dusted, and baked. Every penny his brothers and his father could earn went into the medicines that promised to cure his mother.

As devoted as he was, when his younger brother and sister were old enough to assume responsibility for his mother, Lon left home with an aim to become completely self-supporting. He stumbled through the early years of adolescence attempting to adjust to the differences between things dreamed and truths realized.

He got his first job while in his teens, working from June through September as a tour guide on Colorado's Pike's Peak. Every morning, he set out with a crowd mounted on burros, and led them up 14,000 feet above the sea to the summit where the sunrise greeted his patrons. An hour later, he guided the satisfied spectators downward to eat lunch. He loved the job so much that he hated to see the winter's shroud of snow encase the mountain, bringing to a halt the exuberant elation he felt while on top of the mountain.

His brother was the house manager of a local Grand Opera. When the tourist season ended on Pike's Peak, he secured a position for his younger brother as a prop boy. There, Lon glimpsed the radiance of Richard Mansfield and other stars of the day, as they came through town in various plays. During breathless moments when Mansfield was making up for one of his famous character studies, Lon slipped away from his work and watched through a crack in the dressing room door, his eyes glued on every move made by the great actor. As Mansfield swaggered in as Beau Brummell or slunk along as Ivan the Terrible, the property boy took in everything, and his receptive brain remembered. Lon knew how Mansfield looked before he sat down in front of his mirror, and through that heaven-sent crack in the dressing room door, the property boy could see Mansfield gradually fading away from himself and into one of his roles. Unknowingly, Mansfield served as the future screen star's teacher of disguises. Roles, for which he would later become renowned, could be traced back to these glimpses Lon caught of Mansfield through the crack in the dressing room door.

Later, he found work as a callboy in a mining exchange. The routine work soon left him restless, and he took up tradesman work in the carpet laying and drapery fields. He hung the drapes in the Antlers Hotel at Colorado Springs. His skill with interior decorating led to a position with Cortdez and Feldhauser, the largest drapery house in Denver. For three years, he dutifully did the work required of him. Then, his brother brought him back to the sawdust of the theater.

The local stagehands' union had an opening for a position during the run of a comic opera called *Said Pasha,* and Lon took the job. He closely observed the dancers' routines, watching closely the toes of the dancing vaudevillians. Lon was a natural dancer, and he cultivated the buck and wing, tap, and soft shoe movements he saw performed on the stage. With the perfect bliss of youthful ignorance, Lon became a song-and-dance man.

In 1901, he appeared in the chorus of Gilbert and Sullivan's *The Mikado.* A road tour of an opera called *Fra Diavolo* followed, with prima donna Mabel Day, and her husband, Leslie Stowe, headlining. Lon was listed in the program in a principal comedy role, but he also was in charge of the wardrobe and transportation. He earned $12 a week, a magnificent sum in that day for an eighteen-year-old youth.

Lon and his brother wrote a play called *The Little Tycoon,* and presented it along with other comic operas.

"By all rights, we should have gone broke," he revealed to Harry T. Brundidge, "but we didn't. I guess the town was show hungry, for we made money. After all, it wasn't such a bad little show, and the truth is that I helped John write it. So we decided to take it on the road and worked up a couple of Gilbert and Sullivan comic operas to pad out our repertoire. We played Denver and started for the coast, and then, of course, the inevitable happened, and the show went broke."

The show closed, but Lon remained with the company and toured one-night-stands in small towns located across the Midwest. His brother journeyed to California, and took a job as the stage manager of a local theater in Los Angeles.

Cleva Creighton came into his life the next year, and Lon fell in love with her. They were married on May 31, 1905, and the following year, their son, Creighton Chaney, was born.

Lon joined his brother in California, and took a job as a song-and-dance man with two popular comedians, Kolb and Dill, in their play, *45 Minutes from Broadway.* He had a comedy role in *The Rich Mr. Hoggenheimer,* and then left Kolb and Dill to join a stock company in Los Angeles for several seasons.

By 1914, his marriage to Cleva ended in divorce. The stock company in which he worked closed, and then left for a tour of China. Lon had custody of his son, and knowing the difficulties of taking care of a child on the road, he chose to stay behind.

The burgeoning movie industry offered fairly steady work for those lucky enough to chance an opportunity before the cameras. Lon got a job through his friend, Lee Moran, appearing in some slapstick comedies directed by Allen Curtis and released by Universal-Joker. At that studio, he tried many different kinds of roles, and his versatility quickly impressed producers. When Carl Laemmle opened Universal City in 1915, Lon was hired as a regular member of the studio's stock company.

By the spring of 1915, Lon had appeared in more than fifty

films. He directed a few films with J. Warren Kerrigan, and also wrote several scripts.

"Directing was easy enough, but I failed to see anything of great promise in it," he told Harry T. Brundidge. "In fact, I'd begun to figure out this picture racket to see where I could click best in it. My wife and I argued it over a number of times. I was no longer a young man. Leading men only last a few years, anyway. Screen heavies, too, go out of fashion. The big thing in pictures, I decided, was character work—different disguises, weird roles. It doesn't make any difference how old a man gets when playing these. I began to figure out tricks of make-up I'd seen in the theater . . . "

As an actor, Lon enjoyed the offbeat roles most of all. Director Joseph De Grasse gave him a part in *Hell Morgan's Girl* (1917), a story of the San Francisco earthquake, starring the popular actress Dorothy Phillips.

Variety found the movie exceptional, saying, ". . . in this instance, the scenes depicting life in Frisco just prior to the earthquake rank with the best of that sort of motion picture work. The dive stuff is so vivid that its realism is positively startling. The story is by Harvey Gates, scenario by Ida May Park, direction by Joseph De Grasse, and photography is by King Gray. Their fine work, aided by Dorothy Phillips in the leading role, supported by a company of screen artists, has made of *Hell Morgan's Girl* a feature that could stand state's righting a lot better than several that are being foisted upon exhibitors in that manner at the present time."

Lon's second wife, Hazel Hastings, insisted that he ask Universal for a raise of $10 a week above the $35 he was then getting. The studio manager, William Sistrom, refused his request, so Lon left Universal.

William S. Hart gave him a much-needed part in the Western, *Riddle Gawne* (1918). Lon portrayed Hame Bozzam, a man hunted down by Hart for murdering his brother and eloping with his sister-in-law.

His career reached a new level when George Loane Tucker made a motion picture from George M. Cohan's play, *The Miracle Man*. The story featured a character called "Frog," a fake cripple. Tucker was going to cast a contortionist in the challenging role, but Lon auditioned for the difficult impersonation, and demonstrated his idea of a crippled beggar by imitating one he had known in Chicago. He got the part, and this offbeat characterization gave Lon an opportunity to display some virtuoso acting skills.

An interesting production difficulty involved a scene in which Tom Meighan was required to cry. Meighan was unable to dissolve himself in tears, and the director began to work on him. Finally, the tears began to flow, and the director started the camera. The copious tears recorded were natural, not artifice, and the astonishing footage was cut into the finished film prints.

At the climax of the story, Tom Burke, the "Miracle Man," sets up an elaborate ruse to get people to the little village to be cured by his power. He hopes they will leave rich gifts of thanks. There is one obstacle to this success: a crippled boy who lives in the village.

His father, a scientist, will not let him go to the gathering on the grounds that such curing powers are nonsense. The boy attends, despite being told to stay away. Tom tries to distance the boy from the gathering crowd, while Frog, the fake cripple played by Lon, is set to pretend to let the "Miracle Man" cure him. Before Frog can maneuver into position to enact the fakery, the little crippled boy comes forward. Tom thinks his scheme is ruined because he will be unable to cure the little boy. Up the old pathway to the forefront crawls Frog, while the rest of the people wait behind. Frog stages his fake recovery, and rises to his feet while the amazed crowd watches. Suddenly, the cigarette drops from Tom's mouth, and the others gather around in astonishment, witnessing the little boy as he hobbles forward, drops one crutch and then the other, and runs down the path into the waiting arms of his patriarch who had forbid him to attend the miracle gathering. Then, to the utter amazement of everyone, a girl rises from her invalid chair and slowly follows him.

"The reason for its success is that it states in convincing terms what we would all like to believe, namely, that sins are forgiven, that the afflicted are comforted," said a review in *Variety*. "We cannot believe it, and yet are so anxious to believe that we will pay well to be fooled. Since Ben-Hur nothing approaching this has been seen on stage or screen, and it has Ben-Hur beaten seven ways for real sentiment."

The *New York Times* called *The Miracle Man* "an uncommonly interesting photoplay." When it premiered at the George M. Cohan

Lon Chaney in *The Miracle Man* (1919).

Theater on August 26, 1919, the anonymous reviewer wrote, "The scene where the little village cripple, thrilled by the spectacle of the false cure, casts away his crutches and walks up the path into the healer's arms is a breathless moment from which, as in the play, every atom of excitement is wrung. Unusually good work is done by Thomas Meighan, Betty Compson, and Lon Chaney in a picture which will please all movie enthusiasts and convert a few more."

The Miracle Man created two new stars: Lon Chaney and Thomas Meighan, who had been a reliable leading man since his first film in 1914. Meighan had appeared in thirty-three films before *The Miracle Man,* but this film was considered a breakthrough for him.

Lon was the perfect choice to essay the classic role of a pirate called "Pew" in Maurice Tourneur's *Treasure Island* (1920). In a duel role, he also appeared as "Merry." A review in *Variety* said the film was, ". . . wonderfully photographed and effective acted . . . ."

Two photos from the climax of Lon Chaney's lost film, *The Miracle Man* (1919).
The rest of the cast was remarkable chiefly for really villainous impersonations. If the sons of hell who roamed the Spanish Main as pirates resembled this cast, let us be duly grateful they caught Captain Kidd and his crew and hung them. Fortunately, the movement and story as well as the continually amazing Paramount photography will carry this picture over the line for big money."

The Penalty (1920) was another highly anticipated film; a melodrama featuring Lon as "Blizzard," a man deprived of the use of his legs since a boyhood accident. In the story, a doctor amputates both of the boy's legs below the knee, when he could have saved them. In addition, the same accident also caused a contusion at the base of the Blizzard's skull. In later years, the boy is left with a legacy of evildoing and a supposedly exorbitant intelligence to serve his evil purposes. He becomes the mastermind of the underworld along the Barbary Coast, and dedicates his life to planning revenge on the doctor. A subsequent operation transforms the evil in the man for good, and he weds the woman he loves. His cohorts, fearing religion has taken him over, fire the shot that destroys him. In a gripping, final scene, he utters, "I am interested in death." Seconds later, he pays "the penalty."

As the legless man in *The Penalty*, Lon labored under extreme pain, wearing a leather harness that bound the calves of his legs against his thighs. To complete the appearance of a double amputation, he walked on his knees and wore leather pads as beggars use. So convincing was Lon's characterization, when he took a bow on stage at the premier of the film at the Capital Theater on Broadway, the audience was relieved to see him able to stand at full height, and they greeted him with volleys of applause.

In 1922, First National produced *Oliver Twist,* with Lon again in heavy disguise in the role of Fagin, the old thief who trains the lost little boy for a life of crime. Lon again demonstrated his unique flair for unusual characterizations by playing Fagin as a man of wits who had no particular racial limitation.

Esther Ralston recalled in her autobiography, "In February 1922, I acquired my first personal manager, Mr. Clifford Robertson, of the Robertson-Webb Agency. He was able to get me better parts now, and in April, I was cast as Rose Maylie in *Oliver Twist,* with Lon Chaney. It was a thrill to work with that magnificent actor. He was very kind to me and used to laugh at me for sitting on the edge of my chair in eager anticipation of being called by the great director, Frank Lloyd, to do a scene."

"You must learn to relax, young lady," Chaney cautioned her. "You'll be all worn out by the time they are ready for you. Watch me, I'll show you how to relax."

"Then, Mr. Chaney would slump comfortably in his canvas chair," Esther recalled, "and, taking a small dinner bell out of his pocket, he would place it on his lap. Slowly, he would slide his left leg out in front of him, then his right leg . . . then he would drop his two arms limply at his sides, bow his head until his chin rested on his chest, and almost instantly, fall asleep. The little bell would slowly slip off his lap and fall tinkling to the floor. This would wake him up. Mr. Chaney explained that the one moment of complete relaxation he enjoyed in this fashion would keep him alert and ready to give his best performance all day. It was a trick I gratefully used all through my career."

Lon's portrayal of Fagin won most of the critical acclaim, although the film was intended to be a starring vehicle for Jackie Coogan. Frank Lloyd's excellent direction and the photography ably captured the mood of the pirate caves in true Dickens style.

Worldwide recognition finally came to Lon in 1923 after decades of work in theater and films. *The Hunchback of Notre Dame* offered a bizarre opportunity to amaze audiences with his masterful acting and makeup skill.

Universal and director Wallace Worsley painstakingly recreated the Cathedral of Notre Dame as a setting for the famous tale of Esmerelda and Quasimodo. Lon faithfully recreated a detailed portrait of the hunchback by following Victor Hugo's descriptions in the original book. His disguise consisted of a breastplate covered with skin and chest hair attached to shoulder pads with a rubber hump. The contrivance weighed about seventy pounds, and was attached to the harness in such a way as to restrict the actor from standing upright. A skin-tight, rubber suit affixed with animal hair completed the illusion of deformity. For his head, a wig of matted, filthy hair hung horribly about his face, which was misshapen with protruding cheeks and fang-like false teeth. On one eye, he applied a shell, which he covered with flesh-colored material.

The *New York Times* said of his work in this film, "As the central figure in the film conception of Victor Hugo's *The Hunchback of Notre Dame,* Lon Chaney portrays Quasimodo, the ape-like bell ringer of the famed cathedral, as a fearsome, frightful, crooked creature, one eye bulging but blind, knees that interfere, sharp, saw-edged protruding teeth, high, swollen cheek bones and a dented and twisted nose—a monstrous joke of nature. He gives an unrestrained but remarkable performance in this production, which opened last night at the Astor Theater, where there gathered familiar faces of the stage and screen, literary lights, and men-about-town. Chaney throws his whole soul into making Quasimodo as repugnant as anything human could very well be, even to decorating his breast and back with hair. He is remarkably agile and impressive when showing his fearlessness for a great height, and the strength of his awful hands by climbing down the façade of the cathedral, and on one occasion down a rope, looking like a mammoth monkey on a stick. And yet in this distorted body there was gratitude, for Esmerelda is carried to sanctuary from the gibbet by the muscular ogre."

Victor Seastrom directed Lon in *He Who Gets Slapped* (1924) with Norma Shearer and John Gilbert. As the heartbroken scientist who becomes a clown, Lon had a great opportunity to tell the story of this tragedy. The *New York Times* said, "Never in his efforts before the camera has Mr. Chaney delivered such a marvelous performance as he does in this character. He is restrained in his acting, never overdoing the sentimental situations, and is guarded in his make-up."

The Next Corner was his other 1924 appearance, a film directed by Sam Wood, and starring Conway Tearle, Dorothy Mackaill, Ricardo Cortez, and Louise Dresser.

Lon made two of his most famous films the following year with director Tod Browning. *The Unholy Three* is a story of a criminal ventriloquist, played by Lon without makeup. When masquerading as an old woman, Grandma O'Grady, he is completely believable in manner and appearance. The *New York Times* said it was one of "the finest pictures ever made, due to the able and clever direction . . . ."

The Phantom of the Opera is a vivid tale of great interest to audiences. Lon created unforgettable impressions with his characterization, and again, his mastery of makeup revealed him as Eric, the criminal haunting the catacombs beneath the Paris opera. When Mary Philbin, as the singer, Christine, suddenly tears off his mask while he plays "Don Juan Triumphant" on the organ, audiences are so overwhelmed with the horror of his hideously deformed, skull-like face, they stand up and scream with revulsion.

THE TOWER OF LIES

VICTOR SEASTROM
Director

NORMA SHEARER *and* LON CHANEY
directed by VICTOR SEASTROM
in "THE TOWER OF LIES"

Still *another* proof of Metro-Goldwyn-Mayer's superb genius for selecting Stars and Directors to produce the utmost in motion picture art.

The "*Tower of Lies*" Starring NORMA SHEARER and LON CHANEY
A Victor Seastrom Production. Adapted for the screen by Agnes Christine Johnston. From the novel "The Emperor of Portugallia" by Selma Lagerlof.
A Metro-Goldwyn-Mayer Picture.

LON CHANEY
as Jan

NORMA SHEARER
as Goldie

NORMA SHEARER and WILLIAM HAINES

"THE TOWER OF LIES" is a powerful, heart-stirring drama based on Selma Lagerlof's Nobel Prize novel—"The Emperor of Portugallia"—you will breathlessly await each new unfolding of the plot.

In this picture the art of acting and the art of directing are united as you, who have seen "He Who Gets Slapped", have learned to *expect* in Metro-Goldwyn-Mayer dramas.

Stars that brilliantly dominate the motion picture firmament —the cream of the World's directing genius—these are the factors that have made such pictures as "The Unholy Three", "The Merry Widow" and "Never the Twain Shall Meet" possible.

They stamp *all* Metro-Goldwyn-Mayer screen-plays as undisputed classics.

You who have learned to measure motion picture perfection by Metro-Goldwyn-Mayer productions will find the "Tower of Lies" just another proof of your good judgment.

Metro-Goldwyn-Mayer

"*More stars than there are in Heaven*"

This full-page notice for *The Tower of Lies* **appeared in** *Motion Picture Classic,* **December 1925.**

When the film was first shown at previews in and around Los Angeles, critics praised it, but vehemently called for some comic relief from the unrelenting horror. Universal brought in Chester Conklin from the Sennett lot, and the picture went back into production. Conklin was put through his comic paces, contributing a series of scenes of monkey business for a few laughs. Subtitles were rewritten, and again the film was previewed in San Francisco. Reviews were chilly, and the film was returned to Universal to a new staff of editors who cut it into a new form and revised the continuity. They deleted the comedy, completely reversing the Los Angeles opinion. Chester Conklin and all his scenes were cut, as well as scenes with Ward Crane, who played an important part in the picture's early sequences of garden parties and a duel.

After additional previews, the producers again decided comedy relief was needed, and rather than retrieving the Conklin footage, new scenes were shot with comic Larry Semon bouncing through the opera wings with skittish ballerinas. The final film was successfully released with these additional scenes.

So horrifying was the effect on audiences, the film was boycotted by many exhibitors in England, and the picture was withdrawn from the British market for some years.

Tod Browning again directed Lon in the MGM films, *The Blackbird* and *The Road to Mandalay*. In these later films, he specialized in the grotesque, but was more than just a horror film star. In the latter, Lon played Singapore Joe, keeper of the toughest dive on the whole China coast. The *New York Times* said, "Chaney affects another of those bizarre makeups. This time he plays a gent with a cataract in one eye, and to get the effect of the whole film over the optic, dropped a dangerous preparation into his eye between scenes. This necessitated short scenes to guard against permanent blindness."

In *The Road to Mandalay*, besides the fearsome blank eye created by the use of a chemical formula, the star wore a scar that suggested a knife slash in a fight. This was applied to the face by a mixture that, in drying, shrank up. As the liquid dried on the face, the flesh was drawn together to form a vivid imitation of an unsightly scar.

In *The Blackbird*, Chaney's posture was affected by curving his spine, drawing up one leg and having the tailor accentuate this apparent bodily deformity by making one side of his suit of clothes longer than the other.

The *New York Times* held Lon's film, *The Unholy Three*, in such esteem that it was considered one of the "Ten Best Films of 1925." They said the film ". . . is an enthralling photoplay, thoroughly unique in its idea and equipped with shrewd and imaginative direction."

Tell It to the Marines (1927) showed Lon without gruesome makeup as Sergeant O'Hara of the U. S. Marines, sternly training a wisecracking recruit, played by William Haines. His performance as a tough soldier with a heart of gold was one of the subtlest portrayals of his career.

Lon made four films in 1927, all with interesting disguises calling on extensive use of fantastic makeup. For example, in *Mr. Wu,* he played an ancient Chinese mandarin. He wore clamps on his cheeks to pull them tightly back, and thus give his face the sunken, withered aspect of senility, a painful disguise repeated often during the many days of production.

In *The Unknown,* he was Alonzo, the Armless Wonder, a man pretending to be armless in a knife-throwing circus act. When his love, played by Joan Crawford, refuses his affection because of her psychological revulsion to being touched, he has his arms surgically removed. Hoping to please her, he finds instead that she has been cured of her mental problem, and now readily accepts the touch and affection of a "strong man" in the show. The *New York Times* said, "Like the other Chaney pictures directed by Tod Browning, this has a macabre atmosphere. If you wince at a touch or two of horror, don't go to *The Unknown*. If you like strong celluloid food, try it. It has the merit of possessing a finely sinister plot, some moments with a real shock and Lon Chaney. Besides, Joan Crawford is an optical tonic as Estrellita . . . ."

London After Midnight brought him before audiences as a vampire terrorizing the night. *Mockery* showed Lon as a Russian peasant tortured during the revolution.

"The man himself had to be studied, and not merely his outward appearances," Chaney said to an interviewer with the *New York*

Times in 1927. "The most important thing in being able to enact a character is not to paint the character's face over your own. To learn more about the Russian peasant, I visited a little film theater in San Francisco, watching for a peasant type among the audience that would fit in with the character I was to play. Finally, I came across the man I wanted, and I watched him closely. I first noted that there was in this man a sort of obstruction between perception and reaction. For instance, a thing had to sink in before the face disclosed knowledge of it, as though the message to the brain had been slightly dulled in transit. The character, Sergei, therefore had to be not a little dumb, at least in so far as his physical expressions went. This denseness was reflected also by his gain, a careless shuffle; by his slouchy carriage, his loosely swinging arms and his general air of lethargy and inefficiency." To assemble the elements for this character, Chaney first practiced a shambling walk and a slow response of his physical muscles to his brain. On this foundation, he built his complete characterization, later adding a rough, straggling growth of a beard.

In 1928, as sound revolutionized the industry, motion pictures were in the throes of chaos. Lon resisted appearing in a sound picture, and reunited with Betty Compson in the silent film, *The Big City*. Another silent film, *Laugh, Clown, Laugh,* followed, and Lon later claimed it was his personal favorite. The year was rounded out with two more silent pictures, *While the City Sleeps* and *West of Zanzibar.*

Teaming again with Tod Browning, Lon appeared in 1929 in *Where East Is East* with Lupe Velez and Estelle Taylor.

A growth in his throat undermined his health, and Lon went through several operations. While undergoing treatment, he made his last silent film, *Thunder,* appearing as a retiring railroad engineer on the snowbound tracks of the Chicago Northwestern. While working on this film, he accidentally swallowed a piece of imitation snow. It lodged in his throat, aggravating the condition he already suffered.

Lon believed sound in pictures would diminish the universal appeal of pantomime, and delayed appearing in a "talkie" until 1930, several years after most actors had left behind silent films. For his debut, a remake of *The Unholy Three* (1930), he showed he was as adept at using different voices as he had been with changing his physical appearance. Audiences were amazed at his ability to speak in different voices in the tale of a trio of weirdly assorted criminals. It seemed he would be on a greatly revived career in the new technique of sound films.

Projects were well into the planning stages for Lon, including *Dracula*. When Lon's throat cancer grew worse, he entered a Los Angeles hospital for treatment, but it was unsuccessful. Ironically, he lost the use of his voice, and he spent his last days communicating with only gestures and expressions, as he had done with his mother so many years before. Lon died on August 26, 1930.

Silent Filmography of
Lon Chaney

The Blood Red Tape of Charity (1912)
Poor Jake's Demise (1913)
The Sea Urchin (1913)
Shon the Piper (1913)
The Trap (1913)
Almost an Actress (1913)
An Elephant on His Hands (1913)
Red Margaret, Moonshiner (1913)
Bloodhounds of the North (1913)
The Lie (1914)
The Honor of the Mounted (1914)
Remember Mary Magdalene (1914)
Discord and Harmony (1914)
The Menace to Carlotta (1914)
The Embezzler (1914)
The Lamb, the Woman, the Wolf (1914)
The End of the Feud (1914)
The Tragedy of Whispering Creek (1914)
The Unlawful Trade (1914)
Heart Strings (1914)
The Forbidden Room (1914)
The Old Cobbler (1914)
Hopes of a Blind Alley (1914)
A Ranch Romance (1914)
Her Grave Mistake (1914)
By the Sun's Rays (1914)
The Oubliette (1914)
A Miner's Romance (1914)
Her Bounty (1914)
The Higher Law (1914)
Richelieu (1914)
The Pipes o' Pan (1914)
Virtue Is Its Own Reward (1914)
Her Life's Story (1914)
Lights and Shadows (1914)

The Lion, the Lamb, the Man (1914)
A Night of Thrills (1914)
Her Escape (1914)
The Sin of Olga Brandt (1915)
The Star of the Sea (1915)
The Small-town Girl (1915)
The Measure of a Man (1915)
The Threads of Fate (1915)
When the Gods Played a Badger Game (1915)
Such Is Life (1915)
Where the Forest Ends (1915)
Outside the Gates (1915)
All for Peggy (1915)
The Desert Breed (1915)
Maid of the Mist (1915)
The Grind (1915)
The Girl of the Night (1915)
An Idyll of the Hills (1915)
The Stronger Mind (1915)
Steady Company (1915)
The Violin Maker (1915)
The Trust (1915)
Bound on the Wheel (1915)
Mountain Justice (1915)
Quits (1915)
The Chimney's Secret (1915)
The Pine's Revenge (1915)
The Fascination of the Fleur de Lis (1915)
Alas and Alack (1915)
A Mother's Atonement (1915)
Lon of Lone Mountain (1915)
The Millionaire Paupers (1915)
Under a Shadow (1915)
Stronger Than Death (1915)
Father and the Boys (1915)
Dolly's Scoop (1916)
The Grip of Jealousy (1916)
Tangled Hearts (1916)

THE GILDED SPIDER (1916)
BOBBIE OF THE BALLET (1916)
THE GRASP OF GREED (1916)
THE MARK OF CAIN (1916)
IF MY COUNTRY SHOULD CALL (1916)
FELIX ON THE JOB (1916)
THE PLACE BEYOND THE WINDS (1916)
ACCUSING EVIDENCE (1916)
THE PRICE OF SILENCE (1916)
THE PIPER'S PRICE (1917)
HELL MORGAN'S GIRL (1917)
THE MASK OF LOVE (1917)
THE GIRL IN THE CHECKERED COAT (1917)
THE FLASHLIGHT (1917)
A DOLL'S HOUSE (1917)
FIRES OF REBELLION (1917)
THE RESCUE (1917)
PAY ME! (1917)
TRIUMPH (1917)
ANYTHING ONCE (1917)
THE SCARLET CAR (1917)
THE EMPTY GUN (1917)
THE GRAND PASSION (1918)
BROADWAY LOVE (1918)
THE KAISER, THE BEAST OF BERLIN (1918)
FAST COMPANY (1918)
A BROADWAY SCANDAL (1918)
RIDDLE GAWNE (1918)
THAT DEVIL, BATEESE (1918)
THE TALK OF THE TOWN (1918)
DANGER, GO SLOW (1918)
THE FALSE FACES (1919)
THE WICKED DARLING (1919)
A MAN'S COUNTRY (1919)
THE MIRACLE MAN (1919)
PAID IN ADVANCE (1919)
WHEN BEARCAT WENT DRY (1919)
VICTORY (1919)

Daredevil Jack (1920)
Treasure Island (1920)
The Gift Supreme (1920)
The Penalty (1920)
Nomads of the North (1920)
Outside the Law (1920)
For Those We Love (1921)
The Ace of Hearts (1921)
Bits of Life (1921)
Voices of the City (1921)
The Trap (1922)
Flesh and Blood (1922)
The Light in the Dark (1922)
Oliver Twist (1922)
Shadows (1922)
Quincy Adams Sawyer (1922)
A Blind Bargain (1922)
All the Brothers Were Valiant (1923)
While Paris Sleeps (1923)
The Shock (1923)
The Hunchback of Notre Dame (1923)
The Next Corner (1924)
He Who Gets Slapped (1924)
The Monster (1925)
The Unholy Three (1925)
The Phantom of the Opera (1925)
The Tower of Lies (1925)
The Blackbird (1926)
The Road to Mandalay (1926)
Tell It to the Marines (1926)
Mr. Wu (1927)
The Unknown (1927)
Mockery (1927)
London After Midnight (1927)
The Big City (1928)
Laugh, Clown, Laugh (1928)
While the City Sleeps (1928)
West of Zanzibar (1928)

Where East is East (1929)
Thunder (1929)

Chapter 7
Jackie Coogan

Jackie Coogan is best remembered today as the fat, balding prankster, Uncle Fester, who lit light bulbs by sticking them in his mouth, in the 1960s television series, *The Addams Family*. However, long before playing the role of Uncle Fester, he was the cutest little boy the world had ever seen, a child-star loved all around the world.

Jackie's mother, Lillian Dolliver, was also a child star on the stage. When she grew up, she met Jack Coogan, a vaudeville headliner who also had played a few, small roles in motion pictures. John Leslie Coogan, Jr. was "born in a trunk" on October 24, 1914, to these vaudevillian parents, and spent his first years immersed in a show business background.

As an eighteen-month-old child, Jackie made his film debut in an Essanay motion picture, *Skinner's Baby*. By the age of two, he appeared in his parents' vaudeville act, scampering onto the stage while they took their applause, and winking flirtatiously at the crowd. The Coogans kept Jackie in the finale of their act for several seasons, and later let him clown more prominently on stage with them. He was always a crowd pleaser.

After Charlie Chaplin finished making his film, *Sunnyside*, he was at a loss for an idea for his next comedy. In his autobiography, he recalled, "It was a relief in this state of despair to go to the Orpheum for distraction, and in this state of mind, I saw an eccentric dancer, nothing extraordinary, but at the finish of his act he brought on his little boy, an infant of four, to take a bow with him. After bowing with his father, he suddenly broke into a few amusing steps, then looked knowingly at the audience, waved to them, and

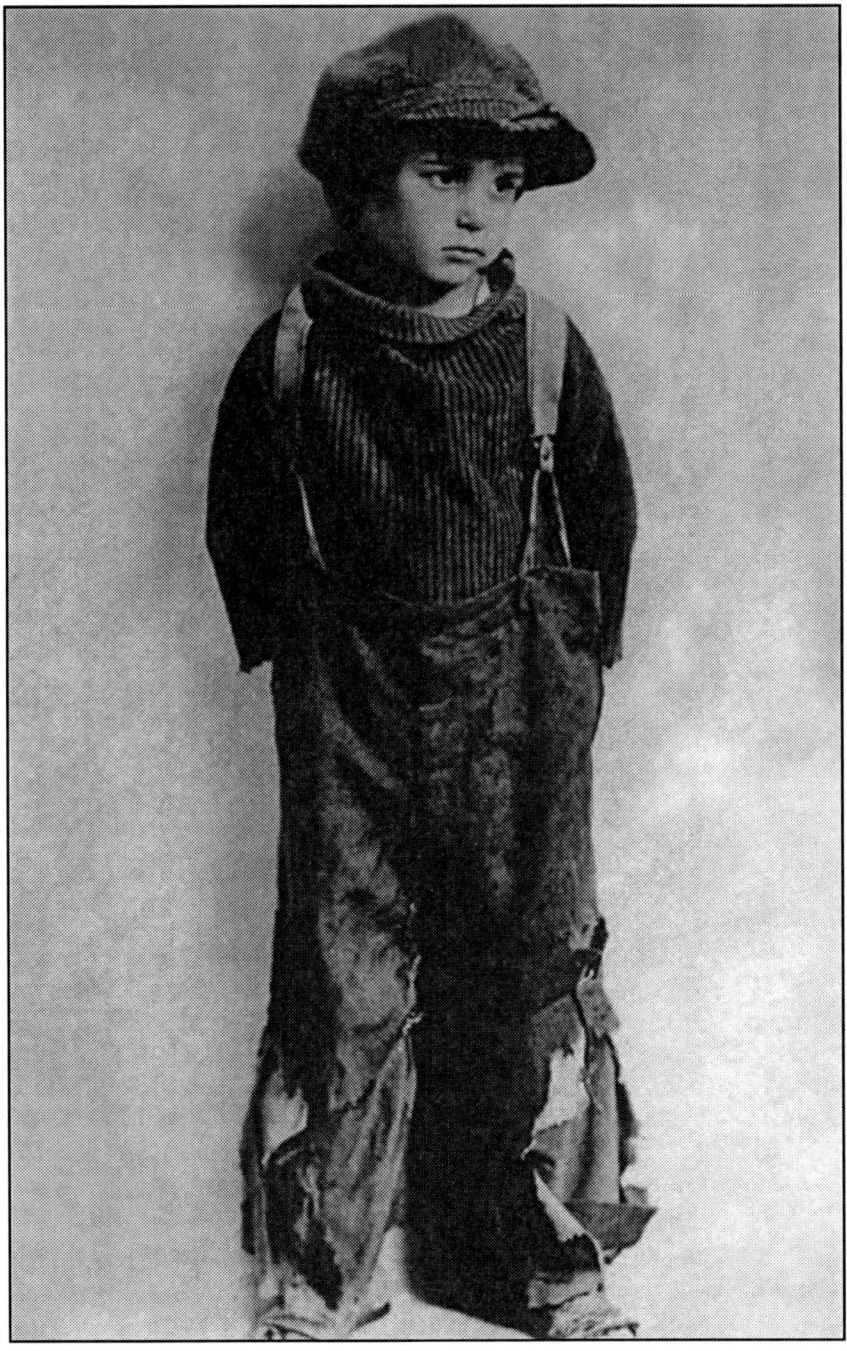

Jackie Coogan, ca. 1923, always played a waif in his early films, patterned after his first starring role in Charlie Chaplin's film, *The Kid* (1921).

Jackie Coogan, on the cover of *Screenland*, April 1923.

ran off. The audience went into an uproar, so that the child was made to come on again, this time doing quite a different dance. It could have been obnoxious in another child. But Jackie Coogan was charming, and the audience thoroughly enjoyed it. Whatever he did, the little fellow had an engaging personality."

Chaplin did not think of him again until a week later. As he faced an open stage filled with the members of his stock company waiting for direction, he still struggled for an idea on which to elaborate his next picture. "In those days, I would often sit before them, because their presence and reactions were a stimulus. That day, I was bogged down and listless, and in spite of their polite smiles, I knew my efforts were tame. My mind wandered, and I talked about the acts I had seen playing at the Orpheum and about the little boy, Jackie Coogan, who came on and bowed with his father."

One member of the stock company mentioned having read in the morning paper an article about Jackie Coogan having been signed by Roscoe Arbuckle for a film. The news struck Chaplin like forked lightning. "My God! Why didn't I think of that?" he remembered shouting. "Of course, he would be marvelous in films!"

Chaplin became fired with enthusiastic ideas. He went on to enumerate the possible gags and the story he could fashion around the little boy. For an entire day, he and his actors elaborated on the story and acted out the possible scenes. Chaplin noticed the cast looked at him askance, wondering why he waxed so enthusiastically over a lost cause. He dejectedly faced the reality that Arbuckle had signed him up and probably had ideas similar to his. Chaplin bemoaned his failure to think of the possibilities sooner.

For the next day, Chaplin could think of nothing but the story concocted for Jackie Coogan. One associate was suggesting getting another little boy when a publicity man suddenly burst into the room. Breathless and excited, he shouted, "It's not Jackie Coogan that Arbuckle signed up, it's the father, Jack Coogan!"

A search party went out to find Jack Coogan, father of the little boy around whom Chaplin wanted to build his next comedy. Once located, Coogan readily agreed to give his little boy to Chaplin for one picture.

Chaplin tested Jackie in a bit part in his short film, *A Day's Pleasure* (1919). He found the boy looked good on film, and plans went forward for a full-length feature film starring Chaplin and Jackie.

The Kid was something of an innovation, as Chaplin elaborated his ideas into a film filled with satire, farce, realism, melodrama, and fantasy. Once filmed and released, it was an enormous success. With this film, Jackie Coogan's star was launched into an orbit where it would remain until 1931.

Jackie's father agreed to sign a contract with First National for more films. *Peck's Bad Boy* (1921) followed the worldwide success of *The Kid*. Then, Jackie appeared in the title role of *Oliver Twist* (1922). Veteran character actor, Lon Chaney, essayed the role of Fagin, the criminal who trained the little boy for a life of crime.

Jackie's father took an active role in producing his next two films. He wrote the scenarios for *My Boy* (1922) and *Trouble* (1922). *Daddy* (1923) was the final film made under his contract with First National.

He made seventeen silent films between 1917 and 1928. Seven of these are missing and presumed lost. Five are available on video and five remain locked in vaults. One of the best of them was *Circus Days* (1923).

The *New York Times* review said *Circus Days* was noted for its strong audience appeal. "This is what is known as an audience picture, with pathos and impossible situations. But the world loves a circus, and lots of people are strong for Jackie Coogan, and one has both in this picture. There are some very pleasing circus scenes in this photoplay, especially those at night showing the procession making its way to the next stand."

In *Circus Days*, Jackie played the part of Toby Tyler, James Otis' character from his popular novel, *Toby Tyler, or Ten Weeks with a Circus* (1881). Toby is one of the good little boys who always thinks of his mother, but continually wanders into trouble with Eben Holt, his mother's brother-in-law.

In one scene, as Holt is about to whip Toby, the youngster presents him with his pipe, tobacco, and shoes to distract him from the expected punishment. In taking off the farmer's big boots, he loses his balance and crashes into a sideboard on which there are plenty of crockery and glass. Jackie flees to the barn, springs from an opening onto a passing hay cart, and lays there until the cart arrives at a circus.

At the circus, he finds work as an assistant to a man operating a lemonade and sandwich stand. A pernicious lad turns up to annoy Toby and steal a sandwich. Toby, who is only half his size, slams the bad boy with a well-aimed wallop and sends him tumbling into the dust.

This advertisement appeared in *Moving Picture World,* August 9, 1923, for Jackie Coogan's film, *Circus Days.*

> *A First National Release*
> **THE FIRST EXPLOITATION FOR CIRCUS DAYS**
> This shows the front of the California Theatre, Anaheim, Calif., for the very first showing of Jackie Coogan in the screen version of Toby Tyler. The clown performed a variety of stunts and kept the kids hanging about the theatre most all day.

This photo appeared in *Moving Picture World*, August 9, 1923, showing the world premier of his film, *Circus Days*.

His next job is to sell ice cream cones in the stands. As he makes his way through the seated crowd, Jeannette, the child bareback rider, begins her exhibition in the ring. Toby becomes distracted by her fascinating performance and pauses to enjoy the show along with the rest of the crowd. At the finish of her act, Toby looks down to the melted ice cream cones in his tray. Luigi, the clown, takes pity on the boy, and gives him enough money to pay for the lost ice cream.

In another sequence, Toby arouses the anger of his boss and takes refuge in the lion's cage. Jackie is splendid in this scene, as he gazes in terror at the lion and then in awe at the lemonade man watching from outside the cage. He is eventually relieved of harm when he discovers the lion is tame, domesticated, and harmless.

The *Variety* film review, August 9, 1923, said, "Judging from the expressions on his little face, Coogan is thinking of what he is doing, and the facial expressions he contrives to achieve are little short of remarkable when one takes his youth into consideration."

The film had its world premiere at the Chicago Theater on July 15, 1923, and the criticisms of the Chicago critics supplemented in every way the excellent reviews published in the trade journals the same month.

In the *Herald and Examiner,* Polly Wood stated: "For the youngsters, *Circus Days* will be a real adventure of a manly little boy; for you and me, *Circus Days* will be the real remembrance of other times."

Rob Reel, writing in the *Chicago Evening American,* said, "There are no 'buts' about it. Jackie Coogan's latest photodrama is a knockout."

Mae Tinee, reviewer for the *Chicago Daily Tribune,* stated: "*Circus Days* is the kind of picture that will, without failure, get old and young. The whole world loves a circus, and the title would gather us in if nothing else would."

Genevieve Harris wrote in *Evening Post,* "This is every kid's dream come true."

As the great child star of the 1920s, Jackie Coogan was cast as a waif in all his early pictures. On January 12, 1923, the *New York Times* announced that the Metro Company had secured Jackie for his next four pictures. Metro sought the services of the little star, and lured him from First National with a contract calling for four pictures during the following two years. A $500,000 bonus check was turned over to his parents, and Jackie was promised the lion's share of the profits in a 60/40 percentage as part of the contract. These earnings were added to the funds his father faithfully stored in a trust fund for his son. Other investments were wisely placed in real estate. Before the age of twenty-one, Jackie was scheduled to become a millionaire several times over.

His first film for Metro was based on Mary Roberts Rinehart's well-known novel, *Long Live the King* (1923). Jack Coogan produced the film for Joseph Schenck. His second picture for Metro was based on the famous Louise de la Ramee book, *A Dog of Flanders.* Released in 1924, under the title *A Boy of Flanders,* the tale of a Belgian boy and his dog followed the successful formula of his earlier films. In rapid succession, *Hello Frisco* and *Little Robinson Crusoe* followed in 1924.

So great was his fame, the nine-year-old sailed on September 6 on a European trip. Tumultuous crowds, matched only by visiting royalty, greeted his arrival in London. In France, more than 16,000 fans besieged the boy. In Geneva, Sir Eric Drummond, Secretary General of the League of Nations, stopped all activity to issue a public thanks for his help in the Near East Relief.

Pope Pius XI received the boy at a private audience in Rome. He asked the young actor to help an orphanage in Athens and gratefully patted him on the cheek. Jackie delivered $1,000,037 worth of cargo relief to the Greek government, and received a decoration of the Silver Cross of the Order of George.

The Rag Man and *Old Clothes* followed one upon another in 1925. All featured the rapidly growing, twelve-year-old, adolescent youth wearing his boyish, trademark "Buster Brown" haircut. Jackie began to rebel, and within days, he was taken for his first short haircut. The event made national news.

It took one barber, one pale mother, one agitated father, one perturbed press agent, one gurgling brother, and eleven news photographers to witness the event. Cameras clicked as the barber's scissors snipped, and Jackie's million-dollar crown of glory fell to the floor. Instantly, the growing boy's shearing turned him from a child into a handsome young man, and one week later, he was enrolled as a cadet in the Urban Military Academy in Los Angeles. There, he trained until someone came along with a good idea for a story. He underwent rigid training at the school while his parent's Rolls-Royce stayed parked in the garage and the restless publicity men twiddled their fingers. Jackie shined his own shoes and made his own bed along with all the other uniformed cadets, as if he were just another boy and not the most famous kid in the world. It did not take MGM long to come up with an idea for a story to feature him in another film.

Johnny Get Your Hair Cut (1926) was hastily written around the event, and Jackie dutifully left the school to shoot another picture, emerging on film with his new image. In rapid succession, *The Bugle Call* (1927) and *Buttons* (1927) were made as the silent film era was reaching its end. It was terribly obvious to everyone that the little boy with the baggy pants and rumpled cap was growing into a stalwart young man. Many wondered whether they could continue to milk his popularity much longer.

Jackie received $5,000 a week for appearing with his father in 1928 at the London Palladium. In 1930, he made his sound-film debut in a remake of *Tom Sawyer* for Paramount. The inevitable sequel, *Huckleberry Finn*, followed in 1931. With these two films, his career as a child actor was all but over. He was no longer "The Kid."

The fortune amassed from his film work, merchandising, and investments amounted to millions of dollars. In October 1935, as he neared the age of twenty-one and his looming birthday heralded the fact that he was soon to come of legal age, Jackie anticipated an adult life enjoying the rewards of his youthful labor. Money was to be paid to him in installments of $250,000 a year. His film career had begun to wane, and he was in dire need of the money.

Unfortunately, Jackie's beloved father passed away on May 14, 1935, after a tragic automobile accident. The next year, his mother married Arthur L. Bernstein, and this man quickly became Jackie's legal adviser and business manager. Within a year, he took full control of Jackie's fortune, and that control was not for the young man's benefit.

Jackie Coogan had earned more than four million dollars as a child star, but was given only a $6.25 weekly allowance. Unknown to him, his mother and stepfather wantonly squandered all but $200,000 of his fortune. On the birthday when he turned twenty-one years old, no money was turned over to him. Jackie trusted them, and set aside any suspicious notions.

His marriage to actress Betty Grable played a powerful role in the discovery of the lost fortune. He now had responsibilities to meet, and no money with which to meet them. According to Norman J. Zierold in his book, *The Child Stars*, Betty Grable commented at that time, "Any other boy would have realized that something was very wrong with his estate when the trust fund he and everyone else believed was there for him was not turned over to him on his twenty-first birthday. Instead, he was given a 'present' of a thousand dollars. And even that had a string to it. He would be given this gift, he was told, on condition that he sign certain papers which, it turns out, signed away just about everything he had. He signed them. It's hard to believe, but he did, because he is, or was, entirely without suspicion."

On April 11, 1938, Jackie faced the fact that he had been swindled. He filed a lawsuit in the Los Angeles Superior Court for what remained of his money. In 1939, he finally was awarded $126,000 of the depleted bank account, prompting the California Legislature to pass "The Child Actors Bill," also known as the Coogan Act, which would set up a trust fund for young performers, holding and protecting their earnings until they reached legal age.

Jackie appeared in several sound films during the Depression of the 1930s. After a stint in the military during World War II, he returned to Hollywood a forgotten and unwanted older man. Minor roles were found in a number of films from 1947 to 1962, but as he aged, interest in his talent had all but died. Then, small parts in a number of television shows brought him to the attention of producers once again. By this time, he was a heavyset, balding, middle-aged man, completely unrecognizable from his image as a child star.

Jackie got the role of Uncle Fester Frump in *The Addams Family* television series in 1964. From the series' debut, he struck a responsive chord with audiences. His often-hilarious antics amused millions of fans, and Jackie found a new career reaching more people than he had ever done in his youth.

Jackie Coogan died on March 1, 1984, of a heart attack. Irving Thalberg, the renowned producer during the golden years of MGM, believed any star, having once found a place in the hearts of audiences, could always find a place again, provided a suitable role could be constructed showcasing their particular talent. This belief was never more profoundly proven than with Jackie Coogan.

Jackie Coogan achieved fame again in 1964 as Uncle Fester Frump in *The Addams Family* television series.

SILENT FILMOGRAPHY OF
JACKIE COOGAN

SKINNER'S BABY (1917)
A DAY'S PLEASURE (1919)
THE KID (1921)
PECK'S BAD BOY (1921)
MY BOY (1921)
OLIVER TWIST (1922)
TROUBLE (1922)
DADDY (1923)
CIRCUS DAYS (1923)
LONG LIVE THE KING (1923)
A BOY OF FLANDERS (1924)
LITTLE ROBINSON CRUSOE (1924)
HELLO FRISCO (1924)
THE RAG MAN (1925)
OLD CLOTHES (1925)
JOHNNY GET YOUR HAIR CUT (1927)
THE BUGLE CALL (1927)
BUTTONS (1927)

Chapter 8
William S. Hart

"What was Custer's last battle like?" William S. Hart asked of "White Bull," the oldest surviving chief of the famous battle.

The ancient Indian stared at the white man, a star of Western motion pictures, and answered truthfully. He said he could not answer, and he would not attempt to do so. "There was too much dust," he said, "and I could see only when I was close to a soldier."

"Well, how did you feel in the fight, and what were you thinking of?" Bill remembered asking.

The old Indian answered with the naïveté of a child and the dignity of his rank, "I was thinking of my sweetheart and how bad it was that on account of the thick dust she could not see me fight."

Bill recalled this conversation with the Indian warrior in his autobiography, *My Life East and West*, appropriately titled to reflect on his incredible career as an actor on the Broadway stage in New York, and later, in films made in California.

Throughout America during the early years of the 20th century, inexpensive, five-cent Western novels proliferated. Boys loved them in the same way a later generation adored super-hero comic books. Bill became the embodiment on film of the strong, long-faced, iron-jawed silent man of the West, and he was idolized by millions of boys around the world. He was also the male ideal for thousands of women. Before this, he was known by patrons of the legitimate stage in the roles of *Ben-Hur*, *The Virginian*, and many other contemporary and Shakespearean dramas.

He was born in a house near a flour mill on the Fox River, and given the name William Surrey Hart, on December 6, 1865, in Newburgh, New York.

Three photos of William S. Hart during his early years on the New York stage: (upper left) *The Man in the Iron Mask*; (upper right) *Romeo and Juliet*; and (bottom) the original cast of *Ben-Hur*.

His father, a miller who traveled throughout what was left of the West, exposed young Bill to life with the Sioux Indians, the open ranges, and the unwritten code of the West that was still in force: the law that killing a man was not as great a crime as stealing his horse or jumping his claim. He wandered with his family through Iowa, Minnesota, Wisconsin, and the Dakotas, while moving from job to job. He was an expert man at his trade, and drew a good salary. His work was to get a mill into good working shape, and then trim and dress the millstones into proper condition for grinding. Then, he would move on. In the back of his mind, he always dreamed of finding the perfect mill where he could settle down and provide a lasting home for his family.

The family had an old Sioux woman who assisted them. From her, Bill learned to speak the language of the Sioux Indians.

One of his earliest memories was the night his newborn brother cried himself to sleep, and then became still. He watched his mother shed bitter tears, while his father put on a haggard look that he always wore when he was troubled. The baby brother Bill had been tickling with a feather to cause him to laugh lay quiet and still. His tiny crib had a block of wood under it so it would not rock. A blanket lay draped over the crib, and as the night wore on, the old Indian woman sat beside it and silently smoked.

The next morning, Bill and his family journeyed in a covered wagon drawn by two yoke of steers in search of consecrated ground in which to bury the baby. After a two-day journey, the family crossed through Red Wing, Minnesota, and gathered on a high hill overlooking the mighty river.

"There was no clergyman; my little brother, being the first, young or old, to be buried there," Bill remembered. "My father did not think himself good enough to read the burial service. He quietly spoke each sentence to Bill's sister and she repeated it over the little open grave."

Far above the giant Mississippi at the place where it commenced its 2,000 mile journey to the sea, Bill and his family stood at the side of the covered wagon led by steers with drooping heads. They lowered into the ground a little plain coffin, fashioned by his father's own hands, and the tiny boy child who had barely lived was laid in the arms of the earth to eternally sleep.

Soon after the boy's death, his mother became ill, and went to heal under the care of some doctors in the East. His two sisters were busily attending school, and his father again longed for a mill where he could place himself and build a lasting home. He took his son, and together, the two journeyed east by way of the Union Pacific railroad.

Bill's father made plans to buy horses and continue their journey into the Yankton, South Dakota Indian territory. He obtained three saddle horses and two packhorses for their trip into the Indian country, and set out on a two-day ride. They passed the Fort Randall army post, and continued northwest into the land of the Sioux.

One morning, the two travelers stopped on a slight rise of ground. Bill's father took a pair of field glasses and looked ahead into the distance. He saw three horses standing and grazing about three miles ahead. They presumed the horses were wild, and continued toward them, watching intently to see how close the horses would allow them to come.

Suddenly, someone yelled and startled the man and boy. With loud whoops, an Indian rose up from behind the horses and leapt onto the back of the animal. He raced toward them, and was followed by dozens of other Indians with war bridles guiding their mounts. Bill watched the Indians dig their bare heels into the sides of the horses as they came within two hundred yards. Then, they made a complete circle around the man and boy, surrounding them, and closing in. Father and son were doomed.

Bill suddenly stood up, took a few steps forward, and began to speak to the Indians in their own sign language. The Indians were flabbergasted. The war circle slowed, and they halted their attack. "When the leader set up his horse and I gaily started to chatter Sioux, not only the leader's right hand, but the right hand of every Indian in the party, followed immediately by the left, went over their mouths; they were astounded."

The visitors were in full war paint and glaring at them, as the helpless pair stood in the middle of the vast, Dakota prairie. The Indians were bent on attacking any incoming white people trying to locate in the Black Hills. They would have stolen their stock and outfit and killed them if they had offered any resistance. Instead, they exchanged humorous looks and smiled to each other, as the boy talked in his childish attempt at the Sioux language.

Bill's father instructed his son to tell them he wanted to see Red Cloud, Spotted Tail, Standing Bear, or any chief. The boy was incapable of interpreting sufficiently, but the Indians understood enough from his sign language to be convinced of their importance. They waved the pair to go straight ahead, and then turned and rode two lightning-fast circles around them, yelling a parting Sioux cry of victory. Then, as quickly as they had arrived, they dashed away, disappearing into the prairie with the sound of their bells jingling in the air, and their feathers blowing straight back in the breeze.

His family later reunited when his mother and sisters returned from the East. Shortly after building a log cabin and setting up a temporary household, Bill's former partner invited him to join him in building a new mill on a site located at Zumbro Falls on the Zumbro River. They moved to the site, and with the help of local Indians, constructed a mill on the great river.

Bill remembered the day when surprising news filtered back to them of the decisive defeat of the leader of all Indian-fighting generals in the Big Horn country. One soldier survived to carry the news of the disastrous battles several hundred miles west of the Hart family home. Their Indian friends knew of General Custer's defeat several days before the news was officially delivered. His father asked the leader of their redskin friends how this was possible.

"John, how do you know this?" his father asked.

The Indian replied, "We knew it one sleep after each fight!"

"But there were no men posted to signal; the country is rough and with many mountains. How could you get information so soon?" asked the astonished man.

The Indian placed his hand upon Bill's head, looked at his father, and then slowly replied, "I will tell you. The Indians have a way of talking through the air that is known only to a few of the older chiefs. No one is admitted to this inner circle until there is a vacancy caused by death. We knew everything two moons ago. We knew our warriors were crying loud in victory, but we also knew our women sang the death song of the Sioux and the Cheyenne. That is why our hearts have all been sad."

Bill's mother again became ill, and with no money coming in from the unfinished mill, Bill's father gave his interest in the mill to the Indians, and moved the family to Rochester, New York, where he hoped to earn much-needed income. There, Bill swam in the Bronx River in the summer, and skated on it in the winter. He attended a private school in Morisania, and studied at public schools after that.

Bill found work as a messenger boy delivering for guests at the Everett House and Clarendon Hotels. The hotel clerks often gave him passes to theaters, and Bill took great delight witnessing performances of the stellar stars of the day, Fanny Davenport, Clara Morris, Sarah Bernhardt, and others.

"I never had but two ambitions. One, to go to West Point; the other, to go on the stage," Bill recalled. "The desire to become a United States Army officer was probably born of my Western life. Soldiers and forts were a part of the West. The stage idea just came, always remained, and will be with me when the final curtain is rung down."

As the old West gradually faded into history, Bill developed a deep appreciation for Western lore, and his affection increased even as he began to pursue a career as an actor in the East.

In New York City, the flourishing theater business offered him the opportunity for a long apprenticeship. "The first lines I ever spoke in portraying a character were those of Friar Lawrence eleven years ago," Bill recalled in an article in *The Silent Picture*. "'The gray-eyed moon smiles upon the frowning night!'"

The Man in the Iron Mask first brought Bill on a tour in 1897 in the role of Louis XIV. The following January, the play opened in New York at the People's Theater.

Other plays quickly followed: *The Bells* opened at the Lyceum Theater on February 16, 1898, with Bill in the role of Matthias. *A Lady of Quality Street* brought Bill to Wallack's Theater, New York, in the role of Sir John Oxon.

Bill played Romeo to Julia Arthur's Juliet at the Grand Opera House in Chicago from April 12, 1899 and during most of the following months of that year.

A tour of *The Christian*, during the latter part of 1901 and the early part of 1902, presented Bill as John Storm in a play based on

Hall Caine's popular novel of the same name. For the remaining months of 1902, a tour of *The Suburban* featured Bill in the role of the villain of the story.

He continued as a popular leading man, opening *Hearts Courageous* at the Power's Theater in Chicago on August 31, 1903. The dramatization went on to New York and opened on Broadway on October 5, 1903. A four-act play, *Love's Pilgrimage*, with Bill appearing as Arthur Conway, played at Wallack's Theater in New York on April 14, 1904.

The Western drama finally claimed Bill in *The Squaw Man*, the famous tale of Cash Hawkins. His power and conviction in the role first excited audiences on a road tour, and then thrilled New York audiences beginning on October 23, 1905.

The Virginian opened on Broadway on September 9, 1907, with Bill taking over the role from Dustin Farnum. He was said to be powerfully effective in his characterization. A tour followed, with a return to Broadway on September 14, 1908.

By this time, Bill had established a reputation as a clever impersonator of Western characters. The role of Dan Stark in *The Barrier* offered him to Broadway audiences at the New Amsterdam Theater on January 10, 1910. As Lonesome Joe in *The Hold Up*, he depicted the rough-and-ready tale of a man handy with his shooting irons.

In the summer of 1912, Bill introduced his vaudeville act, *Moonshine*, appearing as a bad man, Luke Hazy. The tale of a moonshiner in trouble with the law was well received.

After fifteen years of playing lead and support roles to various stars, Bill's stage career climaxed with the opportunity of a lifetime—the role of Messala in the stage version of Lew Wallace's *Ben-Hur*. The play was a sensation on Broadway, complete with thundering horses on a treadmill simulating the famous chariot race.

After the turn of the century, the movie industry ignited with unexpected popularity, and the early Western favorite, Bronco Billy, enthralled a new generation of immigrants with legends of the West that were on a par with the dime-novels so popular at the time, cheap fiction that bore little resemblance to the true West that Bill knew as a child.

When Bill saw his first Western film, he was disappointed. He felt the costumes, mannerisms, and settings were wrong. Still aiming for success on the legitimate stage, he found opportunities for Western roles in the plays *The Squaw Man* and *The Trail of the Lonesome Pine*. Audiences loved him in these parts, and as he took these plays on tours across the country, he found audiences appreciated his attention to detail. "I loved the part of *The Virginian*," he wrote in his autobiography. "It is a beautiful story and a beautiful play—a monument to the fact that a truly great writer can make the moon look like green cheese and get away with it. But I am afraid I offended Owen Wister and lost his friendship in saying so. Owen Wister was a wonderful writer. His stuff was human, simple, and delightful. He loved the West. He loved to write of the West. But there was a lot that he did not know about the West. He was too big a man to hold resentment. Had this not been so, I'm afraid I should have been discharged instead of being engaged for a second season at twenty-five dollars a week advance in salary. I made a big hit as *The Virginian* and the show made money everywhere."

"While playing in Cleveland, I attended a picture show," Bill remembered. "I saw a Western picture. It was awful! I talked with the manager of the theater and he told me it was one of the best Westerns he had ever had. None of the impossibilities or libels on the West meant anything to him—it was drawing the crowds. The fact that the sheriff was dressed and characterized as a sort of cross between a Wisconsin woodchopper and a Gloucester fisherman was unknown to him. I did not seek to enlighten him. I was seeking information. In fact, I was so sure that I had made a big discovery that I was frightened that someone would read my mind and find it out."

Bill saw reproductions of the Old West being seriously presented to the public in a manner reminiscent of burlesque. The films were successful, a fact that made him tremble. He reminded himself that he knew the real West from his first-hand experience, and he was an actor capable of staging it realistically. Soon, knocking on his door was the opportunity for which he had been waiting years. Hundreds of ideas seemed to rush at him from every direction and assumed the form of specific images. In his mind, the die was cast for his future. He felt he had to bend every possible means to earn a chance

William S. Hart, ca. 1920, who brought to films his childhood love of the real West he personally lived among the Sioux Indians.

to make Western motion pictures. He determined to find the opportunity, whether he succeeded, or failed.

"Usually, when stirred by ambition, I would become afraid," Bill later conceded. "But surely this could not be the valor of ignorance. I had been waiting for years for the right thing, and now the right thing had come! I was a part of the West—it was my boyhood home—it was in my blood. The very love I bore for it made me know its ways. I had a thorough training as an actor. I was considered the outstanding portrayer of Western roles on the American stage. It was the big opportunity that a most high Power, chance, or fixed law had schooled me for. It had been many years in coming, but it was here. And I would go through hell on three pints of water before I would acknowledge defeat."

For the remainder of the season, Bill visited all the picture shows wherever he found them, whether at Westport during the summer or on trips to New York. In secret, he cornered his actor friends at The Lambs Club who were working every day playing parts in Western pictures made in New Jersey. He plied them with questions about the work, but told them nothing of his secret, great plans.

So anxious was he to venture into Western filmmaking that Bill hit upon a ruse: when it came time for *The Trail of the Lonesome Pine* to again open, he was reluctant to sign a contract for an engagement. He wanted first to try his pet scheme, so he tried to detour their offer by demanding they raise his salary to $175 a week. He hoped the increase would cause them to refuse his services, and while waiting for the producers to answer negatively, he chanced to meet an actor traveling to California to work in Western pictures.

"I was frightened," he reflected. "They might refuse to give me the part on account of the raise in salary. I was at the point of writing them that I would go for any salary, when they wrote me O.K."

The tour fortunately came west immediately after opening. While in San Francisco, he took the time to learn that all the principal studios were in Los Angeles, and the companies making Westerns was the Universal Picture Corporation, in Hollywood, and the New York Motion Picture Company, in conjunction with the 101 Ranch, in Santa Monica. When he reached Los Angeles, while a friend was registering him at a hotel, he went into a telephone booth, called up the New York Motion Picture Company, and asked for Joe Miller. He spoke with a man who represented Miller.

"I am an actor," Bill said, "and I want to see about making some Western pictures."

The man replied, "Mr. Miller only owns the stock and the

cowboy end of the company. If you want to see about acting, call up Thomas H. Ince. He is manager of the picture company."

Bill went to Thomas Ince, and found the young manager discouraging his interest in films. He continued to push for an opportunity and, finally, Ince allowed him to make a Western.

"My first picture," Bill wrote, "was a two-reeler. It is still playing. Tom Chatterton was the director and also played the hero. Clara Williams was the heroine and I was the villain. Chatterton was and is a clever actor, but he had never directed a picture. I did as I was told, but I felt terrible, and when I saw the rushes on the screen, I knew I was terrible. It was called *His Hour of Manhood*."

Bill was essentially a writer, an important fact in his rise to the highest level of motion picture success. He was one of the first to write explicit details into his scripts, and constructed stories that could be pictured easily by the camera. He was also beyond the age of forty when he first faced the film cameras. This age challenge made it necessary for him to create a character suitable to his appearance.

He was an honest and blunt-spoken man with boundless physical and moral courage on screen and off. He not only wrote many of his films, but also directed dozens of them, all the while playing the lead role, which was no easy feat for any professional.

He was a lonely man who loved animals more than most people. Nearly all of his films contained a scene in which, faced with some problem, he threw his arm around the neck of his horse and confided in the animal. Many people went to a William S. Hart picture for that scene alone. His favorite horse was a little, white-faced Pinto named Fritz. Hardly more than a pony, Bill's feet almost touched the ground as he rode Fritz. The horse did not seem to care, as he gladly took sugar from Bill's pocket, untied knots, and managed to look wonderfully sympathetic while Bill talked to him. Bill often walked into the hills of his ranch with his horses, pouring his heart out to them. He was convinced they understood.

When given the chance to make films the way he wanted, realistic Westerns true to the Old West, success was rapid and immediate. So great was the public reaction to the image he portrayed that Bill continued to make films for Ince at a rapid pace, eventually moving from the two-reel, twenty-four-minute format to longer films.

"My little Western 'horse-opera' company and myself were supreme at camp. When I thought of my freedom and looked at those hills of throbbing hearts, full of the life of my boyhood, I was content, even if I failed to go higher. Success seemed to go with that which was transient. Those hills were mine, and had been mine since my birth. If I had seen farther than I had been able to travel in life, it was the fault of my vision. I had looked and dreamed honestly. If this mimic world of toil where I was earning a living and reproducing days that were dear to me was to be the top of my mountain, I was content. I was surrounded by no greedy grafters, no gelatin-spined, flatulent, slimy creatures, just dogs, horses, sheep, goats, bulls, mules, burros, and white men and red men that were accustomed to live among such things. If we wanted a snake, we could go out in the hills and catch one--one that would warn us that he was a snake, with his rattles . . . I was happy!"

Bill moved on to making feature films at other companies, expanding his popularity to the point where his films were an exhibitor's bread and butter. His popularity was as enormous as that of Mary Pickford and Charlie Chaplin, and both boys and adults loved him. He received as many as two hundred love letters a day from adoring women around the world.

The Testing Block was one of these features, made when the film medium had worked out its full screen syntax, and the

William S. Hart and Eve Novak in an advertising poster for *The Testing Block* (1920).

William S. Hart and Eve Novak in the California hills where they lived and worked on the new motion picture, The Testing Block.

This page from *Moving Picture World* illustrated William S. Hart and Eve Novak in scenes from *The Testing Block* (1920), which was filmed in the California hills.

production was under his personal, full control. It was also a point in the evolution of his film career where the name and his image crystallized.

The story followed "Sierra" Bill, the leader of a band of outlaws in the days of the California gold rush. His physical strength and courage were dominant, but his moral fiber had never stood of "the testing block" of bitter experience. In a raid to collect a reward, he comes upon a poster of Nellie Gray, the violinist in a band of strolling players.

He and his men intercept the players and compel a performance. Nellie's violin plays havoc with the bandit's heart. He gives her a bag of gold and rides away with his followers, but never forgets her. Neither does Ringe, the bandit. The managers take the gold, and they leave the rest of the troupe stranded. The bandits capture the women and draw lots for them. "Sierra" Bill claims first choice and proposes to fight for it. In order to be on a par with his drunken mates, he drinks freely. In the ensuing fight, "Sierra" Bill downs one after another of the band and rides away.

On reaching the hotel, where the players are stranded, "Sierra" Bill encounters a Justice of the Peace. While half-crazed by drink, he forces the Justice up to Nellie Gray's room and compels him to marry the couple. Then, he carries off the girl.

The next scene is two years later, and "Sierra" Bill and Nellie have a little baby boy. "Sierra" Bill is mining gold with fair success when Ringe returns with a Mexican girl he has tired of and plots to steal Nellie. With the aid of others, he induces Nellie to leave her husband, ruins "Sierra" Bill at the gambling table, and wins his Pinto horse. He causes "Sierra" Bill's arrest, and taunts his jailed victim with false stories that his wife had gone and his child was sick. "Sierra" Bill becomes half-crazed and uses his strength to break through the roof of the jail. He manages to send for Nellie, and then inflicts his vengeance on Ringe.

Nellie returns to find the Mexican girl nursing the child and the doctor in despair because the little one cannot sleep. From them, Nellie learns of the conspiracy, and uses her wits to save the child. She soothes the troubled infant by playing her violin. As the child rallies under the mesmerizing strain of her music, "Sierra" Bill returns a changed man. A subtitle claims he was "a nobler one through bitterest sorrow and misery on *the testing block*."

In his autobiography, Bill recalled, "Our location work for *The Testing Block* was done at Ben Lomond, up in the big-tree country. We were there during March and April. Once it rained for over ten days without our shooting a single scene, and we carried in the neighborhood of a hundred people. The first scenes we did were night work, and even then it drizzled intermittently, with big drops of rain constantly dripping from the giant trees. We commenced work at seven o'clock and quit at five in the morning."

He added, "The action of the story (and I could not blame the author) called for me to fight eight men of my bandit gang, one at a time. The battles took place around a campfire. Those who fought first were the lucky ones. They were finished. Those who were kept waiting were unlucky. They nearly perished with the cold. They were in every scene and could only sit there and shiver and watch the fight. It was not so hard on me, as I was getting exercise—exercise that left its mark, too!"

Bill remembered, "The last man I had to tackle was an Indian, Wolf Verduga. The title I spoke and which was to appear on the screen was: 'Come on, Wolf, you're the next.' Wolf and I were very friendly, but Wolf had been there all night, nearly dying of cold. Wolf was twenty-five years of age, a star player on the Riverside Indian School football team, carried two hundred and ten pounds weight, and no excess. In an imbecilic or evil moment I added certain words in Sioux to my spoken title, words which would make a fighting warrior out of an Indian squaw. Allah be praised! And everything else, I was not killed!"

Bill's horse was supposed to be a colt running around the camp loose during these night scenes, and he recalled, "The man who played the villain, Gordon Russell, was supposed to become annoyed at him and hit him with a club. He masked the blow and threw the club at the little fellow as he was running away. In the last part of the story, Russell was to steal Fritz and make a getaway. After following on another horse and being unable to outrun Fritz, I was to call him and he was to stop. The villain was to dismount and run away on foot, and when I came and mounted Fritz he was to jump off at a bank after the villain and trample him to death."

Bill found these to be the easiest scenes to get on film his crew had ever photographed, and he marveled at the intelligence of the horses used in the production. "Russell is a fine, kindly man and a lover of animals, but Fritz had to be held when Russell mounted him, and when I called to him to stop, he not only stopped, but he bucked, and Russell left in a hurry, and the little rascal ran thirty yards toward me in the scene and I changed horses in motion. It was wonderful stuff, and all on account of the resentment the little rascal held for Russell for going after him with a club. Yes! They understand!"

Moving Picture World reviewer, Louis Reeves Harrison, wrote on December 18, 1920, "A picture of strong appeal through the courage and deep suffering of a man of small opportunity, *The Testing Block* is so well constructed and directed that it compares favorably with any previous Hart performance. The rude man of force is not converted by the gentle maid of persuasion to a promise of reform in the final embrace. His wild spirit is never wholly tamed, but it is tested so severely as bring out its noble qualities. Through pain and sorrow it becomes elevated to one of rude dignity. The theme is an evolution of manhood. The idea of the story is Hart's own, developed and directed in production by Lambert Hillyer. The story construction is so strong that more than one condition of high suspense is set up and skillfully maintained. The sets and romantic backgrounds are chosen with keen appreciation of the story's wild and picturesque mood.

"William S. Hart as the tigerish outlaw, 'Sierra' Bill, is a figure so powerful and distinct as to need no other centering of attention than that provided by his own personality. His dress is new, his attitude more intensely animal than ever before, his expression of the lawless male one to be remembered. He has gathered about him a talented support, Eve Novak as the leading woman, Gordon Russell as a fascinating, villainous heavy, Florence Carpenter pathetic in the role of a Mexican girl, and even the baby, little Richard Headrick, is fully imbued with the importance of playing his part. All these contribute to a production bound to hold any motion picture audience, as they did that of the Rivoli Theatre, in a thrall of intense interest."

The Testing Block broke all Sunday records on the opening day of its engagement at the New York Rivoli while the producer-star was on vacation at Victorville, California.

In the film, the picturesque sombrero that Bill wore had an interesting history. This hat of ample proportions, a magnificent specimen of a fully decorated beaver with gold braid, was once owned and worn by the most famous of all bandits of the early days in the old Southwest. His name was Joachin Murieta, and for two decades, his exploits spread from the Rio Grande to San Francisco. Florence D. Yambert of Cripple Creek, Colorado, presented the sombrero to Bill. There was a bullet hole through the upper part of the lofty crown believed to have been made during the bandit's last fight when, surrounded by superior numbers, he was killed in a mountain retreat near the Mexican border. Bill ultimately wore the hat in his portrayal of "Sierra" Bill, a character for whom Murieta was the prototype.

The Testing Block also marked the debut of Eve Novak as Bill's leading lady. She was the younger sister of Jane Novak, who played opposite him in *The Silent Man, Wagon Tracks,* and other pictures. Eva had not been on the screen a great while prior to her engagement with Bill, but seemed to take naturally to the work. In the role of Nellie Gray, the demure little maiden who plays the violin with a band of nomadic players in the Far West, she was said to have scored a genuine success.

Adolph Zukor, in his memoir *The Public Is Never Wrong*, recalled one evening when he and his wife were waiting for the curtain to go up in a New York theater. Two men seated behind them were talking in French. He recognized the deep tone of one of the voices, glanced around, and found that he was looking into the long, tanned face of William S. Hart wearing a dress suit.

"I knew you could talk the Sioux language," Zukor said in greeting, "but I had no idea you spoke French!"

Bill replied with a hearty laugh, "Only fairly well. I'm rusty, and my friend is brushing me up."

Zukor was startled to see the famed Western star in formal attire, but his wife whispered to him, "He's every bit as handsome in dress clothes as in his cowboy outfit." Zukor had never seen Bill on the live stage in his renowned roles as Romeo and Hamlet.

Bill did not marry until he was nearly fifty, but his matrimonial venture was not successful. He and his wife, known as Winifred Westover, a motion picture actress, separated five months after marriage. Divorce proceedings were long and drawn-out, and the union was officially dissolved after Winifred gave birth to a son, William S. Hart, Jr.

Bill was always prepared to meet his fans and give them the man they expected to see. Jane Novak, who had played in one film with him, accompanied him to the opening. After the show, they retired to the lobby where fans filed by in a line to grip and shake his hand. Jane noticed grease spots on his vest and tie.

Later she said, "Bill, your vest is never spotted when you take me out to dinner. What's got into you?"

Bill told Jane his reason for appearing as he did. "It's this way. My public rather expects me to look common."

His devoted sister, Mary, once complained, "I lay fresh clothing out for him whenever he goes to meet his fans. He dips his fingers into the gravy bowl and flicks gravy on his front!"

After finishing his last film, *Tumbleweeds* (1925), Bill retired to his fortress-like, Spanish ranch house in the California hills. His horse, Fritz, died, and was buried there with a raised monument.

By that time, sound films were turning the industry on its head, and Bill wisely left the screen while at the top of his success. He had no fear of speaking because his years of stage work had more than proven how good he was with spoken dramas. In 1939, *Tumbleweeds* was re-released with music and sound effects added. Bill appeared in a spoken prologue introducing the film to audiences, an eight-minute segment showing him in full Western costume, walking slowly up a hill toward the camera. This is the only surviving record of his deep, powerful, and well-modulated voice on film, as he details the importance of the film's theme about the opening of the Cherokee Strip. With tears in his eyes, Bill expresses his love for Fritz, his Pinto pony, and said goodbye to movie audiences in this moving speech:

> "My friends, I love the art of making motion pictures. It is as the breath of life to me. But through those hazards, those feats of horsemanship that I loved so well to do for you, I received many major injuries that, coupled with the added years of life, preclude again doing those things I so gloried in doing: the rush of the wind that cuts your face; the pounding hooves of the pursuing posse; out there in front, a fallen tree trunk that spans a yawning chasm; the animal under you that takes it in the same, low, ground-eating gallop; the harmless shots of the

baffled ones that remained behind; and then, clouds of dust through which comes the faint voice of the director, 'Okay, Bill, okay! Glad you made it! Great stuff, Bill, great stuff! And, say, Bill, give ol' Fritz a pat on the nose for me, will you?' Oh, the thrill of it all. You do give old Fritz a pat on the nose, and when your arm encircles his neck, the cloud of dust is no longer a cloud of dust, but a beautiful, golden haze through which appears a long, phantom herd of cattle. At their head, a Pinto pony—a Pinto pony with an empty saddle. And then, a low, loved whinny, the whinny of a horse so fine that nothing seems to live between it and silence, saying, 'Say, boss, what you riding back there with the drag for? Why don't you come up here and ride point with me? Can't you see, boss, can't you see that the saddle is empty? The boys up ahead are calling for you and me to help drive this last, great round-up into eternity!' Adios, amigos. God bless you all, each and every one."

Later in life, Bill wrote several books on Western history for boys. In addition, he wrote a novel about Patrick Henry. He amassed a great collection of Western paintings, including works by famous artists like Charles Russell and Frederick Remington. He spent a large fortune on his collection of guns, including those from the famous heroes, Billy the Kid and Bat Masterson.

After oil was discovered in the vicinity of his ranch, he remained true to his character and refused to allow any drilling on his personal land. He detested the site of oil derricks cluttering up the view from his ranch house on a hill, and wistfully wished to preserve the natural beauty of the land.

"I am pretty sentimental. The chief reason for my success was my mother. I went to her with all my troubles and came to her for advice all my life," he admitted.

Adolph Zukor recalled his last illness during which Bill briefly emerged from a coma and spoke, saying that he had "been on the other side." There, he had seen green fields, open ranges, and mountains, and there had been bright sunlight, and he had heard beautiful music everywhere.

Bill died at the age of seventy-five on June 24, 1946. He finally caught up with the Pinto pony sporting an empty saddle, and started to ride out on his last, great round up into eternity. At his bedside was his son, William S. Hart, Jr., who had been appointed co-guardian, and a friend, George Frost. Winifred Westover, from whom the actor had been divorced twenty years earlier, had been almost constantly at Bill's side. He bequeathed his money to the county, believing that the people had given it to him and he was giving it back. His will forbade any oil drilling on his ranch.

As a cowboy hero, William S. Hart became one of the most loved idols of the silent screen. His films are so loved that many are still shown today, as new generations discover his depictions of the West as he experienced it during his youth.

Silent Filmography of
William S. Hart

His Hour of Manhood (1914)
The Bargain (1914)
Two-Gun Hicks (1914)
Jim Cameron's Wife (1914)
In the Sage Brush Country (1914)
The Bad Buck of Santa Ynez (1914)
Scourge of the Desert (1915)
The Sheriff's Streak of Yellow (1915)
The Roughneck (1915)
On the Night Stage (1915)
The Darkening Trail (1915)
The Ruse (1915)
Cash Parrish's Pal (1915)
A Knight of the Trails (1915)
Keno Bates, Liar (1915)
The Disciple (1915)
Between Men (1915)
Tools of Providence (1915)
The Taking of Luke McVane (1915)
Pinto Ben (1915)
Mr. Silent Haskins (1915)
The Man from Nowhere (1915)
The Grudge (1915)
The Conversation of Frosty Blake (1915)
Hell's Hinges (1915)
The Aryan (1916)
The Primal Lure (1916)
The Apostle of Vengeance (1916)
The Captive God (1916)
The Patriot (1916)
The Dawn Maker (1916)
The Return of Draw Egan (1916)
The Devil's Double (1916)
Truthful Tulliver (1916)
The Gunfighter (1917)

The Desert Man (1917)
The Square Deal Man (1917)
Wolf Lowry (1917)
The Cold Deck (1917)
The Silent Man (1917)
The Narrow Trail (1917)
All-Star Production of Patriotic Episodes, for the Second Liberty Loan (1917)
Wolves of the Rail (1918)
Blue Blazes Rawden (1918)
The Tiger Man (1918)
Selfish Yates (1918)
Shark Monroe (1918)
Riddle Gawne (1918)
The Border Wireless (1918)
Branding Broadway (1918)
Staking His Life (1918)
The Lion of the Hills (1918)
Breed of Men (1919)
The Poppy Girl's Husband (1919)
The Money Corral (1919)
Square Deal Sanderson (1919)
Wagon Tracks (1919)
John Petticoats (1919)
The Toll Gate (1920)
Sand! (1920)
The Cradle of Courage (1920)
The Testing Block (1920)
O'Malley of the Mounted (1921)
The Whistle (1921)
Three Word Brand (1921)
White Oak (1921)
Travelin' On (1922)
Hollywood (1923)
Wild Bill Hickock (1923)
Singer Jim McKee (1924)
Hello Frisco (1924)
Tumbleweeds (1925)
Show People (1928)

Chapter 9
Tom Mix

The legend of Tom Mix has been a mysterious story. Facts have more often been shrouded by myth, and his legendary, youthful acts of real-life heroism are at times untraceable. Nevertheless, he was one of the first stars of motion pictures, an outstanding screen personality, and an inspiration to millions of young people.

Thomas Hezikiah Mix was born in 1880 in the town called Mix Run, near the city of Dubois, Pennsylvania. The valley of Mix Run was named after his great-great-grandfather, Amos Mix, who settled there in 1804.

His mother, Elizabeth, was very tiny and beautiful, with large, black eyes, and black hair. Tom's father, Ed Mix, worked as a lumberman in the picturesque Bennett's Valley, near Driftwood, Pennsylvania.

Husky lumbermen harvested logs each spring in Pennsylvania, and floated their lumber down the Susquehanna River to mills in the Lock Haven area. At the end of each season, as fall turned into winter and snow piled high over the roadways, homesteaders settled into a routine of mending clothes, bottling food, and socializing with friends. In the winter of January 1880, Tom's six-year-old brother, Harry, was excited to have a new brother join the family. His three-year-old sister, Emma, was hardly aware of the excitement in their little frame house.

At the age of four, Tom moved with his family to Driftwood, a larger town with more opportunities for the lumberman. Tom studied in the first and second grade levels in a one-room school in Driftwood. Then, Ed's employment again moved him to the town of DuBois, Pennsylvania. His expertise with horses gained him a

Tom Mix, ca. 1923, at the time he was making the film, Soft Boiled.

position as superintendent of the stables owned by the DuBois family.

By the end of the 19th century, the old West was vanishing fast. Tom attended school in DuBois, but he dropped out in the sixth grade. The show business seed was planted in him at the age of ten when he saw the *Buffalo Bill Cody Wild West Show* in El Paso. He thought it was important to show people the skills of expert marksmanship, and hard riding.

Tom was eighteen years old when hostilities broke out during the Spanish-American war. President McKinley sent the battleship *Maine* to Havana, allegedly to protect American lives. On February 15, 1898, 260 people were killed when the ship mysteriously exploded. Americans were united in their patriotic fervor to overthrow Spanish oppression and gain some self-government for the island of Cuba. "Remember the *Maine*" became a well-published, national slogan circulated in newspaper stories, as excitement swept through the country and popularized the war.

The tide of patriotism caught up with Tom and his friends. He left school, and then enlisted in the United States Artillery with dreams of joining in the fight he had seen sensationalized in the newspapers. He was assigned to Battery M, 4th Regiment, in the rank of Private, and then ordered to join those guarding the DuPont powder works at Montchanin, Delaware, against a possible attack by enemy naval forces. Battery M was transferred in May 1898 to Battery Point, Delaware, where he drilled and practiced firing the twelve-inch disappearing guns at Fort Delaware on Pea Patch Island. No attack ever came, but during the short Spanish-American war, Tom was promoted to the rank of Corporal.

Tom's outfit was mobilized quickly and thrust into the big land battles for Kettle and San Juan Hills on July 1, 1898. According to his second wife, Olive Stokes, Tom and his men were shaking the Spaniards out of palm trees during a cleanup operation when a Spanish sharpshooter sent the hot sting of lead through his mouth and out the back of his head. Olive said Tom spent a month recovering in a hospital.

There were 1,600 American casualties, and the besieged city of Santiago surrendered when Lt. Colonel Theodore Roosevelt led troops during the tenth week into the Battle of San Juan Hill. Spain granted freedom to Cuba under the Treaty of Paris on December 10, 1898. The war ended, and Tom remained with Battery M until April of the following year. He was promoted to the rank of Sergeant, and transferred to Battery O, stationed at Fort Monroe, Virginia, a receiving center for the returning wounded. Tom trained recruits, visited survivors at the National Soldier's Home, and took part in remodeling activities at the fort's living quarters. He was honorably discharged at Fort Hancock on April 25, 1901.

He reenlisted in January 1902, during the Boer War, and while on furlough, Tom met an attractive schoolteacher named Grace Allin. They were married on July 18, 1902. Tom performed duties at Fort Hancock, and took his last furlough. He was listed as AWOL when he left the military later that year, but the practice was common because in those days, procedures were lax, and men simply left their regiments at the end of a war. No warrant for his arrest was ever issued.

He always wanted to go West, and because he was unsure about whether the Army was still looking for him or not, he took Grace and moved to Guthrie, Oklahoma where she continued to work as an English teacher. While there, Tom developed a physical fitness program for young people.

The couple could not adjust to each other, and his marriage to Grace was annulled. Once again alone, Tom accepted a job with the Oklahoma Cavalry Band as drum major. He was dashing in his colorful uniform, and the band took part in the St. Louis World's Fair of 1904. His friend, Will Rogers, introduced him to a fourteen-year-old girl, Olive Stokes, who would later become his third wife.

He was briefly working as a bartender when he met Kitty Jewel Perrine, daughter of the bar's owner. In late 1905, while he was looking for a better job, Tom joined Colonel Joe Miller and the Miller Brothers' 101 Real Wild West Ranch as a $15-a-month, full-time cowboy. During his first season, Tom and Kitty were married at the Perrine Hotel. This marriage was as brief as his others, and after their divorce, he noticed a champion cowgirl in the Mulhall Wild West Show. Lucille Mulhall was the daughter of the millionaire oilman who ran the show, and Tom joined the cowboys as part of the act.

In December 1908, after his third season with the show, he married Olive Stokes while helping her buy horses in Medora, North Dakota. Olive later recalled that Tom rode on the freighters as they brought the animals to South Africa. Tom impressed the English with his demonstrations of roping and riding. While there, he did little actual fighting, but he did appear as an extra in a motion picture made by an American movie company.

Cripple Creek Barroom, an 1898 film made by the Edison Company, is very likely the first Western film. The same company scored a tremendous hit several years later with *The Great Train Robbery* (1903). This one-reel film was presented in many thousands of nickelodeons as they opened across America. It was the beginning of a new age in the entertainment industry.

He watched these early Western films and thought they looked fake. The wild gestures and exaggerated acting seemed insulting to the young cowboy who claimed to know first-hand about life in the West. In reality, his cowboy experience was limited to rodeos and ranch work, but he looked like a cowboy and exuded a vibrant personality that attracted people to him.

After Tom married Olive Stokes, he planned to get ahead in the Wild West show business. An invitation arrived to join the Widerman Wild West Show in Amarillo, Texas. He took Olive to the dusty, west Texas town, made an agreement with Mr. Widerman, and joined the small show performing riding tricks, somersaulting backward from a galloping horse with precision and grace, and dazzling the audience with a solo lariat act.

With this initial experience, Tom ventured into a partnership with Charlie Tipton and opened his own Wild West show in Seattle at the Western Washington Fair. Forty Blackfoot Indians were engaged to thrill audiences with a spectacular battle attacking a stagecoach. Audiences loved the adventuresome displays, and cowboy Tom was on his way with a new career.

Will Dickey had been touring the country with his own Wild West show in 1909 when he joined the Chicago-based Selig-Polyscope Company under a contract to make Western pictures. He did not know if Tom would like the idea of getting into moving pictures with him when he sent a letter to Olive to ask if she could persuade him to meet him in Flemington, Missouri. To Olive's surprise, Tom enthusiastically agreed.

Ranch Life in the Great Southwest (1910) was the first film in which Tom prominently appeared. He was featured briefly in a bronco-busting scene.

Next, Dickey prepared a two-reel film aiming to realistically portray Western life. *The Range Rider* (1910) was filmed against the natural, outdoor backgrounds of Missouri. All Tom had to do was be himself and refrain from the broad gestures he despised seeing in other Western films. Myrtle Steadman was his leading lady, and William V. Mong enacted the role of the villain in the tale of good winning against evil. *The Range Rider* took almost a month to make, an extremely long time in an era when most films were produced in a matter of days.

The Range Rider proved popular for the Selig Company, and they signed Tom to a contract for one year. He thought the steady income would go a long way to providing a means to buy the ranch of his dreams in Oklahoma.

Tom's films for Selig were enormously successful. He made twelve films in 1910, and Selig's Western films were their biggest moneymakers. Will Dickey believed their popularity lay in the picturing of the winning of the West, the foundation of American life, and Tom agreed.

The company assembled in Jacksonville, Florida, at the Dixieland Park. For the next production, Tom was slated to appear with Kathlyn Williams in a jungle film, *Back to the Primitive* (1911). Kathlyn Williams was a leading star of Selig films in these early one-reel and two-reel productions. Later, in December 1913, Selig would release *The Adventures of Kathlyn*, a fifteen-chapter serial with a new title every two weeks. It would be a sensational hit.

When *Back to the Primitive* was completed, Tom and the Selig troupe left Florida and filmed their remaining pictures in various States.

A patent war was taking place at that time within the fledgling film industry. Smaller, independent producers either went out of business or relocated to California where they could escape the process servers. Mary Pickford and the producers of her company, IMP, resorted to the drastic measure of assembling their entire company off the continental United States in Cuba to escape the threats and violence of the major companies intending to dominate the patents war. The Edison Company constantly badgered other producers for infringement of their patent for the use of the motion picture camera. Selig joined the exodus to the other side of the country, and relocated to California in the spring of 1911.

Tom was signed to a new contract in Chicago, and then made the journey out of town with a contingent of players to make pictures in Canyon City, Colorado. They set up camp in an isolated part of the mountains in a beautiful location invigorated by panoramic views with no patent process servers within sight. They planned their film stories while sitting around a campfire.

After completing their first film in Colorado, Mr. Selig joined the renegade film pioneers and informed them of their new location in the foothills of Los Angeles, California. He mentioned it was near a little place called Hollywood.

Once there, they found a booming city of almost 400,000 people, spread over a flat plain extending from the mountains to the sea. Tom was given a studio in Glendale. It was here that a horse he named Tony joined him. The black colt was purchased from a chicken wagon, trained by Pat Crisman, and later sold to Tom at the age of two. For the next thirty-four years, Tony and Tom were inseparable. Tom was the only person who ever rode Tony.

By 1917, Tom was a top star of Western films. His dream of settling down on a ranch just never happened, and after a daughter was born to them, a wall rose between Tom and Olive, the result of this struggle between the nature of the man and the personality of the movie star. In 1917, they divorced because the fame and pressures of movie stardom separated them from the life they initially shared. The next year, he married Victoria Forde, a leading lady in many of his films.

The Selig-Polyscope Company disbanded in 1917, and William Fox signed Tom to make films for his larger organization. At Selig, Tom often had to create his own stories and had little professional help. Fox fully realized the potential they had with their new star, and they provided an organization to create Western films aimed at youngsters. Work began at a special studio lot covering twelve acres near Edendale, California. The acreage was called Mixville. Tom assembled a team of splendid people, and produced films more elaborate than he had made with Selig. There was an Indian village nestled on a flat piece of land near the rear of Mixville where many convincing raids were filmed. A simulated desert spread over another lot where Tom and Tony wandered looking for bad men in dozens of films.

Tom never rested. When not working on the lot, he could usually be spotted either in conference at the studio's main office on Western Avenue and Sunset Boulevard, or in their private gymnasium.

As Tom's new full-length films made for the Fox Company propelled him to the status of a top-liner, Selig realized the value of these longer films being made with his former star. Selig attempted to create some of his own by editing several of Tom's older short films together into what appeared to be a new full-length film. *Twisted Trails*, for example, was a reconstructed film, and showed considerable ingenuity on the part of the Selig organization. Footage from a film in which Tom did not even appear established the heroine, played by Bessie Eyton, running away from an unwanted marriage. Footage from one of Tom's earlier Selig films was then edited into the story to establish him as a wandering cowboy. To blend the two, a title was inserted announcing, "Thus were the twisted trails of the boy and girl joined together." The remaining footage came from Selig stock of one of their old two-reel films in which both actors appeared together. The reconstructed film was then sold to exhibitors as a new product, although it was entirely made from preexisting scenes released in earlier years. These practices were common among film studios of that era, until exhibitors and actors objected and the practice was largely halted. To halt this trend, Mary Pickford and Charlie Chaplin went to the extreme of buying many of their early short films to prevent their resurgence in new forms that would compare unfavorably with the cinematic advancements in lighting and photography of their later works.

In 1923, Tom made a bold attempt to step out of his cowboy persona in a comedy for Fox. *Soft Boiled* struck against the grain of his typecasted image, submerged his Western regalia, and presented him as a leading man in the first directorial effort of Jack Blystone. Although the film was technically a Western, the film gave him a number of scenes in which to appear in street clothes and formal wear.

The decade of the 1920s was the era when silent films matured. Feature-length films became the standard, and Tom's films were as valuable to Fox as Mary Pickford's were to United Artists. The thousands of small towns across America always welcomed the

This magazine advertisement for the 1923 film *Soft Boiled* appeared in *Moving Picture World*, **August 25, 1923.**

arrival of a new Tom Mix picture. For many youngsters, his films were a great event in their lives. He had a tremendous influence on the youth of America, and took the responsibility seriously. Press agents ground out reams of copy dictating his personal mode of living, his uninhibited enthusiasm, and his dedication to maintaining a clean reputation.

Olive Stokes, in her book *The Fabulous Tom Mix*, recalled how Tom saw himself as a role model. She said he once told a press agent, "I know I've got a reputation to live up to. I *want* to be a good influence on the young people who follow me. I never want to disappoint them. So I've got to live up to what they expect of me. For a long time that used to bother me. I thought I might be missing a lot of fun. I couldn't go places where sometimes I wanted to go, because I was sure the kids wouldn't like it. I felt sort of hedged in. But I changed my mind about that pretty fast . . . after I realized that I really wanted to lead the life the kids expected me to lead."

Tom never varied from his basic qualities, but his lifestyle accelerated far beyond any normal mode of living. His extravagances included a personal yacht and a great mansion in Beverly Hills. He had an arsenal of rifles and revolvers, along with an enormous collection of Western artifacts amassed during his life. The mansion also housed a seven-car garage filled with tens of thousands of dollars worth of automobiles. A special house was built adjacent to the mansion for Tony.

In 1925, Tom made a beautiful Western film of the famous Zane Grey story, *Riders of the Purple Sage*. The full-length production featured sumptuous photography, and is one of the few 35mm films of his silent features that have survived.

Variety reviewed the film and waxed eloquently over Tom's efforts to bring the youth of the world into the film theaters to see him in strong, clean films that showed positive virtues. "All pictures cannot have a Tom Mix, but all pictures of romance may have clean romance, the kind of romance the youth should have in his or her mind and heart, not the vile vamps, the dirty dames, the rotten rogues, and the lustful villains to excite the imagination, or the pictures maybe of adventure or with any subject, but clean—have them clean, for if not, the very children of today, who, as they advance in maturity and observe the kind of licentious pictures now that so many producers are trying to sneak past the censors, those same children, as parents, will wish that their children shall not go to the picture houses."

The *New York Times* said of *Riders of the Purple Sage*, "... it must be admitted that the boys in the Piccadilly yesterday afternoon were very keen about Mr. Mix's ability to outwit the cattle thieves, and their applause demonstrated that they approved of his excellent horsemanship and his manner of polishing off the bad men. In one of the scenes, three men bite the sawdust in a bar, and the redoubtable Jim Lassiter (Mr. Mix) appears rather surprised that he did not kill a fourth bandit. Lassiter's crowning glory is a full-gallon hat. The music in the theater helps Lassiter in his deadly work. When he is about to shoot, there is silence, followed by crack-crack-crack, with a subsequent triumphant air from the organ. Incidentally, Lassiter is ushered on the screen with Elgar's song, *Pomp and Circumstance.*"

Like many people in America, Tom lost millions of dollars in stocks and securities in the 1929 stock market crash, but his career continued unabated as the Great Depression gripped America. When sound films took a hold in the motion picture industry, Tom made *Outlawed, The Big Diamond Robbery,* and *The Drifter.*

He spent the years from 1929 to 1931 as the star of the Sells-Floto Circus, traveling by way of a private railroad car, and touring America. Tumultuous cheering manifested from the crowds in every city where he took his act. While well into his fifties, Tom still radiated a magnetic quality from his position in the center ring with his act, and stirred applause with his trick riding and shooting. He loved signing autographs for the fans before and after each performance, and frequently gave talks to youth groups and charity performances at hospitals.

Tom's daughter, Ruth, grew up in the shadow of her father's fame, but joined him in the circus show in the season of 1931. She was only nineteen years old, but proudly joined the show exhibiting her keen abilities with trick roping and shooting. Tom taught her every trick he knew, and she displayed her prowess with skill. Ruth Mix soon became a star in her own right.

In 1931, Tom made a minor movie comeback with Universal Pictures. Nine talking pictures were made for this popular series.

Tom married Mabel Ward, an aerial performer with the Sells-Floto Circus, and in 1935, he bought the Sam B. Dill Circus, christened it The Tom Mix Circus, and valiantly toured throughout America.

It was a bad year for circuses everywhere, and the misfortunes suffered by his circus during the first season included disastrous weather, an epidemic among the animals, an aerialist's accident, and the usual struggle with wrecks, fires, and financial heartaches. Though he played to capacity crowds, a second tour the following year was proving to be difficult to arrange.

Gone was his mansion in Beverly Hills, his yacht, and his string of Rolls-Royces. A loan was arranged to carry his crew through their winter hiatus in San Angelo, and Tom looked forward to a new season in the spring.

He and his daughter perfected a new routine just before the season was to start. The first weeks were successful, as big crowds turned out in droves to see the circus, but then disaster struck.

Catastrophe came in the form of officials from a small town in Montana. They demanded 200 complimentary tickets for town officials and their families and friends. "It is the law," they said.

Tom told them, "Sounds like a funny law to me. Seems as if the town officials, who have jobs, at least could afford to buy tickets for their families and friends. You see, we keep our admission charge as low as possible so as many persons as possible can see the show. We have a law, too. Our complimentary tickets go to underprivileged children and to charitable organizations."

The officials warned him to change his opinion, or they could not guarantee his show would safely take place. Tom steadfastly refused, and that night, they angrily rounded up a group of men and mobbed the tent. The canvas was ripped and torn down, cars were wrecked, trailers were overturned, and many animals were severely injured. The officials outnumbered Tom's men and ruined the circus, wrecking most of their equipment beyond repair.

Tom pulled the remains of the circus out of town. While in route to their next scheduled stop, a truck towing a trailer filled with horses lost control and plummeted over a mountain road into a ravine, injuring the driver and killing several prized horses. After these horrible events, Tom's financial losses were fantastic. A three-week delay closed the show while new equipment was quickly refinanced.

In Neenah, Wisconsin, the restructured Tom Mix Circus arrived under sunny skies. The crowd had no sooner packed the tent than rain began to pelt against the taut canvas. By the second act, the downpour blew into a raging tornado, and the tent billowing appeared near to collapse. The pummeled, flapping canvas began to sag, and it was obvious that another disaster was imminent. In the ensuing scare, multitudes of animals were cut loose minutes before the tent fell. People panicked, as they raced toward the exits in a frenzied attempt to escape the collapsing canvas. Tom stood in the center ring desperately trying to calm their fears with his persuasive voice over the loudspeaker, while uncontrollable elephants and horses rampaged back and forth among the people. The melee reached surreal proportions when the fire department arrived and slit the tent into long shreds to allow the frightened crowd to escape.

Within minutes, the uncontrollable scuffling passed as the storm passed, and the air was laced with nothing but a gentle, falling drizzle. There was calm after the storm, but by the end of the tragic night, it was obvious that financial ruin hung like a pal over the pitiful remains of the Tom Mix Circus.

Tom led the crew in repairing the equipment, sewing up the tears in the tent, and hoping to carry on with the show, but the spirit of the circus was finished. The circus seemed doomed to close. Strangely, these events got the better of Tom. He ran away from his own circus and left it under the care of his daughter, Ruth, by then enough of a name attraction to draw crowds on her own. She carried on with the show for the remainder of the season, and ended the run with a final performance in Pecos, Texas.

In 1935, Tom came out of retirement to play in a fifteen-chapter, Mascot Pictures serial, *The Miracle Rider,* playing the role of a Texas Ranger braving death in a plot to force his Indian friends from their reservation.

The Tom Mix Radio Show ran from 1933–1950, with various actors playing the role of Tom Mix in fifteen-minute episodes, but no listener ever heard the voice of the real Tom Mix. It did not matter. What they heard sounded like what they presumed was their hero, and the radio show was a popular favorite with both children and adults.

Tom returned from a successful tour of Europe in May 1940, and was filled with enthusiasm for a fresh start with a new motion picture pending and a proposed tour of South America. He called Ruth at her ranch with the great news. He planned to leave for Hollywood the following day.

After hanging up the telephone, he climbed into his green, custom-built Cord convertible to begin the drive from New York to California. A week later, he again called her from Tucson, Arizona, and then resumed the journey on October 12, 1940. On a narrow ribbon of road about eighteen miles from Florence, Arizona, he suddenly came upon a partially constructed bridge with no warning sign about the obstruction. He swerved his car and crashed into the gully at the bottom of the construction where he died.

The Tom Mix Radio Show continued for ten years after his death. Where he died, a Pennsylvania highway marker inscription reads, "The famous cowboy star of silent motion pictures was born a short distance from here on January 6, 1880. He served as a soldier in the Spanish-American War, later becoming renowned for his 'wild west' roles in cinema and circus. Mix died in an auto accident in Arizona on October 12, 1940."

Tom Mix was a legend in his own lifetime. Although his Western films were not as realistically detailed as others, he exuded the type of personality everyone believed was true to cowboy lore. He was greatly loved, and his reputation still fosters admiration today.

Silent Filmography of
Tom Mix

Ranch Life in the Great Southwest (1910)
The Range Riders (1910)
The Cowboy Millionaire (1910)
Indian Wife's Devotion (1910)
Trimming of Paradise Gulch (1910)
Go West, Young Woman, Go West (1910)
The Way of the Red Man (1910)
The Cowboy's Stratagem (1910)
Lost in the Soudan (1910)
Two Boys in Blue (1910)
Taming Wild Animals (1910)
Pride of the Range (1910)
The Man from the East (1911)
Back to the Primitive (1911)
The Rose of Old St. Augustine (1911)
Captain Kate (1911)
Saved by the Pony Express (1911)
Life on the Border (1911)
The Totem Mark (1911)
Dad's Girls (1911)
Told in Colorado (1911)
Why the Sheriff is a Bachelor (1911)
Lost in the Jungle (1911)
Western Hearts (1911)
The Telltale Knife (1911)
A Romance of the Rio Grande (1911)
The Bully of Bingo Gulch (1911)
The Schoolmaster of Mariposa (1911)
Rescued by her Lions (1911)
Outlaw Reward (1911)
A Cowboy's Best Girl (1912)
The Scapegoat (1912)
The Diamond S Ranch (1912)
A Reconstructed Rebel (1912)
The Range Law (1913)

Juggling With Fate (1913)
The Sheriff of Yawapai County (1913)
The Life Timer (1913)
The Shotgun Man and the Stage Driver (1913)
That Mail Order Suit (1913)
His Father's Deputy (1913)
Religion and Gun Practice (1913)
The Law and the Outlaw (1913)
The Only Chance (1913)
Taming a Tenderfoot (1913)
The Marshal's Capture (1913)
Sallie's Sure Shot (1913)
Made a Coward (1913)
The Taming of Texas Pete (1913)
The Stolen Moccasins (1913)
An Apache's Gratitude (1913)
The Good Indian (1913)
How Betty Made Good (1913)
Tobias Wants Out (1913)
Howlin' Jones (1913)
The Rejected Lover's Luck (1913)
The Cattle Thief's Escape (1913)
Saved from the Vigilantes (1913)
The Silver Grindstone (1913)
Dishwash Dick's Counterfeit (1913)
A Muddle in Horse Thieves (1913)
The Schoolmarm's Shooting Match (1913)
The Sheriff and the Rustler (1913)
The Child of the Prairies (1913)
The Escape of Jim Dolan (1913)
Cupid in the Cow Camp (1913)
Physical Culture on the Quarter Circle V Bar (1913)
Buster's Little Game (1913)
Mother Love vs. Gold (1913)
The Wordless Message (1913)
Songs of Truce (1913)
A Prisoner of Cabanas (1913)

Pauline Cushman, the Federal Spy (1913)
The Noisy Six (1913)
Local Color (1913)
How It Happened (1913)
Budd Doble Comes Back (1913)
By Unseen Hand (1914)
A Friend in Need (1914)
The Little Sister (1914)
Shotgun Jones (1914)
In Defiance of the Law (1914)
The Wilderness Mail (1914)
When the Cook Fell Ill (1914)
Etienne of the Glad Heart (1914)
The White Mouse (1914)
Chip of the Flying U (1914)
When the West Was Young (1914)
Out of the Petticoat Lane (1914)
The Going of the White Swan (1914)
The Real Thing in Cowboys (1914)
The Moving Picture Cowboy (1914)
The Way of the Redman (1914)
The Mexican (1914)
Your Girl and Mine: A Woman Suffrage Play (1914)
Jimmy Hayes and Muriel (1914)
Why the Sheriff Is a Bachelor (1914)
The Telltale Knife (1914)
The Losing Fight (1914)
The Ranger's Romance (1914)
The Sheriff's Reward (1914)
The Scapegoat (1914)
In the Days of the Thundering Herd (1914)
The Rival Stage Lines (1914)
Saved by a Watch (1914)
The Man from the East (1914)
The Lure of the Windigo (1914)
The Flower of Faith (1914)
Cactus Jake, Heart-Breaker (1914)

Wiggs Takes the Rest Cure (1914)
Wade Brent Pays (1914)
To Be Called For (1914)
The Soul Mate (1914)
The Reveler (1914)
Me an' Bill (1914)
The Lonesome Trail (1914)
The Livid Flame (1914)
The Leopard's Foundling (1914)
Jim (1914)
If I Were Young Again (1914)
His Fight (1914)
Hearts and Masks (1914)
Finish (1914)
The Fifth Man (1914)
Buffalo Hunting (1914)
Harold's Bad Man (1915)
Cactus Jim's Shopgirl (1915)
The Grizzly Gulch Chariot Race (1915)
Forked Trails (1915)
Roping a Bride (1915)
Bill Haywood, Producer (1915)
Slim Higgins (1915)
A Child of the Prairie (1915)
The Man from Texas (1915)
The Stagecoach Driver and the Girl (1915)
Sagebrush Tom (1915)
The Outlaw's Bride (1915)
Ma's Girls (1915)
The Legal Light (1915)
The Conversion of Smiling Tom (1915)
Getting a Start in Life (1915)
Mrs. Murphy's Cooks (1915)
An Arizona Wooing (1915)
A Matrimonial Boomerang (1915)
Saved by Her Horse (1915)
Pals in Blue (1915)
The Heart of the Sheriff (1915)

With the Aid of the Law (1915)
Foreman of Bar Z Ranch (1915)
Never Again (1915)
How Weary Went Wooing (1915)
The Range Girl and the Cowboy (1915)
The Auction Sale of Run-Down Ranch (1915)
Her Slight Mistake (1915)
The Girl and the Mail Bag (1915)
The Foreman's Choice (1915)
The Brave Deserve the Fair (1915)
The Stagecoach Guard (1915)
The Race for a Gold Mine (1915)
Athletic Ambitions (1915)
The Chef at Circle G (1915)
The Tenderfoot's Triumph (1915)
The Impersonation of Tom (1915)
Bad Man Bobs (1915)
On the Eagle Trail (1915)
The Puny Soul of Peter Rand (1915)
The Parson Who Fled West (1915)
Hearts of the Jungle (1915)
The Face at the Window (1915)
A Mix-Up in Movies (1916)
Making Good (1916)
The Passing of Peter (1916)
Along the Border (1916)
Too Many Chefs (1916)
The Man Within (1916)
A Five-Thousand Dollar Elopement (1916)
Crooked Trails (1916)
Going West to Make Good (1916)
The Cowpuncher's Peril (1916)
Taking a Chance (1916)
The Girl of Gold Gulch (1916)
Some Duel (1916)
Legal Advice (1916)
Shooting Up the Movies (1916)
Local color on the A-1 Ranch (1916)

An Angelic Attitude (1916)
A Western Masquerade (1916)
A Bear of a Story (1916)
Roping a Sweetheart (1916)
Tom's Strategy (1916)
The Taming of Grouchy Bill (1916)
The Pony Express Rider (1916)
A Corner in Water (1916)
The Raiders (1916)
The Canby Hill Outlaws (1916)
A Mistake in Rustlers (1916)
An Eventful Evening (1916)
A Close Call (1916)
Tom's Sacrifice (1916)
The Sheriff's Blunder (1916)
Mistakes Will Happen (1916)
Twisted Trails (1916)
The Golden Thought (1916)
The Way of the Redman (1916)
Starring in Western Stuff (1917)
Delayed in Transit (1917)
The Luck That Jealousy Brought (1917)
The Heart of Texas Ryan (1917)
The Saddle Girth (1917)
Hearts and Saddles (1917)
A Roman Cowboy (1917)
Six Cylinder Love (1917)
A Soft Tenderfoot (1917)
Durand of the Bad Lands (1917)
Tom and Jerry Mix (1917)
Cupid's Roundup (1918)
Six Shooter Andy (1918)
Western Blood (1918)
Ace High (1918)
Who's Your Father (1918)
Mr. Logan, U.S.A. (1918)
Fame and Fortune (1918)
Treat 'Em Rough (1919)

Hell-Roarin' Reform (1919)
Fighting for Gold (1919)
The Coming of the Law (1919)
The Wilderness Trail (1919)
Rough-Riding Romance (1919)
The Speed Maniac (1919)
The Feud (1919)
The Cyclone (1920)
The Daredevil (1920)
Desert Love (1920)
The Terror (1920)
Days of Daring (1920)
Three Gold Coins (1920)
The Untamed (1920)
The Texan (1920)
Prairie Trails (1920)
The Road Demon (1921)
Hands Off (1921)
A Ridin' Romeo (1921)
Big Town Round-Up (1921)
After Your Own Heart (1921)
The Night Horsemen (1921)
The Rough Diamond (1921)
Trailin' (1921)
Sky High (1922)
Chasing the Moon (1922)
Up and Going (1922)
The Fighting Streak (1922)
For Big Sakes (1922)
Just Tony (1922)
Do and Dare (1922)
Tom Mix in Arabia (1922)
Catch My Smoke (1922)
Romance Land (1923)
Three Jumps Ahead (1923)
Stepping Fat (1923)
Soft Boiled (1923)
The Lone Star Ranger (1923)

MILE-A-MINUTE ROMEO (1923)
NORTH OF HUDSON BAY (1923)
EYES OF THE FOREST (1923)
LADIES TO BOARD (1924)
THE TROUBLE SHOOTER (1924)
THE HEART BUSTER (1924)
THE LAST OF THE DUANES (1924)
OH, YOU TONY! (1924)
TEETH (1924)
THE DEADWOOD COACH (1924)
PALS IN BLUE (1924)
DICK TURPIN (1925)
RIDERS OF THE PURPLE SAGE (1925)
THE RAINBOW TRAIL (1925)
THE LUCKY HORSESHOE (1925)
THE EVERLASTING WHISPER (1925)
THE BEST BAD MAN (1925)
THE YANKEE SEÑOR (1925)
MY OWN PAL (1926)
TONY RUNS WILD (1926)
HARD BOILED (1926)
NO MAN'S GOLD (1926)
THE GREAT K & A TRAIN ROBBERY (1926)
THE CANYON OF LIGHT (1926)
THE LAST TRAIL (1927)
THE BRONCHO TWISTER (1927)
OUTLAWS OF RED RIVER (1927)
THE CIRCUS ACE (1927)
TUMBLING RIVER (1927)
SILVER VALLEY (1927)
THE ARIZONA WILDCAT (1927)
LIFE IN HOLLYWOOD N. 4 (1927)
DAREDEVIL'S REWARD (1928)
A HORSEMAN OF THE PLAINS (1928)
HELLO CHEYENNE (1928)
PAINTED POST (1928)
SON OF THE GOLDEN WEST (1928)
KING COWBOY (1928)

Hollywood Today No. 4 (1928)
Outlawed (1929)
The Drifter (1929)
The Big Diamond (1929)

Chapter 10
Antonio Moreno

Antonio Moreno was the first Latin lover of the silent screen. He brought to early films a powerful sexuality and a lean, masculine way of moving that fascinated women. This demeanor, coupled with an aura of Spanish poetry and romance, made him one of the most colorful and interesting figures on the silver screen. He had one of the longest careers of motion picture actors.

Born on September 26, 1886, as Antonio Garrido Monteagudo y Moreno, in Madrid, Spain, he was the only son of Juan Moreno, a career officer in the Spanish Army. Juan died while his son was a child, and he left behind an impoverished widow in the town of Seville.

His mother, Ana, moved to Algeciras, and then, later, took residence in Gibraltar, where her growing boy became friendly with the English soldiers. "Although I was only a little boy," Antonio recalled many years later, "I tried to learn English, but didn't make much progress." Antonio was fascinated with everything American, and while at an early age, set his heart on journeying to the land across the sea.

Each year in Gibraltar, the annual town fair attracted people from all over Spain. Antonio found work as a teenage laborer on the fairground's buildings. One day during the fair, Enrique de Cruzat Nanetti, a Spanish attorney and graduate of Harvard, was ambling about the grounds with his American friend, Benjamin Curtis. The two men noticed the attractive youth, and while questioning him in light conversation, discovered that he could speak a smattering of English and was interested in anything American.

Antonio Moreno, ca. 1918.

Antonio mentioned he would be looking for another job when the fair ended, and Nanetti offered Antonio a position as an interpreter and companion-nurse for his ailing American friend during their remaining weeks of travel in Spain.

From his earnings as an interpreter, Antonio was able to move with his mother to better surroundings in the small, coastal town of Campamento. Zanetti and Curtis did not forget the Spanish youth who assisted them during their Spanish travels, and after they returned to New York, they cabled him the fare for his passage to America. Antonio quickly made the journey. At the age of fifteen, he walked up the gangplank from the Gibraltar docks to the American steamship, in effect, crossing the bridge from nonentity to fame. He did not know that the door to his future was about to open.

Aboard the boat was one of America's most distinguished actresses, Miss Helen Ware. Her attention riveted on the handsome lad with the fiery eyes, and she engaged him in conversation.

"What do you intend to do when you reach America?" inquired Miss Ware.

"Make a fortune," promptly replied young Antonio.

Miss Ware smiled at his confidence, and replied, "I think you will find both fame and fortune in the theater if you chose to become an actor." Her words left an indelible impression on him, and he brimmed with enthusiasm to make his way to the center of theatrical activity in the world of the New York Theater. For Antonio, Broadway beckoned.

In 1902, he enrolled in a Catholic school and studied English with dogged determination. Within a year, he knew enough of the new language to attend a New York high school. Adeline Moffet, a Manhattan social worker, often staged entertainments at downtown schools. Antonio met Adeline, and she later introduced him to a wealthy Manhattan widow, Mrs. Charlotte Morgan. Mrs. Morgan was equally taken with the young man, who was the same age as her recently deceased son. She took Antonio into her Northampton home, and then enrolled him in the nearby Williston Seminary to educate him for the priesthood. "I know that my mother never meant more to me than Mrs. Morgan," said Tony. "Why, I even used to call her 'Mummy.'"

Though Mrs. Morgan was willing to financially provide for Antonio, he was independent by nature, and insisted on working. He found jobs as a laborer at a Northampton silk hosiery factory, as an employee of the New England telephone company, and as a meter-reader for the local gas company. He also found work playing small roles with a resident stock company in Northampton. This first taste of the theater whetted his appetite for acting. When the summer's engagement ended and the company moved onto other cities, Antonio went to New York, and there, found work as an electrician. He had a burning desire to be near Broadway, the center of the theatrical profession, where he hoped he would find success.

Maude Adams, then hard at work with rehearsals for *The Little Minister*, was having electrical trouble with the lighting switchboard at the Empire Theater. Antonio was sent to help with the repairs, and after completing the tasks, he asked the stage manager if there were any jobs available. Fortunately for the ambitious young man, there was a position open for a "super." Antonio took the job, and as the first weeks passed, he was given a few lines to speak in a small role in the play. This first taste of Broadway set him on a course he would follow for the rest of his life.

During the next five years, he found many roles in the professional theater: he played with Mrs. Leslie Carter in *DuBarry* and *Two Women*, with Constance Collier and Tyrone Power, Sr., in *Thaïs*, with Wilton Lackaye in *The Right to Happiness*, and with Beatrice Ingraham in vaudeville. He acted with the Manhattan Players for a season of stock at the Lyceum Theater in Rochester.

Antonio found people noticed his unique, devil-may-care personality, and the graceful air of Latin romance surrounding him only added to his allure. Helen Ware encouraged him to stick to his ambition to become an actor. After a season with E. H. Sothern playing Shakespearean repertory, Antonio met Walter Edwin, an elderly English actor, who encouraged him to try his luck in motion pictures.

In 1912, motion pictures were taking a firm hold on neighborhood audiences all across America and, in many small towns, replacing the traditional live theater. Even Sarah Bernhardt had appeared in several motion pictures, raising the prestige level of what was once considered a low form of cheap amusement to a level considered respectable. Motion pictures also offered an easy way to make quick cash, always a necessity for any actor. Antonio looked into the curious, new business by visiting the Rex-Universal Studios on Eleventh Avenue and 43rd Street.

He was quickly cast into a Marion Leonard film, *The Voice of the Million*. He played a young mill striker in a small town, and photographed so well that he tried working in several other films for rival studios. D. W. Griffith used him in small parts in a number of his best Biograph one-reel films: *Two Daughters of Eve* and *The Musketeers of Pig Alley*, both with Lillian Gish, and *So Near, Yet So Far*, with Mary Pickford.

"About two years ago, a handsome, dark-complexioned young man appeared in a Biograph play, and his unique personality attracted considerable attention," wrote a reporter in 1914 for *Photoplay Magazine*. "He stood five feet ten in height, weighed about 168 pounds, and was gracefully put together. His dark brown eyes flashed under his long, black lashes, and his manner was graceful and pleasant. He at once attracted attention, and when different companies began to bid for him, the Reliance Company made him the best offer, which he accepted."

He was always quick to make friends, and he built valuable and lasting friendships among men who thought highly of his acquaintance. One friend was a young actor who would later change his name to Ramon Novarro. One day, Antonio smuggled him in the trunk of his car past the guards at Vitagraph to enable the ambitious youth to get a part as an extra.

When asked if he had become an American citizen, Antonio told one reporter in 1914, "I tried to fill out some naturalization papers, but I had trouble in finding out the name of the steamer that I sailed on, and met with so many other difficulties that I gave up the idea of becoming a citizen of the United States, although I suppose I should be a citizen, and I would certainly be proud to be one." Antonio was an inalienable Spaniard, intensely patriotic, and loved his country passionately.

By 1914, Antonio had developed a strong following all over the world. Men liked him because of his forthright masculinity and all-American spirit, and women adored him for his handsome, dark looks and romantic Spanish flavor. Albert E. Smith, president of Vitagraph, eagerly put Antonio in the role of Norma Phillips' "country lover" in a fifty-two-chapter serial, *Our Mutual Girl*. Each episode featured Norma visiting historic and popular sites in New York, or encountering a famous celebrity of the day.

That same year, D. W. Griffith supervised his appearance with veteran actors Lionel Barrymore, Henry B. Walthall, and Blanche Sweet in *Strongheart*.

Norma Talmadge, Vitagraph's reigning ingénue, quickly realized his potential. In 1914, Antonio played in *John Rance, Gentleman*, the first of at least seven films he would make with her that year. Norma's sister, Constance, snapped him up to star with him the following year in the film *In the Latin Quarter*, a tale of an artist falling in love with a pretty model who saves his paintings from a jealous woman.

Edith Story was the next female star to win Antonio for her films. In more than a dozen titles, she played opposite him, and they became very close during the association. "I think we would have married if we had stayed together any longer," Antonio remarked in *Films in Review*. "I don't think I'll get married until some lady makes up her mind otherwise. Then, I'll be lost, of course."

Pathé signed Antonio in 1917, and with that studio, he experienced two of his biggest early hits. *The Naulahka*, directed by George Seitz, and based on the fascinating book by Rudyard Kipling, follows Antonio as he travels to India in a quest for a famous girdle of wonderful gems, the "naulahka," which is possessed by a Maharaja. *Variety* reviewed the film with a glowing tribute to the acting prowess of Warner Oland as the Maharajah, and concluded with the comment, ". . . Mr. Moreno is naturally manly." Women seated dreamily in audiences all over the world thought the same, while Hollywood's biggest female stars vied with each other for his services.

The House of Hate (1918) paired Antonio with Pearl White, fresh from her tremendous, worldwide success in the serials *The Perils of Pauline, The Exploits of Elaine,* and *The Romance of Elaine*. This new, twenty-chapter serial cast Antonio as a young scientist in love with the daughter of a munitions king. Each weekly episode followed the young lovers as they escaped the perils of "The Hooded Terror."

Antonio went immediately to work in fifteen episodes of yet another serial, *The Iron Test* (1918), as a circus acrobat hounded by the menacing "Red Mask."

CHAPTER 10: ANTONIO MORENO | 203

An advertisement showing Pearl White and Antonio Moreno in the 1918 serial, *The House of Hate*.

    The final chapter of *The Iron Test* had no sooner ended its run in theaters than another serial, *The Perils of Thunder Mountain*

(1919), pummeled Antonio with storms, floods, forest fires, and snow drifts over the course of the next fifteen weeks. Antonio was piling one serial success upon another. Although he made a fortune for the Vitagraph Company, he began to long for work in feature-length films.

In 1920, Albert Smith put Antonio through fifteen weekly episodes of more danger in the serial, *The Invisible Hand.* This was immediately followed by another fifteen-episode serial, *The Veiled Mystery.*

Antonio Moreno in the Vitagraph serial, *The Invisible Hand* **(1920).**

James R. Quirk, editor of *Photoplay* magazine, in his 1920 review, noted Antonio's tremendous drawing power, declaring him the "king of serial actors," superior to others because of his onscreen prowess as a romantic idol.

Frederick James Smith, editor of *Shadowland* and *Motion Picture Classic,* called Moreno, "the most picturesque personality of the screen," and predicted he would be numbered among the feature stars with the greatest popularity.

Pictureplay magazine placed Antonio along side Douglas Fairbanks, Wallace Reid, and John Barrymore as one of the ten most popular male stars of the coming year.

Feature-length films were attracting most of the attention by 1920, and although Albert Smith, president of Vitagraph, offered Antonio an attractive incentive to continue as a star of serial films, Antonio wanted to rejoin producers of longer, full-length features. After nearly 200 serial episodes, he was reluctantly entrenched as a "king of serials." He wanted to spread his wings, and was forced to leave Vitagraph to accomplish this ambition. In December 1920, no move by a film star was hailed with greater excitement than the return of Antonio Moreno to feature productions after years in serials. The serials established him in a premier position of popularity, and Antonio was thrilled to at last find a promotion to more distinguished work in feature-length films.

After working with Gloria Swanson at Paramount in *My American Wife*, Samuel Goldwyn hired him for two films in 1923, *Lost and Found* with Pauline Stark and *Look Your Best* with Colleen Moore.

Via the serial route, Antonio had built a worldwide popularity comparable to that of Pearl White, with whom he appeared at one time. In spite of this success, he excelled as an actor in more human dramas. He earned distinction with his romantic fire and physical magnetism, and his feature films of the 1920s perfectly captured his charm.

On January 27, 1923, Antonio finally married the woman of his dreams. Daisy Canfield Danziger, daughter of oilman Charles Canfield, was an intelligent, witty, and a socially-accomplished divorcee. The Morenos traveled to Europe on their honeymoon, and he returned to his hometown to visit his mother in Campamento and introduce his wife. Practically the entire village turned out to welcome the local boy who made good.

Daisy and Antonio returned to Los Angeles and built a magnificent Mediterranean villa on a six-acre estate mounted on the crest of a hill. Christened "Crestmount," it was originally a lonely estate nestled among the hills looming over Los Angeles. In time, it became a packed subdivision known today as Moreno Highlands.

With serials now behind him, Antonio went to Paramount, MGM, Warner Bros., and First National for one exciting film after another. When Rudolph Valentino broke his Paramount contract, *The Spanish Dancer*, a vehicle prepared for him and planned for production after he made *The Young Rajah*, was rewritten as a starring role for Pola Negri and Antonio. It provided him with a dazzling role, one of the best of his work during the 1920s.

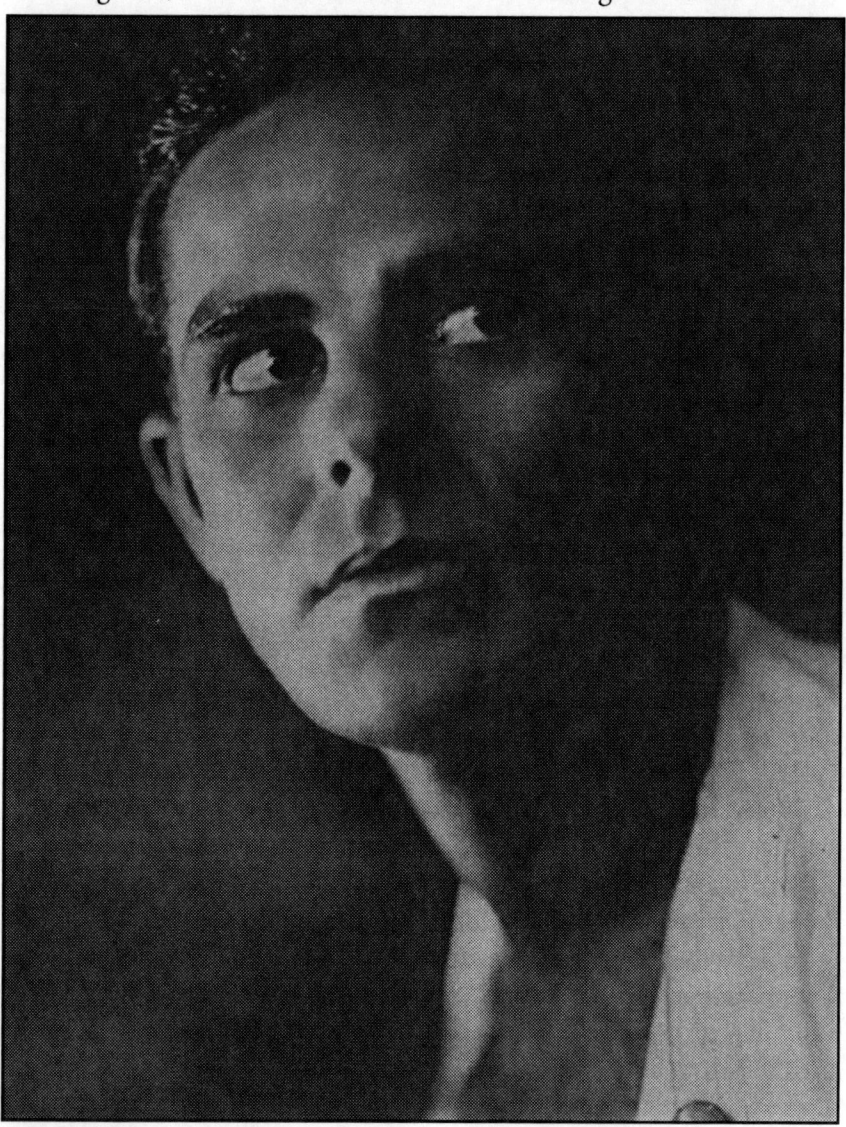

Antonio Moreno, ca. 1925.

Photoplay Magazine **described this photo as showing "Pauline Starke and Antonio Moreno illustrating the cosmic urge" in their June 1925 issue.**

His old friends from Vitagraph kept recalling him. Constance Talmadge featured him in her bright comedy, *Learning to Love*, and director Rex Ingram gave him the male lead in *Maré Nostrum*. This 1926 picture was made in Europe, and became the favorite of Antonio, Ingram, and his co-star, Alice Terry. In *Maré Nostrum*,

An advertisement for *Maré Nostrum* appeared in *Motion Picture Classic*, **August 1926.**

they were splendid as ill-fated lovers, she as a Canadian spy who ultimately faces a firing squad, and him as a Spanish sea captain claimed by the sea. *Maré Nostrum*, with its lush, Mediterranean backgrounds, the romantic legend of Amphitrite, the sea siren, and careful, luxuriant photography, gave Antonio a chance for a rich characterization few of his other roles offered.

Variety reviewed the film, and gave particular notice to Antonio's capable performance and the direction by Rex Ingram. "Ingram has allowed his sense of the dramatic to run rampant at times . . . Ingram remained abroad a long time to make this one, and few will deny that he has turned out a picturesque gem."

The *New York Times* said of *Maré Nostrum*: "Mr. Moreno has plenty of character in his countenance, but he does seem to be a ready victim to a pair of blue eyes. His path is filled with weird coincidences over which he, of course, has no control."

MGM now wanted him, and they trusted his support of their Swedish discovery, Greta Garbo, in her second film. *The Temptress* gave Antonio one of his most colorful roles. About Garbo, he later said she was ". . . the most aloof, yet fascinating actress I ever worked with. In her love scenes she was all glacial fire."

Author Elinor Glyn, famous for her lurid novels and tales of romance scripted for Paramount, dubbed the doorman of the Ritz Hotel and three Hollywood stars as the only people with "It," a word she coined to describe the previously indefinable attraction certain personalities had for both men and women. The Hollywood recipients of this accolade were Clara Bow, Antonio Moreno, and Rex the Wonder Horse. Paramount capitalized on the worldwide publicity generated by this moniker bestowed from Miss Glyn's imagination, and thrust Clara and Antonio into *It* (1927). The sparkling comedy proved to be one of the biggest hits of the year.

In 1927, Constance Talmadge again played with Antonio in one of her last films, *Venus of Venice*. It was made when the motion picture industry was in the middle of the first, chaotic change from silent films to "talkies." With his years of stage experience, Antonio had no qualms about appearing in talking pictures. His bilingual ability paid off well, as he easily shifted from English films to Spanish versions of the same stories. He even starred in the Spanish-language versions of films made in English with other actors. William Powell played the lead in *The Benson Murder Case* (1929), and Antonio starred in the Spanish-language version, *El Cuerpo Del Delito*. Walter Huston starred in *The Bad Man* (1930), and Antonio starred in the Spanish-language version, *El Hombre Malo* (1930). Neil Hamilton headed the cast of *The Cat Creeps* (1930), while Antonio duplicated the same role in *El Gato* (1930).

He helped launch the burgeoning Mexico film industry by directing *Santa* (1932), Mexico's first all-talking film, and *Aguilas Frente Al Sol* (1932), the country's second all-talking film. For Fox, Antonio starred in several Spanish-speaking features during the 1930s.

In 1933 his wife died in an unfortunate crash of her chauffeur-driven limousine during a foggy night on Mulholland Drive.

Antonio went to Spain to act in three films, and would have stayed, had a civil war not broken out and ended film production for several years.

He never remarried. Adrift in Hollywood during the 1940s, not entirely forgotten, but too old for leading man roles, he continued to work in supporting roles in several films. When World War II began, he assumed the responsibility of air raid warden for his Hollywood residential district. He met and formed a strong friendship with Mrs. Mary G. Westbrook, who would later figure into his personal life in a significant way.

During the war, Antonio played a Mexican justice of the peace in *Tampico* (1944), a Spanish commandant in *The Spanish Main* (1945), a villainous South American agent in Alfred Hitchcock's *Notorious* (1946), and Tyrone Power's father in *Captain from Castile* (1947). He was as busy as he wanted to be, and enjoyed staying involved in motion picture work.

He continued to play occasional roles in films during the 1950s, but his considerable wealth enabled him to enjoy a comparative life of leisure. He bought a Beverly Hills home on South Peck Drive where he lived for the rest of his life.

Antonio appeared prominently in the 3-D film, *The Creature from the Black Lagoon* (1954), a huge hit with teenage audiences, and later, a perennial on the "late shows" on television. His last America film was in John Ford's *The Searchers* (1956), where he played a Spanish-American trader. His final film, *El Senor Y La Cleopatra* (1958), was never released in the U.S.

In May 1965, he suffered a stroke, but recovered under nursing care during the next two years. His three children, born to his wife from her first marriage, thought he remained too ill to manage his own affairs properly. Antonio petitioned the courts to appoint Mrs. Mary G. Westbrook conservator of his estate. His children objected stringently, and Mrs. Westbrook withdrew. Antonio appointed Leon P. Scammon, a longtime friend and accountant, to handle the task.

The following year his health took a turn for the worse. He suffered two strokes, and then died on February 15, 1967.

Antonio Moreno was the first Latin male to become a motion picture star. He radiated excitement, passion, and masculinity, attributes admired by both men and women around the world. Many of his best pictures have survived, and in them, the boy from Madrid with the smoldering eyes, dark lashes, and bronze skin continues to elicit sighs from viewers discovering him for the first time.

Silent Filmography of
Antonio Moreno

Iola's Promise (1912)
The Voice of the Millions (1912)
His Own Fault (1912)
An Unseen Enemy (1912)
Two Daughters of Eve (1912)
So Near, Yet So Far (1912)
The Musketeers of Pig Alley (1912)
Oil and Water (1913)
A Misunderstood Boy (1913)
No Place for Father (1913)
A Cure for Suffragettes (1913)
By Man's Law (1913)
The House of Discord (1913)
Judith of Bethulia (1914)
Strongheart (1914)
Too Many Husbands (1914)
The Accomplished Mrs. Thompson (1914)
Fogg's Millions (1914)
Memories in Men's Souls (1914)
Men and Women (1914)
The Loan Shark King (1914)
Under False Colors (1914)
Sunshine and Shadows (1914)
The Song of the Ghetto (1914)
Politics and the Press (1914)
The Persistent Mr. Prince (1914)
The Peacemaker (1914)
The Old Flute Player (1914)
The Ladies' War (1914)
John Rance, Gentleman (1914)
In the Latin Quarter (1914)
His Father's House (1914)
The Hidden Letters (1914)
Goodbye Summer (1914)
The Island of Regeneration (1915)

The Dust of Egypt (1915)
A Price for Folly (1915)
On Her Wedding Night (1915)
Youth (1915)
The Quality of Mercy (1915)
The Park Honeymooners (1915)
The Night of the Wedding (1915)
A 'Model' Wife (1915)
Love's Way (1915)
The Gypsy Trail (1915)
Anselo Lee (1915)
Kennedy Square (1916)
The Supreme Temptation (1916)
The Shop Girl (1916)
The Tarantula (1916)
The Devil's Prize (1916)
Rose of the South (1916)
Susie, the Sleuth (1916)
She Won the Prize (1916)
The Magnificent Meddler (1917)
Her Right to Live (1917)
Money Magic (1917)
Aladdin from Broadway (1917)
Captain of the Gray Horse Troop (1917)
A Son of the Hills (1917)
By Right of Possession (1917)
The Angel Factory (1917)
The Mark of Cain (1917)
The Naulahka (1918)
The House of Hate (1918)
The First Law (1918)
The Iron Test (1918)
Perils of Thunder Mountain (1919)
The Veiled Mystery (1920)
The Invisible Hand (1920)
Three Sevens (1921)
The Secret of the Hills (1921)
A Guilty Conscience (1921)

My American Wife (1922)
Look Your Best (1923)
Lost and Found on a South Sea Island (1923)
The Trail of the Lonesome Pine (1923)
The Exciters (1923)
The Spanish Dancer (1923)
Flaming Barriers (1924)
Bluff (1924)
Tiger Love (1924)
Hello Frisco (1924)
The Border Legion (1924)
The Story Without a Name (1924)
Learning to Love (1925)
Her Husband's Secret (1925)
One Year to Live (1925)
Maré Nostrum (1926)
Beverly of Graustark (1926)
The Temptress (1926)
Love's Blindness (1926)
The Flaming Forest (1926)
It (1927)
Venus of Venice (1927)
Come to My House (1927)
Madame Pompadour (1927)
The Whip Woman (1928)
Nameless Men (1928)
The Midnight Taxi (1928)
Adoration (1928)
Synthetic Sin (1929)
The Air Legion (1929)
Careers (1929)
Romance of the Rio Grande (1929)

Chapter 11
Jack Pickford

Mary Pickford's success as one of the first female stars in films was a phenomenon unequaled in the history of motion pictures. So widespread was her popularity, the name "Pickford" spelled magic at the box office. Her brother, Jack, easily rode the first wave of her popularity to gain entry into the motion picture business, and with the strong guidance of his mother, managed to find a niche for himself in roles as a country youth. He had many fans at the height of his personal success in films, and was one of the first boy actors to rise to prominence in the fledgling industry.

Before they were known by the stage name "Pickford," his family lived by their real name, Smith. The little Smith family from Toronto traveled a long and painful road before they found a good fortune in motion pictures.

Jack's father was one of twelve children, a very handsome, charming man, gay and lovable, with a head of curly, golden-brown hair. On August 16, 1896, his only son, named after himself, was born to his wife, Charlotte. Jack was the third of their three children, following his sisters, Lottie, and Gladys.

To support his growing family, John Smith worked all night in a local theater pulling scenery. This extra money barely helped take care of his wife, Charlotte, and his three children.

By day, he worked as a purser on the Toronto to Lewiston steamship line near Niagara Falls. One day, while the steamship was on its regular route along the St. Lawrence River, he rushed down the stairs to a lower deck, failed to see a dangling pulley overhead, and struck it with his head. A blood clot formed near his brain, and he died soon after the accident.

His body was removed to the family home, and then buried the following day. While only in her middle twenties, Charlotte Smith became a widow with three children to support. She first attempted to provide for her three little ones by sewing dresses at home, scraping together what meager money she could from her skill.

There was a master bedroom in their home, and Charlotte decided to rent the room, as there was plenty of space in the rest of the house for her and the children. One of the renters, a stage manager with the Cummings Stock Company of Toronto, was producing a play called *The Silver King*. He asked Mrs. Smith if she would consider letting her two little girls appear in a schoolroom scene. After investigating the theater backstage and leaving impressed by the behavior of the people in the company, she consented to allow Lottie and Gladys to make their theatrical debut in the play.

The Cummings Stock Company finished the run of *The Silver King* and moved on, and Mrs. Smith found other roles in plays and variety shows for her children, especially her daughter, Gladys. Hal Reid, father of Wallace Reid, came to Toronto to try out a play he had written, *The Little Red Schoolhouse*. Charlotte arranged roles for all three children in the play, and Jack made his professional debut as an actor.

A road tour of *The Little Red Schoolhouse* took the entire family away from Toronto when Lillian Gish, another child actress in the touring version of the play, became ill. Gladys had played the same part in the original production in Toronto, and was quickly recruited to take her place on the tour. Her brother and sister were with her, and Jack began a lifetime of travel that would continue until his death. Charlotte met Lillian's mother, Mary Gish, and for a few years, the Smith family and the Gish family threw their lots in with each other, sharing rooms, advice, and dreams.

While the two families lived together, they attempted to earn some extra money one summer. Mary Gish and Charlotte opened a candy and popcorn stand on the grounds of the Fort George amusement park. One day while they were away from the stand for a brief time, little Jack fed the entire stock of the candy stand to their dog. The dog died, and the Gish and Smith families were out of business. With no recourse to take, they returned to work in the theater. They were driven by desperation.

The Little Red Schoolhouse was renamed *A Human Life*, and a tour in that play took them from theater to theater along a path of small theaters leading from Buffalo to New York.

Charlotte wanted to get to New York for another reason: to apply for work the following season. She had resolved to take roles herself, where her now-matronly appearance could be used in small parts. Once in New York, she pulled her children through the intensive and discouraging rounds of theatrical agencies, the endless hunt for another job that all actors dread.

Years later, Mary Pickford remembered the agony of these applications. "No one can have an idea of what this means who has not personally looked for work on the stage. The motley crews of the fly-by-night theatrical companies of those days; the merciless summer heat of New York; the rudeness of the receptionists; the sight of starving actors with their celluloid collars and brave faces; the overly bleached blondes with their inevitable turquoise jewelry and one lingering piece of soiled finery, like a blouse or jabot, and the lip rouge that would begin to wear off as the heat grew and the day lengthened. The picture of Mother, Lottie, Johnny, and me trudging along to these offices will stay with me to my dying day."

Charlotte managed to find work for her and the family. A famous play of the time, *The Fatal Wedding*, offered roles for all four of them, and they were soon rehearsing for the first performance in Pottsville, Pennsylvania. Charlotte went on in the first act and had the first line of the play. She was not an actress, and struggled to give her best impersonation of one. A hectic schedule followed, consisting of nineteen weeks of one-night-stands, averaging eight to nine performances each week for five-year-old Jack, seven-year-old Lottie, and eight-year-old Gladys. In-between performances, Charlotte kept constantly busy, staying up into the middle of the night making new dresses and fur coats for her girls, and sewing shirts for Jack.

They often had to rush out of their hotel in the dark, early hours of the morning to catch a train to the next town. Charlotte had all she could manage rousting her children from their beds, tired and sleepy as they were, and forcing them out into the cold to march like rigid toy soldiers down crumbling hotel stairs to their rendezvous with a train at the next station. Gladys was always ready, but the other two children only wanted to sleep.

One morning, Jack was unable to wake up when rousted at three o'clock in the morning while Charlotte rushed them to pack for the train to their next one-night stand.

"We've got to get up, Johnny!" Charlotte gently urged.

Jack ignored her plea, fell back into the large bed, and went to sleep with his little back curled against the wall. He mumbled, "I'm so sleepy, Mama, I want to stay here. I don't want to go."

It tore at Charlotte's heart to force the sleepy-eyed boy to his feet, and then compel him to dress and stumble out into the cold night in a race to leave on the smoky train journey. She sat down and cried over the unfortunate situation their lives had become. She found a career in the theater was anything but glamorous. Lottie and Gladys went after Jack, forced his long-ribbed stockings onto his weak legs, and got him dressed despite his protests.

They led him from the hotel into the freezing snow. While trudging through the drifts, Charlotte continued to weep silently. Suddenly, Jack revolted again. This time, he refused to move.

"I won't go, Mama. I want to go back home to bed; I'm too sleepy!" Jack wailed. No amount of coaxing or pleading would make him move. He planted his feet in the snow and refused, crying, "I won't go!"

Gladys and Lottie were carrying their own suitcases, and Charlotte was carrying both her suitcase and Jack's. Their livelihood depended on catching that train, and the job it provided was the only means Charlotte had of keeping her family together. Close to the breaking point, Charlotte suddenly dropped the two bags to the sidewalk and, without another word, picked Jack up and threw him over the railing into the soft, deep bed of snow. Then, she stubbornly trudged on, with Lottie and Gladys trailing behind. Thinking they were leaving him, Jack scrambled to his feet and rushed to rejoin the troupe. As they marched through the cold wind and darkness, tears silently streamed down Charlotte's face.

Times became increasingly difficult for her. During 1904–1905, she was forced to send Gladys and Lottie out on the road alone in a play called *The Child Wife*, while she and Jack took roles in another production. The separation was excruciating.

The following season, she was more determined than ever to keep the family together. She obtained roles for all three children

Chauncey Olcott in *Edmund Burke* (1906), with Gladys, Lottie, and Jack Smith, before they changed their names to Mary, Lottie, and Jack Pickford.

with Chauncey Olcott. The opportunity was a Godsend. Olcott was a stalwart of the American theater, and the play was called *Edmund Burke*.

In the new play, Gladys played the role of Lord Bertie, Lottie took two of the older boy parts, and Jack was tagged to play Lady Phyllis. It was an utter humiliation for him to lower himself to appear in a girl's wig, pantalets, and brocaded pannier dress. To add to the insult, he was forced to wear a sweeping, organdy petticoat under which was a pair of pantalets. It took all of the family's powers of persuasion to coax him into the costume every night, often succeeding only minutes before the performance.

During the next five years, Jack attended some school in Toronto while Gladys went on the road as a child star of *In Convict's Stripes*. She finally made her Broadway debut in *The Warrens of Virginia*, playing with an up-and-coming actor, Cecil B. DeMille. For this play, producer David Belasco changed Gladys' name to the better-sounding "Mary Pickford." In a short time, all four members of the Smith family would be known only by the last name, "Pickford," in order to capitalize on the growing renown the name afforded.

Mary wrote in her autobiography that she believed Jack would never have been in the theater or films if their father had lived. In fact, she said he would probably have never left Toronto. By the time he was twelve and his older sister was sixteen, the era of the traveling stock shows was rapidly coming to an end. A new amusement called "the movies" gave birth to thousands of nickelodeons across America. These tiny, storefront theaters replaced many of the cheap, live theaters, and stage actors found themselves struggling for jobs.

The more desperate of these actors found temporary work in the movies, earning from $2 to $5 posing for the motion picture cameras. Mary, as Gladys was now known, was shocked when her mother suggested a solution to their dwindling funds.

"Would you be very much against applying for work at the Biograph Studios, Gladdie?" she said to her one day. To calm her objections, Charlotte assured her the easy money would only be used to tide the family over until they could get another job in the theater.

In 1909, Mary Pickford made her debut in motion pictures in D. W. Griffith's *The Violin Maker of Cremona*. During the following weeks of additional work, the regular pay was so good that Charlotte quickly joined Mary with Lottie and Jack in tow. She secured work for the whole family in Biograph films, producing something their family had never known before: a savings account.

Linda Arvidson Griffith, in her book *When the Movies Were Young*, remembered the atmosphere of the Biograph studio at 11 East Fourteenth Street: "Actors—graduates from various trades and professions of uncertain standing, and actors without acting jobs, lounged all over the place, from the street steps where they basked on mild, sunny days, into the shady hall where they kept cool on hot days; and had they made acquaintance with studio life, they could be found in the privacy of the men's one dressing room shooting craps—the pastime during the waiting hours."

Boy actors were in little demand at Biograph in 1909. When Griffith needed one, Jack was usually handy. The twelve-year-old thought it was great fun to play in his sister's films and in those of the other stars. He created quite a stir about the old studio. People often looked at him and wondered if he would have the same success as his popular sister. Jack appeared in at least five films in 1909: *The Message, Pranks, Wanted, a Child, In a Hempen Bag,* and *To Save Her Soul.*

He was so natural acting in his roles that the following year he appeared in at least twenty-two Biograph films. Jack got his first leading part in a comedy directed by Frank Powell, *The Kid* (1910). The story followed the impish pranks of a boy resisting his father's second wife.

After shivering through an icy Eastern winter, the Biograph Company found it increasingly difficult to get their outdoor scenes photographed in the frozen parks surrounding New York. The producers concluded it would be advantageous to haul wardrobe, cameras, stories, and a troupe of actors to the city of Los Angeles, where conditions were considerably improved.

News spread quickly around Biograph of the impending trip to the west coast and the guarantee of steady employment during the winter. A flurry of excitement swept through their ranks. Some husbands chaffed at leaving their wives in New York and declined to go. Some of the women had other family members they could not abandon. Others simply did not want to leave New York. Those left behind wept and begged to be on the train.

A few days after Christmas, the selected gang of theater gypsies landed at the train station, exuberant at the thought of four luxurious days on the rails, as they headed for the palm trees and poinsettias beckoning to them from California.

While Griffith, his wife, and a few other Biograph members first left New York via the *Twentieth Century Limited,* the rest of the company was scheduled to embark on *The Black Diamond Express* to the city of Chicago. Once there, the company was to shift to the *California Limited* for an eight o'clock departure that evening.

Mary still had no theatrical job for the coming season, and she took Griffith's offer to join the journey to California for forty dollars a week.

While Griffith was nervously waiting for the arrival of his two leading men, the actors came running into the station. Arthur Johnson and Charlie West arrived breathless and hatless just as the last gong rang for the train's departure. Griffith had not counted on a smooth departure, knowing the nature of his vagabond performers, and one was destined not to happen. Unknown to him, Charlotte had made up her mind to stage a last minute hold-up for an increase in Mary's salary.

As the pandemonium of boarding the gaggle of actors onto the train began, their luggage, equipment, and supplies hastily lodged into their proper compartments, Charlotte cornered Griffith on the loading dock with her daughter in tow. As Mary wept goodbye to her boyfriend, actor Owen Moore, Charlotte accosted the director with her demand for the salary increase. In the midst of all the excitement, Jack began to cry as if on cue, wailing because he was not going on the trip with his sister. Mary tore herself away from Owen to implore the director for the extra ten dollars a week. They hurled good reasons in his face, facts which he could not deny. Griffith steeled himself for the onslaught, and then brought their lobbying efforts to a quick halt.

"Now, I've got little Gertie Robinson all ready to come on at a moment's notice," he threatened, referring to another up-and-coming child actress poised to step into the leading ingénue roles. "Mary goes without the raise or not at all!"

Griffith's challenge worked. The Smiths gave in. Mary took her place on the train, little Jack began to bawl at the top of his lungs, and their parting caused a terrible pall to fall over the already-confused scene.

Griffith soothed the desperate expression on Charlotte's face by agreeing to take little Jack at $15 a week. He agreed to pay his fare, resigning himself to stowing the small boy in one of the extra coach seats Biograph had wisely appropriated for unforeseen needs. Charlotte, satisfied with the arrangement, was willing to let Jack go despite Mary's argument that her brother had no luggage. Mary was annoyed at the way the turn of events had played out. They were still arguing even as the train began to pull from the station. Mary stood in the doorway protesting over the hissing steam and chugging engine. Her mother waved farewell and deposited Jack on the moving train steps calling, "Look after your sister, Johnny!"

On arrival in California, Mary joined with Dorothy West and Effie Johnson, two other actresses on the trip, along with her brother Jack, in securing lodgings at a rooming house on South Olive and Fifth Streets. The accommodations proved unworkable, and they soon moved to the New Broadway Hotel on North Broadway and Second Street, setting up comfortably with two rooms and a connecting bath.

The male actors of the company adopted Jack with devotion. He would sit with them during the evenings and watch them play poker until three o'clock in the morning. The fifty-cent allowance doled out by his sister for his supper fell happily into his pockets each night. Then, Jack connected up with his older male pals on their way out to a night on the town. Jack grew wise in the ways of the world at an age when most boys were still learning how to tie their shoes.

The company set immediately to work. The quaint Spanish missions dotting the lush California hills served as scenic backgrounds for many of the films made that summer. They quickly turned out *In Old California, Love Among the Roses,* and *Gold Is Not All,* among other films made during those first weeks.

Jack played in one of the most important films Griffith made that summer. The director had been possessed all the while they journeyed from New York to make a film based on the poem *Ramona,* Helen Hunt Jackson's famous Indian romance. $100 had been paid to the publishers, Little, Brown & Company, for the rights to adapt the novel into a film. The company went all-out for the production, and it went on record as the most expensive picture put out by any manufacturer up to that time, and one of the most creative.

For *Ramona*, the actors traveled to Camulos, a part of Ventura County, seventy miles from Los Angeles. There, they found a beautiful old adobe house, herds of sheep for the shearing scenes, a little flower-covered outdoor chapel, where Ramona's family worshiped, and a bleak mountaintop for the scene where Alessandro and Ramona bury their little baby. An old Spanish bell was found to ring out the news of the wedding scene. Biograph was proud of the finished film, and advertising folders were widely circulated with photos and descriptive information about this highly admired effort. It was Griffith's most artistic production at that time.

Happy Jack, a Hero (1910) featured Jack in a story fashioned with him as the star. He appeared in many films made that summer, and then returned with the company in the fall to New York. There, they faced another icy winter, but this time, with a steady income.

Once he had returned to Biograph's New York studio, Jack was featured in a number of films, including several built around his personality. *For Her Brother's Sake* (1911) and *A Boy of Revolution* (1911) pictured him prominently in stories styled to take advantage of his boyish enthusiasm and happy Irish face. In all, Jack appeared in more than twenty-two films in 1911.

The IMP Company of actors, ca. 1911. Jack Pickford is seated front and center, and his sister, Lottie Pickford, is seated to his immediate right. Mary Pickford is just above him, and Charlotte Smith, their mother, just above her in the top row.

Unknown to her family, Mary had secretly married Owen Moore. Owen then left the Biograph to work for the Independent Motion Picture Company (IMP), later to evolve into what is now known as Universal. Mary was anxious to be with him, and left Biograph for their offer of $175 a week. Motion picture camera patent infringement rights were still a hot issue between competing companies. The lawsuits reached a bitter pitch at this time, and violence frequently erupted. IMP found themselves receiving threats from competitors. They decided to remove their production to the comparatively safer locations available off the mainland of the United States.

An expedition was arranged to sail cast and crew to Cuba. Charlotte, Mary, Lottie, and Jack joined director Thomas Ince, and the pilgrimage sailed to the island of Cuba on the *S. S. Havana*. It was a disastrous mistake. While on the boat, Mary confessed her secret marriage to her mother and family. Jack wept bitterly, Mary felt she had betrayed her family, Owen began to drink heavily, and the troupe landed in Cuba dejected and depressed. It was only the beginning of their troubles there.

The IMP films failed to approach the high standards achieved by Griffith at Biograph. Operations were set up in a converted jail on the outskirts of Havana. They were humiliated when forced to act with carpenters and mechanics hastily filling out the ranks of performers because there was no local talent pool from which to draw. The photography of the films was less than the image-conscious Mary found acceptable, and the Pickfords were completely miserable. The final straw was the assignment to her of the part of a mother to a nine-year-old child in a picture called *A Quarter Before Two*. To make matters worse, IMP fired both Owen Moore and her sister, Lottie. The situation had become intolerable.

Although the films were successful, the Pickfords left IMP and Cuba as soon as her contract expired, and after a brief stint with another firm known as Majestic, they returned to Griffith and Biograph. The break with IMP and Majestic was not easy. Mary had to file a lawsuit claiming her contracts with the two companies were invalid due to the fact that she was only nineteen years old, a minor according to the law. Supreme Court Justice McCall dismissed an injunction served against her by the two companies.

In 1912, Jack appeared in at least twenty-five films, and was rapidly growing into a young man of fifteen. People were watching him as his sister's star rapidly rose, still wondering if he would have the same success as she.

In the early months of 1913, Griffith was growing restless with the restrictive Biograph management. He quietly maneuvered to find artistic freedom. At this time, Jack appeared in six more films. *For the Son of the House* (1913) was the last Biograph film in which Jack played a prominent role before Griffith announced that he was leaving to start his own company.

Griffith broke with Biograph in a trade announcement in the *Dramatic Mirror* on September 29, 1913. He joined a new company under the name of Reliance-Majestic to distribute several films each year under their banner for distribution by Mutual.

In October 1913, Griffith's move from Biograph set him as head of production of Reliance-Majestic. He took with him as many of the best of the Biograph actors as he could. Those loyal performers who made the transition with him included Jack Pickford, Bobby Harron, Lillian and Dorothy Gish, Blanche Sweet, Mae Marsh, Edward Dillon, Henry Walthall, Donald Crisp and George Siegman. Mary did not go. Realizing her full potential, Charlotte made a deal with Adolph Zukor to star her in feature films.

As the head of production, Griffith supervised *The Gangsters of New York, Dope, Ruy Blas, Frou Frou, Sapho, Moths, The Great Leap, The Mountain Rat, The Floor Above,* and other films.

At the same time, Mary's tormented marriage to Owen Moore climaxed with Charlotte and Adolph Zukor compelling her to move to California before she had a nervous breakdown. Mary recalled in her autobiography, "The Pickford caravan, consisting of my mother, my sister Lottie, her baby Gwynne, and my brother Jack left New York in January 1917 to take up a temporary residence in California, which proved to be permanent.

Griffith also moved his Reliance-Mutual operation to California, leaving behind both New York and the one-reel format for pictures. He had already produced a number of full-length films, and the first film he produced there was *Home Sweet Home.*

This six-reel film forecast his later masterpiece, *Intolerance.* It was made up of several stories with a common theme: the sentiment of the title song by composer John Howard Payne. Jack Pickford, now back at work with Griffith, appeared as one of Mary Alden's sons in the third, tragic episode.

Jack became fast friends with Constance Talmadge and Dorothy Gish, two young actresses just beginning to find their footholds with audiences. Constance had completed work in Griffith's *Intolerance*, as the "Mountain Girl" who rode a chariot to the rescue of the king of Babylon, and Dorothy was starring in smaller program films for his organization. The three shared a devil-may-care attitude and a profound sense of fun.

Constance's mother recalled in her autobiography, "No sooner had I breathed freely once more at Constance's escape from death in the *Intolerance* chariot than Jack Pickford came along with a sporty new roadster presented to him by Mary, and filled me with a new fear. Jack made boon companions of Constance and Dorothy, and their favorite amusement was to have him race up a steep hill at full speed, reach the top, quickly reverse the gears, and let the car slide backwards all the way down. Constance assured me that she could recommend this as an A-1 thrill and invited me to join. Needless to say, I found a number of important things to do around the house. But Jack and the girls thought it a marvelous hair-raising sensation, and seemed to think that my anxiety was the finishing comedy touch—if their shrieks of mirth at my terrified face meant anything."

Jack became entrenched in a lifestyle of excess. He worked, when his mother and sister arranged parts for him, and he was successful. Audiences took to the happy young man because of his natural manner and easygoing style. He had roles in two of Mary's films, a George Sand fantasy, *Fanchon the Cricket* (1915), and *Poor Little Peppina* (1916), an immigrant comedy.

In *Freckles* (1917), Jack played a one-armed boy who escaped from an orphanage, in a screen adaptation of a book by Gene Stratton-Porter.

What Money Can't Buy (1917) featured Jack with an all-star cast, including Louise Huff, Theodore Roberts, Hobart Bosworth, and James Cruze. The story of a mythical kingdom and a royal romance prompted a reviewer from *Variety* to say, "Jack Pickford puts the same youthful ingeniousness in his part that distinguished his former successes and he is ably assisted by Louise Huff in a part that gives her ample opportunity for charm and loveliness . . . beautiful and artistic settings both in exteriors and interiors help thoroughly to give the proper air of royal romance that is needed. There is admirable restraint in all the players. Nothing is overdone. Everything is in complete good taste, even to the king's magnificent chess board."

Jack would have had even greater success if he could have been known as someone other than Mary Pickford's brother. Mary believed he was a much better actor than herself, and later went on record to applaud the stark simplicity and directness of his talent. She also admired his keen, shrewd sense of humor. She believed he would have gone farther if he had been known as simply Jack Smith. Jack did not care. To him, making pictures was a way to make fast money, on a par with shooting craps.

He came into his own with *Tom Sawyer* (1917) and the sequel, *Huck and Tom* (1918).

One of the greatest successes of Jack's career, *Tom Sawyer* is also significant as one of the rare surviving films by director William Desmond Taylor. As the boyish and appealing figure penned by Mark Twain, Jack is at his best. One sees the youthful Pickford boy vibrantly charming, a far cry from the ravaged figure visible in his later 1920s films when alcoholism—as well as the later tragedies of his personal life—had stripped him of his charisma and charm.

In the role of Becky Thatcher, actress Clara Horton was a perfect choice. At the age of thirteen, she appears in the one major role of her career that has been acclaimed as her best. Clara had been in films for some years, having been known as the "Éclair kid" at the Éclair Film Company as an eight-year-old. She had risen to notable popularity from 1915 to 1917 in roles at companies like Powers and Universal, and by the time director Taylor cast her as Becky Thatcher, she was capable of lending a distinctive flair to the part that remains remarkably fresh today.

A review in *Variety* said of *Tom Sawyer*, "There are very few of us who haven't read of the mischievous adventures of Tom Sawyer and Huck Finn, hence the screen adaptation of Mark Twain's *Tom Sawyer* should be of great value as a feature attraction not only for its intrinsic value, but as a title to conjure with. It should prove potent attraction to the family trade, and should therefore stand a more extended run than is usually allotted most pictures in a town. One's first observation would be that so simple a tale would be

Four scenes from *Tom Sawyer* (1917) and *Huck and Tom* (1918), with Clara Horton, Jack Pickford, Robert Gordon, and Antrim Short.

insufficient entertainment to the patrons of such a house as the New York Strand, and when the picture first starts you become fearful it won't hold up for five reels. As it progresses, however, the comedy grows apace until it winds up in a blaze of glory, blotting out the scene where Tom, Huck Finn, and Joe Harper, after living several days on an island and believed to have been drowned, enter a church while funeral services are being held for them. There is

Tom's first love affair, with little Becky all dressed up in her pantalets; his first smoke and its consequences; the yanking out of his aching tooth with the aid of a piece of string, and so on. All very trivial to be sure, but it is clean, wholesome amusement, and try to be as dignifiedly grown up as you can, you will enjoy it. Jack Pickford is the star, and looked and acted in a sufficiently youthful manner to admirably visualize the hero. The young men portraying Huck Finn and Joe Harper were equally effective in their respective roles. Becky was a sweet little thing and the entire company aided in creating the proper pictures. William D. Taylor, as director, fulfilled his mission. This production will never grow old. It can be repeated at regular intervals by exhibitors for generations."

By comparison, The *New York Times* commented on the many, highly humorous moments in *Tom Sawyer*, but was unimpressed with Jack. "In the event of the filming of additional scenes it might be well to entrust the title role to someone other than Jack Pickford, who, in addition to being too large for the part, acts quite without inspiration or sympathy. Huckleberry Finn suffered from a similarly uninspired performance, but Joe Harper lived and had his being somewhat as Twain would have wanted him. In short, the film is good entertainment for those who do not know their *Tom Sawyer* too well."

Tom Sawyer was the third of seven films Jack would make for William Desmond Taylor, and the only one out of their association that is known to have survived. Taylor also played an important role in the career of Mary Pickford, directing her in three films: *How Could You, Jean?* (1918), *Johanna Enlists* (1918), and *Captain Kidd, Jr.* (1919).

The same week of January 25, 1918, while Mary was proving to be a revelation to her many followers in *Stella Maris*, Jack appeared in the Paramount production of *The Spirit of '17*. A review in *Variety* said the film was ". . . calculated to arouse any latent patriotism that may exist in the breast of the youth of America. It is so divided throughout the five reels and the story so disjointedly and disconnectedly told, that one has more or less difficulty in gathering a clear idea of what it is all about. The main plot isn't absolutely planted until practically the end of the fourth reel, and when finally it is set, it is the sort of tale usually devoured by twelve-year-old boys anxious to accomplish heroic deeds." Jack seemed to have risen above the mediocrity of the film, for the review went on to say, "The star has been very happily cast for the romantic role of the boy scout who is fortunate enough to be the direct medium for the exposing of an alien plot. It is exactly in his line, that of a winsome youth fired with the spirit of patriotism. When he affects that far-away expression he resembles more than at any time his famous sister."

Jack's success the previous year with *Tom Sawyer* prompted Paramount to produce the inevitable sequel, *Huck and Tom*, in 1918. According to *Variety*, "Director William D. Taylor has added another acceptable Paramount visualization of the immortal Tom Sawyer stories to the screen. Jack Pickford and Robert Gordon are again Tom and Huck respectively and this particular feature is built around the murder of a doctor by Injun Joe. The kids are in a graveyard at midnight when it happens and aid in the eventual apprehension of the culprit. The culmination of the story comes with the discovery by the boys of hidden treasure, which makes them rich. The whole thing is very human and as it recalls one's early reading, carries with it just the proper romance for both the present and last generation of theatergoers. There is no particular point upon which to dwell, other than to record the comedy registered strongly in the Paramount projection room, where it was screened for a bunch of hardened trade paper reviewers."

His Majesty Bunker Bean brought Jack into a popular springtime comedy the week of April 12, 1918. The Paramount release told an interesting story of a young man who needed nothing but the power of suggestion to make him a success. *Variety* said, "Pickford is the boy, and he handles the title role wonderfully well. The production end, as far as sets and locations are concerned, demand nothing extraordinary, but those there are, are adequate. The photography is well handled and there are a number of doubles used as fade-ins that are very well worked out . . . a comedy picture that gets laughs on its action as well as its titles, and it is action all the way with a real fresh love story carried along at a speedy clip. That is enough for any picture audience."

Jack Pickford, ca. 1920.

Mile-A-Minute Kendall (1918) again paired Jack with Louise Huff the same week Mary Pickford was appearing in *M'Liss*. His other sister, Lottie, was the co-star of this story that had more than a few traces of personal reality in it. William D. Taylor directed for Paramount the screen adaptation of Owen Davis' play of the same name. Jack was typecast as a millionaire's son who had a strong liking for fast living, chorus girls, and a penchant for mechanical invention. As Kendall, Jack invented something worth millions, and then marries the sweetheart of his childhood. *Variety* said, "There are some specially fine character portrayals by members of the cast, among them a vampire bit by Sister Lottie, that will surprise those who have been accustomed to seeing her in more respectable roles. Somehow the idea of a sister vamping her own brother is not exactly palatable . . . "

Sandy (1918) was a simple, straightforward tale of an Irish stowaway on a ship bound for America. Jack was ideally suited for the role of a boy with keen wit and an honest and wistful look in his eyes who makes his way to Kentucky with a heart full of love for the little girl who begged her family not to report the boy to the authorities. He arrives in their town in the middle of a storm and falls unconscious from hunger in the middle of the street. A passing Judge picks up the youth and takes him home. After a shooting with the drinking brother of the girl, who has become involved with fixing a horse race, Sandy fixes the situation and ends up marrying the girl. "Not startlingly original," said the review in *Variety*, "but the picture is replete with excellent character portrayals and makes for a thoroughly enjoyable hour's entertainment."

The Little Shepherd of Kingdom Come (1920) was based on a novel considered by many to be great when it was first released. It was the story of a boy brought into the environment of the South after walking down the mountains of the Blue Grass country. *Variety* said, "Jack Pickford's work in this feature, while giving him the benefit of most of the scenes, is hardly the kind of vehicle suitable for his talents. Rather is he better adapted for the role calling into services the light comedian, the flippant American youth who, in the early stages of existence, throws all caution to the winds and finally winds up with a sensible outlook on life."

Jack may have tired of playing so many country boys when he was, in fact, quite the opposite. When World War I broke out, he was still under the age of twenty-one, but he gave up a $2,500 a week movie contract, and enlisted as an ordinary sailor. Doctor Doe, a Navy induction officer, became friends with Jack. He entered his life by cultivating a friendship with flattery and attention, then moved into his apartment, and even had full use of Jack's limousine.

While in the navy, Jack served as a go-between for Lieutenant Benjamin Davis, Dr. Doe, and an assortment of worried bluebloods from New York, who had enough money to pay for soft positions in the Naval Reserve, guaranteeing their military duty would be far away from the front lines. All three men were caught in the scam.

Davis was court-martialed and found guilty. Charlotte rolled up her sleeves and went to work pulling strings to avert a complete catastrophe and deflect negative publicity from the family name. She compelled Jack to turn State's evidence and testify for the prosecution. The navy's lawyer recommended a dishonorable discharge for lying about his use of intoxicants. Charlotte arranged a letter from Joseph Tumulty, the personal secretary to President Wilson, to have the discharge changed to the more conventional "honorable" type. She claimed this was a necessity because he was scheduled to appear in a propaganda movie for aviation called *The Brood of the Bald Eagle*. The discharge was arranged, the movie was never made, and Jack left the navy free to once again enjoy the high-life of New York City and showgirls.

In 1917, he met the former Olive Elaine Duffy, who only a few years earlier had been a shop girl working for $3 a week in McKee's Rocks, a suburb of Pittsburgh. She was born at Charleroi, Pennsylvania, in 1898. At the age of seventeen, she was married to Bernard Krug Thomas, whom she divorced in 1915. Known as Olive Thomas, a legendary beauty with lovely, violet-blue eyes fringed with long, dark lashes, she rapidly rose to fame and fortune in the theatrical world. Florenz Ziegfeld recognized her particular allure and featured her in his productions. In 1917, she left the stage, attempted a career in motion pictures, and attained some prominence as a star for the Triangle Studios. Jack fell hopelessly in love with Olive. When his mother and sister learned of his infatuation, they were fearful she would have a negative influence on his life and his struggling career. His mother was vigilant of the Pickford name and reputation, and frowned heavily on this latest addition to her growing entourage.

Charlotte thought him too young for marriage, especially to a musical comedy performer. Olive was accustomed to the fast life of rich, eligible, young men swirling in the social world of the theater.

Olive was several years older than he, and Jack was madly in love with her. He followed his heart, ignored his mother, and proposed marriage.

In August 1920, Olive and Jack embarked on a journey to Europe with several of their friends, calling it a second honeymoon. After a night of drinking and partying, Olive said she had a headache, and went to the bathroom where several bottles were strewn around the area. She accidentally took pills from a bottle of dichloride of mercury tablets, a recommended cure for syphilis, instead of aspirin. As the pills burned in her stomach, she discovered the accident and screamed. Jack came running, and forced her to drink twelve to fifteen glasses of tepid water mixed with milk and butter.

By the time an ambulance arrived, precious time had been lost. Olive lived for one week thanks to Jack's quick thinking, but her last week was one of agony. By September 9, she had lapsed into a coma. She finally died in Jack's arms on September 10 at 10:15 in the morning. The French authorities spent a week investigating the case, and finally concluded that her death was an accident and not a suicide. The medical report ascribed her death to "acute nephritic inflammation." The incident made front-page news.

Headlines in the *New York Times* screamed from their September 11, 1920 publication, "Paris Authorities Investigate Death of Olive Thomas." The article said the police were actively seeking evidence on rumors of cocaine orgies intermingled with champagne dinners often lasting into the early hours of the morning. A former army captain by the last name of Spalding, sentenced just days before Olive's death, was closely questioned for supplying cocaine to the revelers.

The French police were anxious to interview Jack. Immediately after her death, he left the Ritz Hotel, and took up quarters under the care of his physician at the Hotel Crillon. He declined to receive any visitors, including the authorities that were turning their investigation directly on him. He and another woman were said to have been observed leaving the Ritz Hotel and accompanying Olive during her last pilgrimage to the Montmartre district on the Saturday evening before her death. While waiting an opportunity to question Jack, Police Commissioner Docrocq and Captain

Catrou of the First District had received the testimony of the waiters, porters, and chambermaids at the Ritz Hotel where Miss Thomas was said to have taken the poison. Due mainly to Charlotte's direction during the crisis, Jack escaped the country.

He solemnly crossed the ocean with her body on September 18, 1920. He later confessed to Charlotte that he had come to the brink of suicide while on the boat. He never fully recovered from her death.

Mary hired Jack to co-direct her film, *Through the Back Door*. This job was more of an attempt to jog him out of his depression over Olive Thomas and her death than to start him on a new career as a film director. As always, Mary did most of the directing on her films. Jack served the purpose of "calling the shots" as the camera turned.

Mary again hired Jack to co-direct *Little Lord Fauntleroy* with senior director, Alfred E. Green. Jack's contributions were to suggest various gags and comic business, while Green handled the acting and camera planning.

Jack never had the same sense of ambition as his sister. One day, while they were in the middle of producing *Little Lord Fauntleroy*, he sat beside Mary while she was brushing her curls before going on the movie set. He studied her intently in the mirror until their eyes met. For a moment, he thought of the lives the three had led, Mary, their sister Lottie, and himself.

"You poor kid, you've never lived, have you?" Jack said.

"Certainly I have," Mary replied. "I'm doing exactly what I always wanted to do."

"Well, I don't know. You see, if Chuckie and I were bumped off tomorrow, the world would owe us nothing. We've had a million laughs. You've had everything, yes, but, Mary, you've never really lived. And you don't know how to play."

Jack knew how to play, and for him, the playground was New York City and the showgirls from the Ziegfeld Follies. For Jack, a second marriage to Marilyn Miller was ill-fated. She was another career-minded Ziegfeld showgirl. The marriage quickly ended in divorce in 1927.

In March 1923, both Jack and Lottie were investigated by a federal grand jury for violations of the Volstead Act, the law governing Prohibition. Since many people around the nation were also in violation of the Prohibition laws, Jack paid little attention. According to Eileen Whitfield, in her book *Pickford the Woman Who Made Hollywood,* "Charlotte's basement was renowned for its abundant stash; it is said she kept the door locked to prevent her son from making unexpected raids . . . Jack could drink and be forgiven, for he drank with style. He ran wild but in the company of Hollywood's top-drawer alcoholics, wits-about-town, with proven talent." Charlotte and her attorneys kept the charges as quiet as possible, and they continued with their careers.

Jack married a third time, again to a Ziegfeld girl. Mary Mulhern grew to dislike being married to him within three months, and she divorced him in 1932.

The Goose Woman (1925) brought Jack into a film based on a story by Rex Beach about a goose woman who was once a famous opera singer. She accidentally involves her son in a murder for the satisfaction of seeing her name in lights again. The story was based on one of the most famous trials in New Jersey. In this film, despite his personal problems, Jack appeared quite confident and was very effective, but the strain of his life was showing in his face.

Jack's last work in a motion picture was in *Gang War* (1928), an independent film made for FBO Pictures.

A few years later, Jack visited Mary at her home in California. He looked ill and emaciated, and his clothes hung on him as if he were a clothes hanger. Mary recalled a wave of premonition that came over her while watching her brother leave.

As they started down the stairs to the automobile entrance, Jack called back to her, "Don't come down with me, Mary dear, I can go alone."

As Mary stood at the top of the staircase, an inner voice spoke to her. "That's the last time you'll see Jack," she remembered hearing.

Jack died in Paris on January 3, 1932, at the age of thirty-six, of what was called "progressive multiple neuritis which attacked all the nerve centers." The room in which he died was one from which he could see the window of the hospital room where Olive Thomas had died thirteen years earlier.

Silent Filmography of
Jack Pickford

The Message (1909)
Pranks (1909)
Wanted, a Child (1909)
In a Hempen Bag (1909)
To Save Her Soul (1909)
All on Account of the Milk (1910)
The Call (1910)
The Newlyweds (1910)
The Smoker (1910)
The Kid (1910)
The Tenderfoot's Triumph (1910)
An Affair of Hearts (1910)
Ramona (1910)
The Modern Prodigal (1910)
Muggsy Becomes a Hero (1910)
In Life's Cycle (1910)
Rose O'Salem Town (1910)
Examination Day at School (1910)
The Iconoclast (1910)
The Broken Doll (1910)
Two Little Waifs (1910)
Waiter No. 5 (1910)
A Plain Song (1910)
A Child's Stratagem (1910)
Happy Jack, a Hero (1910)
The Lesson (1910)
White Roses (1910)
His Trust Fulfilled (1911)
Fate's Turning (1911)
The Poor Sick Men (1911)
A Decree of Destiny (1911)
Sweet Memories (1911)
For Her Brother's Sake (1911)
A Boy of Revolution (1911)
The Stuff Heroes Are Made Of (1911)

A Convict's Heart (1911)
The Lost Necklace (1911)
A Temporary Truce (1912)
Katchem Kate (1912)
A Dash Through the Clouds (1912)
The School Teacher and the Waif (1912)
Man's Lust for Gold (1912)
An Indian Summer (1912)
The Speed Demon (1912)
The Would Be Shriner (1912)
Black Sheep (1912)
What the Doctor Ordered (1912)
A Child's Remorse (1912)
The Inner Circle (1912)
Mr. Grouch at the Seashore (1912)
A Pueblo Legend (1912)
A Feud in the Kentucky Hills (1912)
A Ten-Karat Hero (1912)
The Chief's Blanket (1912)
The Painted Lady (1912)
The Musketeers of Pig Alley (1912)
Heredity (1912)
My Baby (1912)
The Informer (1912)
Brutality (1912)
The New York Hat (1912)
My Hero (1912)
A Misappropriated Turkey (1913)
The Massacre (1913)
Love in an Apartment Hotel (1913)
The Unwelcome Guest (1913)
Fate (1913)
The Sneak (1913)
The Work Habit (1913)
For the Son of the House (1913)
The Gangsters of New York (1914)
The Mysterious Shot (1914)
Home, Sweet Home (1914)

The Eagle's Mate (1914)
Wildflower (1914)
His Last Dollar (1914)
Liberty Belles (1914)
The Love Route (1915)
The Commanding Officer (1915)
Fanchon, the Cricket (1915)
The Pretty Sister of Jose (1915)
A Girl of Yesterday (1915)
Poor Little Peppina (1916)
Seventeen (1916)
Great Expectations (1917)
The Dummy (1917)
The Girl at Home (1917)
Freckles (1917)
What Money Can't Buy (1917)
The Varmint (1917)
Ghost House (1917)
Jack and Jill (1917)
Tom Sawyer (1917)
The Spirit of '17 (1918)
Huck and Tom (1918)
His Majesty, Bunker Bean (1918)
Mr. Fix-It (1918)
Mile-a-Minute Kendall (1918)
Sandy (1918)
Bill Apperson's Boy (1919)
Burglar by Proxy (1919)
In Wrong (1919)
The Little Shepherd of Kingdom Come (1920)
The Man Who Had Everything (1920)
Just Out of College (1920)
A Double-Dyed Deceiver (1920)
Garrison's Finish (1923)
Hollywood (1923)
The Hill Billy (1924)
Waking Up the Town (1925)
My Son (1925)

THE GOOSE WOMAN (1925)
THE BAT (1926)
BROWN OF HARVARD (1926)
EXIT SMILING (1926)
GANG WAR (1928)

Chapter 12
Wallace Reid

"Wallace Reid had inherited his father's gift for storytelling, had a keen sense of humor, a good singing voice, played the saxophone and piano, and was altogether the most magnetic, charming, personable, handsome young man I've ever met. And the most co-operative," wrote Jesse Lasky in his book *I Blow My Own Horn*.

William Wallace Reid was born in St. Louis, Missouri, on April 15, 1891, the son of actor/playwright Hal Reid and his wife, Bertha Westbrook. His first experience as an actor was in St. Louis in 1896. Wally was four years old, and he took the part of a little girl in a melodrama written by his father, *Slaves of Gold*. Hal Reid had more than a hundred plays crisscrossing the country in those days before motion pictures.

When Wally was ten years old, the Reid family moved to New York. He attended public schools, and later studied at the New Jersey Military Academy. In 1909, he worked as a surveyor on the Shoshone Dam in the Big Basin district of Wyoming. There, Wally also worked as a ranch hand, and as a clerk at the Irma Hotel owned by Buffalo Bill Cody, the Western stage and event star.

As a young man, he came back to New York, and worked as a reporter for one of the city's newspapers. His return to the stage was in a vaudeville sketch written by his father, *The Girl and the Ranger*.

He was also something of an artist. He loved to paint, an ability born from an early stint as a cartoonist with a Newark newspaper. J. Wilson MacDonald, the renowned sculptor, was his great-uncle. There were those who thought he inherited the family talent for working with clay and could have been a successful sculptor, had acting not taken a firm grip on his life.

Wallace Reid ranked as the most popular leading man in the movies, ranking equally with Mary Pickford and Charlie Chaplin.

His father worked on film scenarios at the Chicago-based Selig-Polyscope studio in the 1910s. Hal Reid was a close friend of President Taft, and he was able to bring the first motion pictures of the President signing a document in the White House to Vitagraph, another film company. There, Reid was the head of the company's scenario department, and wrote many of the melodramas produced by the pioneering film company. Wally's strapping good looks caught the eye of Milton Nobles while the writer/director was preparing a one-reel film. *The Phoenix* (1910) was planned to star Nobles and his wife, Dolly. He asked Wally, who had worked in journalism, to play the part of a young reporter in the film. The six-foot-tall youth moved with a naturally athletic gait and projected a strong presence in the finished film.

Hal's son was handsome, he excelled in music and athletics at school, and when away from his studies, he often accompanied his father when he went to work at Vitagraph. Albert Smith, president of Vitagraph, remembered that Wally's first acting job was a bit part in James Fenimore Cooper's *The Pathfinder*, in which his father also played a part. Another source claimed his first film role was as a female impersonator with John Bunny. He earned $25 dollars a week playing small roles, operating cameras, and occasionally writing films during the nine months when he worked at Vitagraph, but he had no desire to be an actor. His interests were wide and varied.

He also had a hand in accidentally starting the practice of using mood music during the making of a film. This happy inspiration came at the Vitagraph in 1910 while Florence Reid was finding the surrounding atmosphere prevented her from feeling the right emotion for a scene. Dick Rosson picked up a violin and played music for her, moving her emotions so she could play the scene with the needed feeling. While watching this moment, Wally became touched by the musical tone of the instrument. Before a few months passed, he had learned to play the viola, and earned additional money as an off-camera mood musician to add to his earnings as an actor.

In addition to the viola, he could also play the violin and saxophone. His mother later recalled, "He was a good violinist, to me a wonderful violinist, and he spent a good many hours of his scant leisure with his instrument."

He left motion picture work to take a position on the editorial staff of *Motor Magazine*, but soon returned to acting where a steady income was available. Hal Reid had moved to Universal, and in 1912, Wally went with Universal when that company made their first filmmaking trip to California. There, he met a beautiful seventeen-year-old, Dorothy Davenport, with whom he acted in a one-reel melodrama, *His Father's Son*.

In 1913, at the age of twenty, Wally and Dorothy married. Her family was well known in the theater. Her aunt, Fanny Davenport, was considered one of the great actresses of the American stage, and her father, Harry Davenport, was also a star. Dorothy was in her early teens when she started playing bit parts in films. By the time she was seventeen, she was a star at Universal. She appeared with Wally in many films during 1913. They had one son, Wallace, Jr., and later in 1922, adopted a little girl.

Wallace Reid in *The Deerslayer* (1912), an early one-reel short film produced at Vitagraph.

Wally worked for several other studios releasing through Universal, but his interests lay with the technical areas of writing and directing. To his dismay, the studio wanted him in front of the camera, not in the behind-the scenes work. Wally wanted to direct films. As with his previous experience, he was good in front of the camera, and audiences responded warmly to him. He was forced to continue as an actor, but he achieved the difficult feat of writing, directing, and acting in several dozen pictures during 1912–1914.

The early movies took full advantage of Wally's physique and athletic prowess. "To be sure, I wore a string of beads and a leopard skin at Vitagraph when I made a series of Indian pictures, but it seemed all right," he mused. "Funny what a psychological effect a coat of tan makes. Brown like an Indian, the primitive costume seemed wholly appropriate, but with white skin, you feel so darn undressed prancing about." In many pictures, Wally appeared as a miner or mining prospector saving the heroine from being taken advantage of by ruthless thieves.

He appeared in more than ninety films by 1914, including a few uncredited roles in pictures made by D. W. Griffith. At that time, Griffith had left his original studio, Biograph, and ventured into making feature films. In his mind, he secretly planned to make an epic picture about two families struggling to survive in the Civil War.

In May 1914, Wally left Universal for Mutual, and his long awaited opportunity to work with D. W. Griffith arrived. Mutual and their two subsidiaries, Majestic and Reliance, were producing some of the most outstanding pictures at that time. Wally gave up the backbreaking schedule Universal had him strapped to, writing, directing, and starring in two films a week, and he gladly went to work for Griffith for less money, which was a significant bow to the great director's ability. Salaries were not very big for actors at most studios, and the little house he and Dorothy owned just off Hollywood Boulevard was not yet paid for. His earnings were not the issue, at that time. Being in quality pictures made by the industry's foremost producer was the point of making the move. The prestige and creative excellence that came with working for Griffith meant more than money. Wally also harbored a continual wish that he would get to write and direct exclusively. For him, being an actor was just a means to hopefully reach that goal, but he was so loved as an actor that they kept him in front of the camera. He lamented in more than one interview that his "face kept me from getting a chance to be a writer or a director." Nothing annoyed him more than the thought that he was just getting by on his looks, but to Wally, it seemed that he was doomed to be an actor, a fate he did not want.

Wally went to work for Griffith in a string of films pairing him with Dorothy and Lillian Gish, Mae Marsh, Blanche Sweet, and others. Griffith's dream of an epic Civil War film became a reality, and at first, the film was titled *The Clansmen*. Griffith rehearsed the film for six weeks, and he began filming on July 4, 1914, America's Independence Day, in the countryside outside Los Angeles. Henry B. Walthall was set to play the leading role of the "Little Colonel," but he turned up missing just as filming was to begin. Griffith replaced him with Wally, and nearly five hundred feet of film was shot with him in the role. Then, Walthall recovered, and Griffith went back to him as his original choice, and put Wally into the role of Jeff the Blacksmith. Griffith thought Wally embodied the spirit of a white, Southern male, full of masculine energy, and strong enough to feel the fury he needed to pit against the Negro, Gus, in a rough and realistic fight scene at White-arm Joe's gin mill.

Photography continued from July to October of 1914. Elmo Lincoln played at least three roles in the film, and in a 1948 interview with Seymour Stern, author of *Griffith: The Birth of a Nation Part 1*, he pointed out that rehearsals for the big fight scene had to be stopped and abandoned. "The fight was terribly realistic," he said. "Round tables were used; one table was smashed. The Negroes got badly banged up in the fracas. Several persons were injured and hospitalized. The fight started in rehearsal with such ferocity that Griffith stopped it and said he would take the close-ups first. After the close-ups were taken, the fight resumed for the camera. All thought of further rehearsals was abandoned."

Lincoln went on to relate that Wally was in good shape in those days and packed a punch. Reid knocked Lincoln almost senseless. Rosin bottles were used for the fight; however, the prop department made the mistake of filling the bottles with water to represent gin.

Wallace Reid (top) in the close-up that made him a star, portraying Jeff the Blacksmith in D. W. Griffith's epic, *The Birth of a Nation*. (Bottom) Wallace Reid in the famous fight scene from the same film.

As the players began swinging, the result was carnage on the set and, ultimately, a rousing, realistic, no-holds-barred fight. The finished fight scene made an incredible impact, and was one of many highlights in the final film.

The Clansmen was released on February 8, 1915, at Clune's Auditorium, Los Angeles. The title was changed to *The Birth of a Nation*, and Wally's one fight scene in the hugely successful film pushed him into unheard-of popularity and, along with many others in that picture, he became a star overnight. Worldwide fame fell at his feet. Still, he did not want to be an actor.

"Eventually, I want to direct," he confided to Maude Cheatham, at that time. "I know well enough that my popularity will not always last, and though I intend to stay in motion pictures just as long as the public wants me, I shall leave them as soon as I feel myself slipping. Lord knows, when you have eaten a big dinner, no matter how enjoyable it may have been, it is terrible for the hostess to urge you to eat more. Well, I'm not going to force my pictures when the public feels they have had enough."

In the wake of *The Birth of a Nation's* success, Jesse Lasky signed Wally to a contract with Famous Players-Lasky *as an actor*. With this agreement, his ambitions to direct and write were forcibly ended. Lasky paired him in three films with international opera star Geraldine Farrar. *Maria Rosa, Carmen,* and *Joan the Woman* were the highly successful films featuring him with the exciting, international singing sensation. With this work, he grew in stature as an actor, even though his heart was never in it.

Cecil B. DeMille, the director of these three films with Farrar, thought back in his autobiography to his first impression of Wally. "When Jesse Lasky and I had gone to see *The Birth of a Nation*, I had noticed in it a young man playing a very small part as a blacksmith. He stayed in my mind. He was handsome and clean-cut; he knew how to behave in front of a camera, making even his brief appearance memorable. His name, I made it my business to discover, was Wallace Reid. He had a few years of experience in films, but in parts so small that he welcomed the extra dollars he could make playing mood music for the big stars. I sent for him, and our conversation confirmed my belief that he was star material himself. I felt, as I have often felt since about stars and stories, that the public would like what I liked in Wally Reid; and I backed my judgment by giving him the lead in *Maria Rosa*, his first starring role."

Geraldine Farrar was new to films, and DeMille smoothed the process of adapting her talents from the stage to film by first producing *Maria Rosa*, and then filming *Carmen*, her well-known success from the opera stage. The films were released in reverse, with *Carmen*, the film made after she had experienced the full process of film work, shown first, and *Maria Rosa* released some months later. The public first saw Wally in a starring role in a feature-length film in *Carmen*. DeMille directed Geraldine Farrar and Wally in five pictures made for Lasky during 1915–1917: *Maria Rosa, Carmen, Joan the Woman, The Woman God Forgot*, and *The Devil Stone*.

During World War I, he wanted to join the military. He was young, healthy, a crack rifle shot, and a true patriot, but the studio refused to allow him to enlist. His wife and mother echoed their sentiments. They hurled every possible reason at him to persuade him from enlisting, finally making him feel guilty for even considering the idea of abandoning his work and his family. They finally argued that if and when those first recruits were exhausted, he could then consider enlistment. "Wait until then," they reasoned. Wally relented, and instead, toured with the *Blue Bungalow Band*, performing at benefits for the war effort and providing much needed funds to aid the various relief efforts. Wally remained good-natured about it despite his deep humiliation at being out of the war when so many other able-bodied men were dying. The hardest thing to swallow was when he put on make-up every morning and stood around posing for pictures, when, all the while, other men were dying. Despite the front he put on that he was comfortable with the arrangement, he felt intense guilt. "Had a great time up north," he told Maude Cheatham, in an article in *Motion Picture Magazine*, putting on a mask of happiness when inside, he was full of shame. "You know, I was appearing in a stage production, *The Rotters*, and it seemed mighty good to hear my own voice again, to receive the immediate response to my work. Believe me, it was just pure joy to hear an encore. You can't imagine how it spurs a fellow on to the highest tension. That is one of the things we miss in pictures."

Wally did as the studio told him to do, dutifully appearing in every film they offered, and staying true to his professional and family obligations.

He was not the only person in films who stayed out of the war while daily reports of the battles shattered the peaceful valley of Los Angeles like a cannon. Citizens were actually urged to be prepared for an invasion. To deflect any criticism over the fact that so many healthy men then appearing in films were oddly at home, DeMille earnestly offered the city seventy-five men with machine gun rifles and ammunition. They were recruited from several studios with the expressed purpose that they would protect their homeland as part of a Home Guard unit under his command. His brother, William, was positioned as the unit's top sergeant. These civilians were drilled, and carefully outfitted with real uniforms. When the troupe was sworn into the California militia, the colors were ceremoniously presented by Mary Pickford and proudly borne by Color Sergeant Wallace Reid. The Lasky Home Guard never saw any active duty, and was largely ceremonial, designed more for publicity than actual preparedness for any so-called invasion. The film magazines of the day were rife with photos of the men in this Home Guard unit.

Wally was kept out of the war. He worked as a face-painted actor. He provided for his family. He fulfilled his obligation to Paramount and Jesse Lasky. No one knew that inside he was crumbling with indignity and embarrassment.

Jeanie MacPherson, an actress who abandoned her thespian career to work as a writer for Jesse Lasky, delivered a splendid original story to her producers called *The Golden Chance*. Lasky thought the story was made to order for Wally. Wishing to establish a bright new star on the roster of his new company as an actor "above the title," the story called for the finest production effort his people were capable of giving. This predestined the proposed film for their finest director, Cecil B. DeMille.

DeMille took the chore of directing the film at the same time he was directing Sessue Hayakawa and Fannie Ward in *The Cheat*, accomplishing the impossible by starting one crew and cast at nine o'clock in the morning and shooting until five o'clock in the evening. After dinner at his desk, he slept until eight o'clock, and then rose to meet the fresh-as-a-daisy cast and crew of *The Golden Chance*, working the second picture crew until their quitting time at about two o'clock in the morning. After breakfast and a short nap, he resumed the routine again until both pictures were completed on schedule. He then took a well-deserved three-day vacation.

At five o'clock in morning on November 11, 1918, the official armistice was signed bringing an end to the war in Europe. It also brought an end to the fearful, deep feeling haunting Wally that he had shirked his full responsibility to the war effort. During this time, his life had taken on a fairy tale dimension: on one hand, he was working regularly and supporting his family, as a grown man should; on the other hand, he was like Peter Pan, the boy who never grew up. Wally was a very young man still in his twenties, a youth to whom life had always been kind; the proverbial boy born with a silver spoon in his mouth. Despite his wishes, it was his charm and good looks that opened every door for him and gave him a comparatively easy path to take in life. It also brought around him other people who were too quick to forgive him anything and everything, including those things that should not be forgiven. He was regarded as an idol, something larger than life, and the acclaim bewildered him when it became undeniable.

Wally was the most popular actor in America. Only Mary Pickford and Charlie Chaplin exceeded him in popularity, according to polls taken after the war. He ground out a steady output of titles released every few weeks. Paramount kept the public supplied with an endless flow of Wallace Reid pictures. He hardly had a break between each film.

While making the film *The Valley of the Giants* (1919) in Oregon, disaster struck. Wally was on a train bound for the location in the High Sierras. The train crashed, and Wally injured his sciatic nerve, gashed his head, and tore cuts into his arm. The accident left him with blinding headaches, and the pain threatened to prevent him from finishing the film. Lasky sent their company doctor to Oregon with a supply of morphine so that he could continue working without feeling the full brunt of the pain. After the picture was finished, he was rushed into another picture with no break. Doctors kept supplying Wally with morphine for the pain from the injuries long past the time the drug should have been discontinued, but no one thought his use of it would ever become a problem. In time, well after he had recovered from the accident, the repetitious use of the narcotic led to an addition. He thought he could control it, and secretly took the narcotic in small, regular doses. He never stopped working. In fact, Paramount hit a nerve with the public when they first paired him with Byron Morgan racing stories. *The Roaring Road* (1919) was a smash hit, and spawned many other pictures of its type.

Jesse Lasky commented in *I Blow My Own Horn*, "Wallace Reid was the easiest actor to cast and work with in the whole of my experience. He had a terrific vogue in automobile-racing pictures—the audiences couldn't get enough of him behind a steering wheel. We virtually turned these road-racing items out on an assembly line and every one was a money maker. But that didn't type Wally. He was believable in almost any role we gave him."

Lasky found Wally struck a responsive chord with the daredevil auto movies in which he was most popular. The films were said to have featured flashing cars and dangerous roads, and usually built to a climactic race. The studio reaped a fortune with *The Roaring Road* (1919), *Excuse My Dust* (1920), and *Double Speed* (1920). They kept him busy moving from one film to the next, often with no more than a day's break between productions. The actor appeared in *six films* in the first year of his Lasky contract, and the following year he was seen in *ten*. Lasky determined to get the full value of his popular star during the seven-year period of his contract. During these years, Wally continued his secret use of morphine. He still believed his use of the narcotic was justified, and did not realize he was caught in the grip of an addiction.

Cecil B. DeMille cast Wally as Anatol DeWitt Spencer, a Park Avenue dandy, in *The Affairs of Anatol*, a new film pairing him with Gloria Swanson. Wally portrayed a husband who became tired of his wife because she kisses him too much. He complained to a friend that his honeymoon had "too much honey in it."

"I could not complain of the New York office's generosity in making talent available to me," said DeMille, "and one of the bit players was the lady who deserves more credit than I do for inventing sex appeal—Elinor Glyn, the priestess and prophetess of 'It,' whom Jesse Lasky had brought from England to write a screenplay which he hoped would outdo her sensational novel, *Three Weeks*. Madame Glyn, as she liked to be called, happened to be at the studio and condescended to join Lady Parker, the wife of Sir Gilbert Parker, at a bridge table in a scene for *The Affairs of Anatol*."

"Nothing is so deadly to a husband as a surfeit of sentiment," DeMille went on to explain. "Sooner or later, in every man's life there comes an ending to the honeymoon. Not that he loves his wife less, but he has passed the springtime of his love and he is anxious to be accomplishing things—he wants to progress for his wife's sake as well as his own, and kisses at breakfast, luncheon and dinner begin to thoroughly sicken him—just as too much candy is apt to do."

In the bittersweet film, Gloria Swanson, playing the amorous wife, fails to realize this until her husband, quite by accident, is thrust into a close association with four girls. The tempting affairs first include one with Wanda Hawley, then another with a simple country girl from his youth, now a gold digger singing in a cabaret. The third kiss involves Agnes Ayres, a girl he meets in the country attempting to drown herself, and the fourth pairs him with Bebe Daniels in the role of the wickedest woman in town. Anatol discovers the wrong of his ways, and settles down to love his wife forever.

The original working title was *Five Kisses*. To an interviewer from *Motion Picture Magazine*, director DeMille explained, "It takes five kisses to make a man. The most enchanting kiss is with the eyes open—eyes in whose depths the man imagines he sees all sorts of mystery."

The Affairs of Anatol, as the film was later titled, was said to be merely suggested on a play by Austrian writer Arthur Schnitzler, and was made at the height of Wally's popularity. Unknown to most people, the actor was constantly on morphine during the film production.

Gloria Swanson recalled beginning the film thinking it would like a thrilling reunion with a large cast of actors with whom she was familiar. She was comforted by the arrangement, having just endured the difficult birth of her daughter, Gloria. "It turned out instead to be torture," she acknowledged. "First of all, shooting began before I really felt up to it. I was worried that my figure wasn't quite back to normal, but more than that, I had been torn rather badly during the final stages of labor." She was pestered daily by the publicity department to bring little Gloria to the studio for exploitation photos. She refused, and word spread that she had become cross and irritable since her confinement. In spite of her condition, Gloria was a professional and entered work on the film in a spirit of enthusiasm. Her dedication was worth the effort.

The picture was one of the smash hits of 1921. The production was first-class, even to the hand tinting of the prints in a variety of handsome colors, including scarlet, gold, and blue.

The *New York Times* heralded the film when it premiered in New York at two theaters simultaneously, an unusual marketing ploy used for the time. "Here is Mr. DeMille at his best," the newspaper review said. "Whether you will like it is another matter. If you like a glorified movie that you can take as a movie and are not asked to take as a genuinely human photoplay, you will probably be among the large number who will find enjoyment in Anatol and his innocent escapades. Mr. DeMille, it appears, must be ornate and artificial, theatrical at all times, and his style is not suited, therefore, to stories of real people and serious import—but the case of the present offering is different. Here is an extravagant story that never by any chance could be taken seriously, ornamented by elaborate and expensive sets, and such an assemblage of screen favorites as has never before been brought together in one picture for the worship of idolatrous fans. And, incidentally, a number of the screen's best pantomimists are among them. So it's a magnificent puppet show, legitimately and logically excessive in every way. For once Mr. DeMille's theatricalities are in harmony with his subject. He is free, for example, to indulge his love of trick furniture and bizarre costumes to his heart's content without giving offense. They're all part of the show."

The review went on to point out, "Wallace Reid, as Anatol, farces some of his scenes delightfully."

This was Wally's final picture with DeMille. According to Lasky, Wally began to show a change in his appearance at this time. He wrote in his autobiography, "He wasn't believable as a heavyweight fighter in *The World's Champion*, taken from a Broadway play.

Wallace Reid discussing the production of *The Affairs of Anatol* (1921), with director Cecil B. DeMille.

He was rapidly losing weight and couldn't stand on his feet for more than a short time. He made a valiant struggle to get through his scenes, but it was obvious that something was wrong."

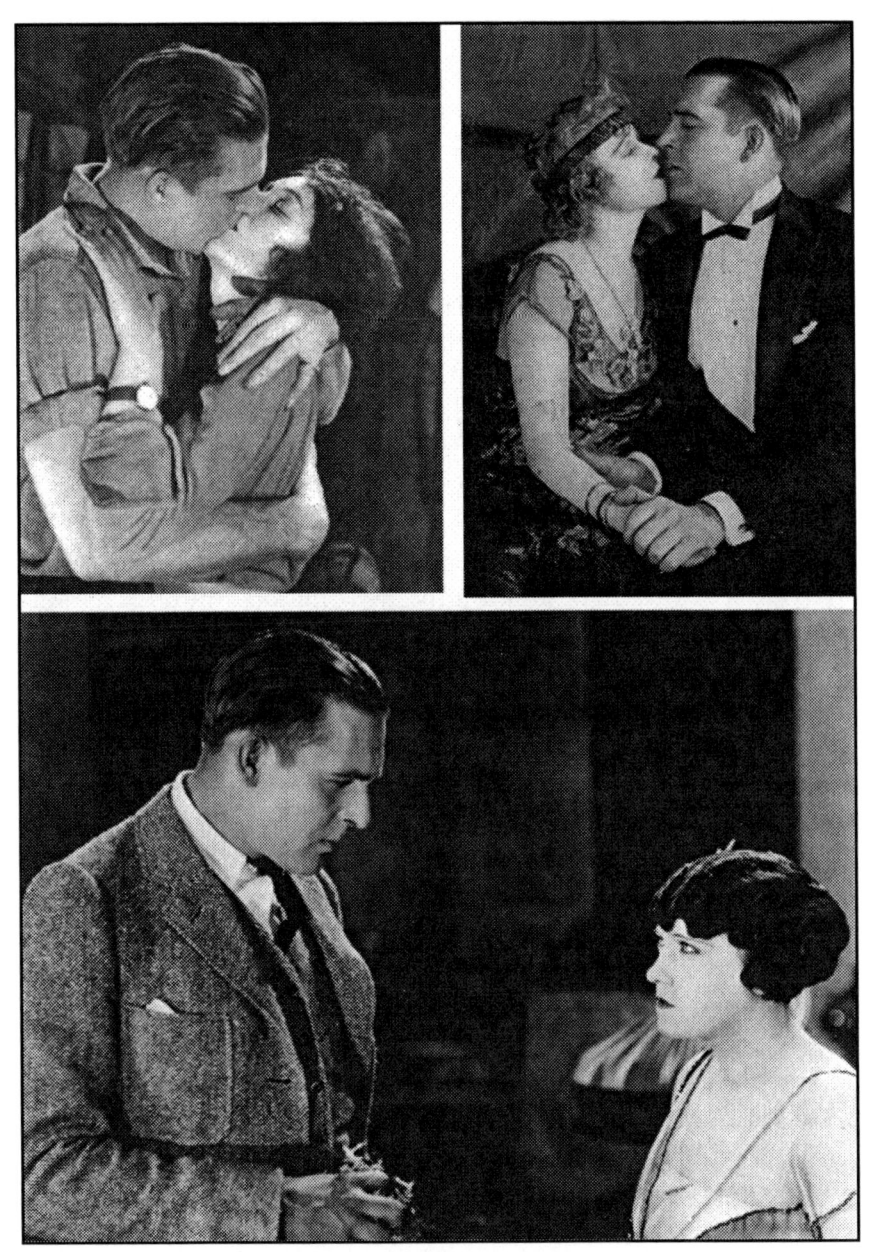

Three scenes from *The Affairs of Anatol* (1921), starring Wallace Reid with Agnes Ayres (top left), Wanda Hawley (top right), and Gloria Swanson (bottom).

As Wally's career was reaching a creative climax, there were ominous rumblings of wrongdoing erupting in the press. On November 25, 1920, the show business newspaper, *Variety*, reported a mysterious incident concerning the arrest of a strange man:

> "Had Dope for Sale"
> *Los Angeles:* Thomas H. Tyner, alias Claude Walton, alias Bennie Walton, was taken into custody here on a local lot with seven bundles of heroin on his person, according to the arresting officer. He was arraigned before U.S. Commissioner Long and held for $1,000 bail for a preliminary examination. It is said Tyner declared he was delivering the dope to one of the best-known male picture stars on the coast and that it had been the second time he was engaged to deliver to the same star, whose wife, in the hope of having him break the habit, informed the authorities."

Rumors were brought to Lasky that Wally was taking dope. Lasky heard of people murmuring these innuendos throughout the whole country. He found himself sitting on a public relations powder keg.

On December 8, 1921, Saul Rogers and Lewis J. Selznick visited Will H. Hays, an Indiana lawyer who had been the Republican national chairman, then Postmaster General. They represented ten of the leading motion picture producers and two additional companies. They presented a letter asking him to become head of an association they felt it urgent to form. They told Hays of a series of unsavory incidents in Hollywood which had given the responsible-minded producers as much concern in their capacity as good citizens as in their professional status as picture-makers. Not the least of these incidents was the Roscoe "Fatty" Arbuckle trial on rape charges.

The Hays Office, as the association soon became known, was to assist producers in the self-regulation of themes and stories used by the film industry. Although Arbuckle had been acquitted of the criminal charge against him, Adolph Zukor, President of Paramount, had recently decided to shelve their unreleased Arbuckle comedies rather than release them and add impetus to the public outrage over the Arbuckle scandal. Zukor sacrificed hundreds of thousands of dollars invested in the completed but unreleased films. Jesse Lasky wanted to avoid a similar crisis with Wallace Reid.

Lasky called Hays long-distance and told him he would have to do something about the situation. The two men formulated a plan. Then, Lasky sent for Wally. As fond as he was of him, the producer found it very difficult to tell him he knew of the rumor swirling into a whirlwind of gossip. As head of production, Lasky was responsible for his actions.

According to Lasky, Wally looked him squarely in the eye and said, "It isn't true! And don't you believe it!"

Lasky replied, "I want to believe you, Wally, but the only way the rumors can be stopped is by absolute proof that they're false. Would you mind if I got a doctor to examine you?"

"Why should I? Go as far as you like," the actor challenged.

Lasky gave him the benefit of the doubt, but the actor's loss of weight and unnatural fatigue during the shooting of his current film were symptoms that were known to accompany an attempt to break a narcotic habit. Lasky arranged for the studio's manager, Charles Eyton, to bring a physician from the Southern Pacific railroad in for the examination. The doctor was apprised of the suspicions prompting the examination and charged with the duty of living with Wally for a time to observe his habits.

In her book, *Swanson on Swanson*, Gloria Swanson remembered the studio's difficulties with Wally while working on *The Affairs of Anatol*. "Wallace Reid, the male star, was a cause of constant anxiety to me. I heard endless rumors that he was an addict, and although I never saw him take drugs, his behavior never seemed quite right during *Anatol*. He was forever offering me rides, and once he sent his valet to my dressing room to ask for a photograph of me. I always found ways to refuse him politely, but he gave me the jitters."

Lasky told Wally of the plan to end the rumors, and informed him if his behavior led no further evidence, the studio would have the ammunition needed to squelch the rising whispers of drug addiction. Wally agreed to the constant observation by the doctor. Two weeks passed during which the actor appeared to be the perfect image of a man with nothing to hide. The doctor reported back to Lasky.

"To the best of my knowledge, Mr. Lasky, Wally Reid is not using narcotics," he said. The doctor had eaten meals with the star, accompanied him to the golf course, and even went to the extreme of searching his belongings while Wally co-operated. "I don't know anyone else I could live with like Siamese twins for two weeks without wanting to murder, but he is unquestionably the nicest chap I've ever known," was the doctor's final conclusion. Wally had been given a clean bill of health.

Lasky, relieved to learn his profitable star was free from narcotics, notified both Will Hays and Adolph Zukor.

While making his last film for the studio, *Thirty Days* (1922), Wally was barely able to stand, let alone act. Lasky, Hays, and Zukor were shocked a few weeks later when Wally voluntarily admitted himself to the Banksia Place Sanitarium determined to kick the drug habit he had been carrying in secret.

Lasky and Hays visited him in the sanitarium. Barely over thirty years old, the young man with the magnetic personality that charmed the whole country had tried to salvage his reputation on his own. While charming the railroad doctor during the two weeks of close scrutiny, he had taken himself to the torturous extreme of attempting to kick his habit by the sheer force of his own will power. He was too late.

Cecil B. DeMille remembered many years later the brave determination in Wally's voice just before he entered the sanitarium. "I'll either come out cured," the heroic man said, "or I won't come out."

He was under treatment for more than a month, attended by Dr. G. S. Herbert. As the weeks passed, his normal weight of 185 pounds had reduced to 135 pounds. "I'm winning the fight, Mama," was his invariable greeting when his wife visited him.

Doctors told him the only way to live would be to take small doses of morphine. Once addicted, it was impossible to break the morphine habit. He chose to quit and die rather than face a life enslaved to the drug. He died at the sanitarium in the arms of his wife on January 18, 1923, a few months before turning thirty-one.

According Richard Koszarski, in his book *An Evening's Entertainment, Film Daily Yearbook of Motion Pictures*, in 1923, shortly after Wally's death, the Russell Sage Foundation, the National Board of Review of Motion Pictures, and Associated First National Exhibitors surveyed 37,000 high-school students in seventy-six cities across the country. When asked who they considered their favorite actors, Wallace Reid came in second on both lists compiled by boys and girls, unique in his ability to appeal strongly to both sexes.

After his death, Dorothy Davenport Reid rallied to campaign around the country aiding social reform groups to fight the growing problem of drug use in America. She produced a film called *Human Wreckage*, released in 1923, starring Bessie Love. The story attempted to pull the veil of silence from the problem of drug addition. The film revealed in graphic detail the horrors of drug addiction and served to stimulate public reforms. She often accompanied the film to deliver lectures to the film audience.

Human Wreckage was criticized by the *New York Times* in a 1923 review: "To deliver a lecture through a motion picture against the traffic in drugs, Mrs. Wallace Reid appears in this film that might appeal to an audience of those who need narcotics, but to the average person who has a night off and goes to the theater for entertainment, it is not pleasing. A valiant attempt has been made to render this production effective, and James Kirkwood's performance in certain sequences is unusually good. The story, however, wanders along until it becomes tiresome, and the dramatic climax is spoiled."

Variety noted in its review: "The best impression left by the film is that of a ghost-like hyena stalking through every scene where drugs come in to wreak their worst. This was frequent. A title said the hyena is the ugliest of animals, inferring the drug habit is the ugliest of the diseases."

Moving Picture World, August 11, 1923, said, "Crowds that flocked to the theater on the opening date were so large that it was necessary to build an extra box office on the sidewalk, for which a special permit had been granted by city authorities."

Dorothy Davenport Reid appeared as an actress in at least ninety-four motion pictures, beginning with *A Mohawks Way* (1910) and ending with *The Road to Ruin* (1934). She contributed as a writer to seventeen films, produced two others, and directed *Linda* (1929), *Sucker Money* (1933), *Woman Condemned* (1934), and *The Road to Ruin* (1934).

Wally earned the affection of the millions of people who adored watching him in the movies. He gave them his best, even though he did not want to be an actor. His personal descent into the secret agony of morphine addiction was accidental and born from the insistence of the film producers, who initially plied him with the drugs to keep film production moving at the required pace. The public understood the tragedy of his decline, and wept all the more because of the unfortunate circumstances. After his death, they still thought he was the most magnetic, charming, personable, and handsome young man in the movies.

Silent Filmography of
Wallace Reid

The Phoenix (1910)
The Leading Lady (1911)
The Reporter (1911)
War (1911)
The Pathfinder (1911)
Leather Stocking Tales (1911)
A Red Cross Martyr; or, On the Firing Lines of Tripoli (1912)
Chumps (1912)
Jean Intervenes (1912)
Indian Romeo and Juliet (1912)
The Telephone Girl (1912)
The Seventh Son (1912)
The Illumination (1912)
At Scrogginses' Corner (1912)
Brothers (1912)
The Victoria Cross (1912)
The Hieroglyphic (1912)
Diamond Cut Diamond (1912)
Curfew Shall Not Ring Tonight (1912)
His Mother's Son (1912)
The Gamblers (1912)
A Man's Duty (1912)
At Cripple Creek (1912)
Making Good (1912)
The Secret Service Man (1912)
An Unseen Enemy (1912)
Indian Raiders (1912)
His Only Son (1912)
Every Inch a Man (1912)
Early Days in the West (1912)
Hunted Down (1912)
The Cowboy Guardians (1912)
The Tribal Law (1912)
An Indian Outcast (1912)

All for a Girl (1912)
The Seepore Rebellion (1912)
Kaintuck (1912)
Hidden Treasure (1912)
Before the White Man Came (1912)
All for a Girl (1912)
The Fires of Fate (1913)
The Wall of Money (1913)
The Mystery of Yellow Aster Mine (1913)
The Animal (1913)
Man's Duty (1913)
The Picket Guard (1913)
The Powder Flash of Death (1913)
In Love and War (1913)
Their Masterpiece (1913)
Pirate gold (1913)
When the Light Fades (1913)
Near to Earth (1913)
When Jim Returned (1913)
The Kiss (1913)
The Deerslayer (1913)
The Spirit of the Flag (1913)
Woman and War (1913)
Mental Suicide (1913)
The Harvest of Flame (1913)
The Cracksman's Reformation (1913)
A Cracksman Santa Claus (1913)
Dead Man's Shoes (1913)
A Rose of Old Mexico (1913)
The Harvest of Flame (1913)
The Spark of Manhood (1913)
The Gratitude of Wanda (1913)
The Heart of a Cracksman (1913)
Cross Purposes (1913)
Retribution (1913)
The Lightning Bolt (1913)
Youth and Jealousy (1913)
When Luck Changes (1913)

The Ways of Fate (1913)
Via Cabaret (1913)
The Tattooed Arm (1913)
Price of Lonesome (1913)
Modern Snare (1913)
Love and the Law (1913)
A Hopi Legend (1913)
Her Innocent Marriage (1913)
Hearts and Horses (1913)
A Foreign Spy (1913)
Dead Man's Shoes (1913)
The Picture of Dorian Gray (1913)
The Menace (1913)
The Intruder (1914)
The Countess Betty's Mine (1914)
The Wheel of Life (1914)
Fires of Conscience (1914)
The Greater Devotion (1914)
A Flash in the Dark (1914)
Breed o' the Mountains (1914)
The Mountaineer (1914)
Regeneration (1914)
The Voice of the Viola (1914)
Heart of the Hills (1914)
The Way of a Woman (1914)
Who So Diggeth a Pit (1914)
The Spider and Her Web (1914)
Women and Roses (1914)
Cupid Incognito (1914)
A Gypsy Romance (1914)
The Test (1914)
The Skeleton (1914)
The Fruit of Evil (1914)
The Daughter of a Crook (1914)
The Quack (1914)
The Siren (1914)
The Man Within (1914)
Passing of the Beast (1914)

Love's Western Flight (1914)
A Wife on a Wager (1914)
'Cross the Mexican Line (1914)
The Den of Thieves (1914)
The Avenging Conscience; Thou Shalt Not Kill (1914)
For Her Father's Sins (1914)
The Odalisque (1914)
Over the Ledge (1914)
At Dawn (1914)
The Exposure (1914)
Sierra Jim's Reformation (1914)
The Second Mrs. Roebuck (1914)
The Niggard (1914)
A Mother's Influence (1914)
Moonshine Molly (1914)
The Little Country Mouse (1914)
Her Awakening (1914)
For Those Unborn (1914)
Down the road to Creditville (1914)
Down by the Sounding Sea (1914)
The City Beautiful (1914)
Baby's Ride (1914)
Arms and the Gringo (1914)
Another Chance (1914)
Home Sweet Home (1914)
The Birth of a Nation (1915)
The Lost House (1915)
Enoch Arden (1915)
A Yankee from the West (1915)
The Chorus Lady (1915)
Carmen (1915)
Old Heidelberg (1915)
The Golden Chance (1915)
The Three Brothers (1915)
Station Content (1915)
Sheriff for an Hour (1915)
The Craven (1915)

To Have and to Hold (1916)
The Love Mask (1916)
Maria Rosa (1915)
The Selfish Woman (1916)
The House with the Golden Windows (1916)
Intolerance (1916)
The Yellow Pawn (1916)
The Wrong Heart (1916)
Joan the Woman (1917)
The Golden Fetter (1917)
Buried Alive (1917)
The Prison Without Walls (1917)
The Penalty of Silence (1917)
The World Apart (1917)
The Brand of Death (1917)
Big Timber (1917)
The Squaw Man's Son (1917)
The Hostage (1917)
The Woman God Forgot (1917)
Nan of Music Mountain (1917)
The Devil-Stone (1917)
Rimrock Jones (1917)
The Things We Love (1918)
The House of Silence (1918)
Believe Me, Xantipee (1918)
The Firefly of France (1918)
Less Than Kin (1918)
The Source (1918)
The Man from Funeral Range (1918)
Too Many Millions (1918)
The Dub (1919)
Alias Mike Moran (1919)
The Roaring Road (1919)
You're Fired (1919)
The Love Burglar (1919)
The Valley of the Giants (1919)
The Lottery Man (1919)
Hawthorne of the U.S.A. (1919)

Double Speed (1920)
Excuse My Dust (1920)
The Dancin' Fool (1920)
Sick Abed (1920)
What's Your Hurry? (1920)
Always Audacious (1920)
The Charm School (1921)
The Love Special (1921)
Too Much Speed (1921)
The Hell Diggers (1921)
The Affairs of Anatol (1921)
Forever (1921)
Don't Tell Everything (1921)
Rent Free (1922)
The World's Champion (1922)
Across the Continent (1922)
The Dictator (1922)
Nice People (1922)
The Ghost Breaker (1922)
Clarence (1922)
Thirty Days (1922)
Night Life in Hollywood (1922)
Hollywood (1923)

Chapter 13
Rudolph Valentino

Rudolph Valentino has become an icon of the silent cinema through his roles in the films *The Sheik* and *Son of the Sheik*. To those unfamiliar with silent films, images of him as a hot-blooded, burnoose-shrouded man of the desert have come to symbolize the romanticism and mystique they believe is typical of silent films. For some aficionados, a posthumous passion for his photographs and films continues its ongoing growth more than eighty years after his death. Even though critics have scorned many of his films, his cult of admirers keeps his legend alive. The public, not movie press agents, made him a star unequaled by anyone except Mary Pickford and Charlie Chaplin.

There was a young man behind the makeup, a human being largely forgotten by the trappings of his film roles. The man behind the myth is a sad story, for he led a life of loneliness and struggle. He was born Rodolfo Alfonzo Raffaelo Pierre Filibert Guglielmi di Valentina d'Antonguolla on May 6, 1895, in Castellaneta, Italy, a small village just north of Taranto. He was the third of four children: the eldest, a sister named Beatrice who died at the age of eight, an older brother, Alberto, and a younger sister, Maria.

His father was Giovanni Guglielmi, and his mother was Beatrice Barbin. After his father died of malaria, the Guglielmi children helped their mother with her struggle to provide the bare necessities of life. They were extremely poor and owned no property. The miserable hopelessness of their lives was contrasted by the constant news of work and good wages gained by immigrants who had gone to America. Rodolfo heard these tales, and to the young Italian, America was where he wanted to live.

In 1908, at the age of thirteen, Rodolfo attended a military school, and he completed the course within two years. His mother urged him to apply for admission to a naval academy, but he failed the physical examination. He turned his passion toward his ache to reach America, and resolved to make the ocean voyage despite a lack of funds.

Rodolfo begged his mother to help him find some way of making the journey across the sea. Finally, borrowed money barely made possible his passage in steerage class for the trip. After buying the cheapest ticket, he converted the remaining money to American currency, and found it equaled exactly one dollar. With the bill safely pinned to the inside of his shabby coat, and the prayers of his widowed mother at his side, the eighteen-year-old set out for America on December 13, 1913.

Rodolfo came down the gangplank to American soil alone, landing among the teeming immigrants of New York City. Knowing little English, he first found work in the dead of winter as a dishwasher and waiter. He paid one dollar a week for nightly refuge in a bare, cold room in a boarding house. Like many immigrants of the early 20th century, he found the American dream enticing and difficult to realize.

His initial good luck came with a job as a gardener's helper on the Long Island estate of Cornelius Bliss. There, he observed the easy, confident manners of the rich, and imitated the way they lit their cigarettes, handled tennis rackets, and rode horses.

He developed the habit of attending the dance halls and cabarets of Manhattan where he first learned to dance the popular steps of that day: the Castle Walk, American and Continental tangos, and waltzes. He made extra money dancing for hire to women without partners.

A job dancing at the popular nightspot, Maxims, brought him to the attention of a professional dancer, Bonnie Glass, then a headliner in the swanky nightclubs of America's largest cities. After losing Clifton Webb as her partner, she offered Rodolfo the job. He toured with her, using the name "Signor Rodolfo," in appearances at the Winter Garden, the Palace, supper clubs, and vaudeville.

During the first four years after he left Castilleneta, the

In the short span of seven years, the young man who sailed from Italy with one dollar pinned inside his coat became a Hollywood star, and changed his name from Rodolfo to Rudolph Valentino.

William Morris Agency booked him for $150 a week at the New York Roof on Broadway and 55th Street. Then, he was paired with another professional dancer, Joan Sawyer. They made appearances in New York, Washington, and Philadelphia. Ambitious, determined, and hard working, his heart was set on an unlimited future, but he did not know that he had only eight more years to live.

He found work in the chorus of two musicals, *The Merry Monarch*, and *The Masked Model*. When the shows closed, he traveled to San Francisco, and briefly worked as a dance instructor. A chance acquaintance with the film actor, Norman Kerry, brought encouragement and advice for breaking into films. Rodolfo joined the cast of *The Passing Show*, a play starring Al Jolson, and arrived with the tour in Hollywood in 1917.

Many people admired the handsome, foreign-looking young man, but it was Hayden Talbott, who was working for film director Emmett J. Flynn, who offered him $50 a week and a chance to break into pictures. The lure he extended was a small part in the role of a contemporary thug.

"The picture was called *The Married Virgin*, and I played the stellar role—a heavy, which is somewhat of a novelty," Rodolfo remembered, in an article in *Movie Weekly*. "I thought that when it was released, perhaps someone would see possibilities in me. There were difficulties, and the picture was tied up. It was not released until three years later! Thus did luck take another backhanded slap at me. But I managed to exist."

Rodolfo continued to work as a dancer, and while he was on the east coast, he went to The Vitagraph Company located in the wilds of Flatbush. Vitagraph was the gateway for many fledglings in the motion picture industry, including Norma Talmadge, Florence Lawrence, Florence Turner, Agnes Ayres, Carlyle Blackwell, John Bunny, Francis X. Bushman, Dolores and Helene Costello, Maurice Costello, Sidney Drew, Dustin Farnum, Oliver Hardy, Hedda Hopper, and Hoot Gibson. Rodolfo sought out the pioneer film company, not as an actor, but as a tradesman.

Albert Smith, the President of Vitagraph, remembered in his memoirs, *Two Reels and a Crank*, that the young man had been recommended by a friend as a possibility for their set decorating department. On the day of his first visit, the slim, dark youth visited Smith to apply for work, and claimed to have had some experience in the decorating field.

"But no experience with motion pictures?" inquired Smith.

"No, sir," replied the youth.

"Then, how are we to know whether you can do the work here?" Smith asked.

"I'm sure I can do it," Rodolfo answered with grim resolve.

"You're young, and decorating is highly specialized work. Will you permit me to test your knowledge? Take a look around the room and tell me what you think of it."

Smith watched, as the young man's gaze swept around the office. Then, Rodolfo began to recite the changes he would make in the framed artwork, the dark drapes, in fact, everything in the room. He commented that the room was in very bad taste with shocking conflicts in the periods of furniture. "Many decorators choose the works of artists who lived in the period reflected by the furnishings," Rodolfo told Smith.

Smith felt satisfied that he would be a good addition to the decorating department at Vitagraph, and sent Rodolfo to work. Within a week, he was thrust by their directors *in front of the camera* as a foreign-looking extra. He caught the eye of Rex Hitchcock, a beginner in the scenario department with ambitions to direct. Some years later, Rex Hitchcock would change his name to Rex Ingram.

Rodolfo made his acting debut at Vitagraph in *My Official Wife*, a Russian story made with the advisory assistance of Leo Trotsky, then several years away from his involvement in the future of his homeland.

Samuel Goldwyn frequented the social rooms at the Hotel Alexandria where he often met other workers from the film community. In his book, *Behind the Screen*, he remembered frequently seeing Rodolfo stand around the hotel lobby. "He was very dark and slim," Goldwyn recollected, "and his eyes had the somberness of the Latin. I was especially struck by the grace of his walk and of his gestures. Even when he leaned up against a cigar-case he did it with a certain stateliness, and you felt that the column of some ruined temple overlooking the Mediterranean would have been much more appropriate than his present background. Quite evidently he was looking for a job. In fact, before I was introduced to him, I heard him approaching various people in the industry."

"Anything doing today?" Goldwyn heard him ask one man. "Have you finished casting so-and-so? When do you start shooting?"

These questions were the type that was all too familiar in the hotel lobby at the Alexandria, and made more touching in Rodolfo's case by his naïve manner and foreign accent. Rodolfo asked the questions with a look of eagerness, and could scarcely hide his disappointment when the answers were discouraging.

In 1918, he appeared in a supporting role in the film *A Society Sensation*, starring Carmel Myers. The light, improbable comedy was about a sea captain who has a hallucination that he is of noble blood, and brings up his daughter, Sydney, like a duchess. Sydney visits her family friend who introduces her to society as a duchess, and then she becomes the rage of the town. Rodolfo plays Dick Bradley, the son of a rich and climbing mother, and falls in love with Sydney, to his mother's delight. But exposure comes, and Sydney goes back to her fishing village. Dick follows her, and they end up marrying just before the final fade out. A review in *Variety* said, "Rudolpho De Valentina, a very American Dick, despite the fact he is a fairly recent arrival from Italy. The scenes, taken on or near the water, are all cheerful and pretty. The support and direction contribute to the good result."

1919 was a busy year for Rodolfo. In *The Delicious Little Devil*, he starred with Mae Murray, and billed himself as Rudolph De Valintine. A small part with his friend, Norman Kerry, in *A Rogue's Romance* (1919) did little for him, and a tiny part again with Kerry in *Virtuous Sinners* (1919) brought a paycheck, but little notice from the press.

Dorothy Gish, the enormously popular star of a long series of comedies produced by D. W. Griffith, noticed him. Her sister, Lillian, recalled in her autobiography, "Dorothy had an instinct for picking potential stars. She discovered another young man, slender and dark-haired, and had him cast as a gigolo in one of her pictures, *Out of Luck* (1919). In one scene, the gigolo was supposed to be making love in a café to a rich woman. Mr. Griffith came over to watch rehearsals and was pleased with the young man's performance. As he often did, he suggested a bit of 'business' for the scene. The gigolo is sitting beside the woman, who is wearing pearls. As she turns her head to watch the dancers, he picks up her strand of pearls, singles one out, and tests it with his teeth to see if it is real. It was a perfect touch for the character and has since been copied many times with equal success."

When Griffith saw the finished film, he was so impressed with Rodolfo that he hired him to dance in an on-stage prologue preceding the premier screening of his new film, *The Greatest Question* (1919). The dance paired him with Carol Dempster, and was such a hit that Griffith extended it for three weeks. At this time, he called himself Rudolpho Di Valantina, a slight variation of his real name, one he thought had a more romantic and pleasing sound.

He succeeded in obtaining other roles in two Universal pictures and two at Paramount. Griffith tested him for the lead in his film, *Scarlet Days*, but ultimately favored his protégé, Richard Barthelmess. Although Dorothy Gish thought her discovery would make a better Latin than Richard Barthelmess, Griffith told her,

"I agree with you, Dorothy. But women are apt to find him too foreign-looking." Clearly, Griffith miscalculated.

Lillian Gish remembered her friend and co-star in many films, Bobby Harron, brought Rodolfo into their group of intimate friends because he was a newcomer to films and shy. She, her sister Dorothy, and Bobby rode horses with him. They found his two great loves were horses and dancing. In addition, he designed riding clothes for both Lillian and Dorothy, and was a good cook.

Rodolfo married a young actress, Jean Acker, who sought a movie career of her own. The marriage was never consummated, and was later rendered invalid by a civil district judge.

A prominent part in *Eyes of Youth* with Clara Kimball Young followed. "I was selected for villains because of my dark complexion and somewhat foreign aspect, I presume," Rodolfo lamented, in an interview in *Italian-American Digest.* Young's position as a contender for first honors as a screen star had been on the wane by 1919. In this film, she displayed hitherto unsuspected histrionic talent. The story restored her to top honors. She earned rave reviews for a role requiring her to present three ages in the life of one woman. Rodolfo made a brief appearance as a slimy underworld rat, called in the film, "a professional correspondent."

Once to Every Woman (1920), supporting Dorothy Phillips, offered another role as an Italian heavy.

Rex Hitchcock, at that time known as Rex Ingram, finally achieved his ambition to be a director. He remembered the dark-eyed Rodolfo he had known from Vitagraph, and thought of him for the lead in his film, *The Four Horsemen of the Apocalypse.* At that same time, Rodolfo met and strongly impressed screenwriter June Mathis. She also thought Rodolfo would be ideal for the lead role, and brought him to Ingram.

Ingram recalled this convergence of opinions about the Latin youth's ability in *Behind the Screen.* "I was attracted at once by Valentino's face and by his remarkable grace of movement, and I made immediately a mental note of him . . . of course, it was obvious that he was the exact type for the young tango-dancer hero of the story. Even after I started work with him, though, I had no idea how far he'd go—not at the very first."

Ingram remembered preparing for a tango dance sequence. "But when we came to rehearsing the tango, 'Rudy' did so well that I made up my mind to expand this phase of the story. I did this by means of a sequence in a Universal picture I had made several years before. The sequence showed an adventurous youth going into a Bowery dive and taking the dancer after he had first floored her partner. Bones and marrow, I transposed this action to South America—yet only a few of my wise Universal friends recognized it. This bit of acting not in the book gave Rodolfo a chance for one of his showiest pieces of work. I rehearsed it very carefully for three days right on the set, and I think the result showed it."

Rudolph Valentino, ca. 1922.

Rudolph Valentino in the title role of *The Sheik* (1921).

Alla Nazimova, the famous Russian actress, had ventured into silent films and met with great success. She hired Rodolfo to play Armand Duval opposite her role as Marguerite Gautier in a modern adaptation of Alexander Dumas' classic, *Camille*. Shooting began in January 1921.

His breakthrough success eventually came with the release of Rex Ingram's *The Four Horsemen of the Apocalypse*. For this role, he finally changed his stage name to Rudolph Valentino. Producer Samuel Goldwyn thought back in his autobiography to a conversation he had with Griffith at the time of this enormous success. Goldwyn asked Griffith for his opinion of Rudolph.

"I declare I don't know," replied Griffith. "All the time I was looking at him in *The Four Horsemen* I kept asking myself, 'Is this fellow really acting or is he so perfectly the type that he doesn't need to act?'"

Jesse Lasky had a secretary, Jeanne Cohen, who was fascinated with a new novel titled *The Sheik*. She told her boss the manuscript "left her quivering." She insisted Lasky read the story, but the busy producer had little time. He trusted his secretary's instinct fully, and bought the rights to the book for $12,500 based on her opinion. When he finally did read a synopsis of the story, Lasky found that he was unable to envision any of the current actors at his studio to be suitable for the role of the Arabian lover. "Wallace Reid was too much the good-natured, big-brother type," Lasky pondered, "Rod La Rocque was too suave and sophisticated, Thomas Meighan was too wholesome and casual, and Jack Holt, a two-fisted cowboy, was unthinkable." Then, he attended the opening of *The Four Horsemen of the Apocalypse*. Lasky was overwhelmed by all of the elements in the picture, especially the unknown Italian actor discovered by June Mathis, giving one of the best silent-screen performances he had ever seen. Rudolph played the Argentine, tango-dancing gaucho with the grace and movement of a panther. Lasky envied Metro, which he presumed had Valentino under contract, and wished the actor had been his own find.

A few weeks later, Rudolph visited Jesse Lasky's office. The producer learned that the Metro studio had never secured any option on the actor's services. Rudolph was then one of the industry's greatest "overnight stars." Incredible as it seemed, neither Rex Ingram nor the Metro studio had signed the young Italian actor to a binding contract. Lasky seized the opportunity, and Rudolph left his office with a five-year contract.

Within a short time, the story of *The Sheik* came back to Lasky's attention, and the producer realized he owned the perfect story for

Rudolph, one that seemed tailor-made for him. He also owned the bullfighting saga, *Blood and Sand*, a story rife with a main character that exhibited smoldering passion and wore picturesque costumes. Several more stories were lined up to make magnificent use of the sensual appearance Rudolph radiated.

Lasky's partner, Adolph Zukor, shepherded Rudolph through the films *The Sheik, Blood and Sand, Monsieur Beaucaire,* and *The Sainted Devil.* He fully expected the power at Paramount would see to their success, but the producer was unprepared for the resulting phenomenon. "We certainly did not expect him to convulse the nation," Lasky recalled in his autobiography. "Valentino was as strange a man as I ever met . . . Valentino rarely smiled on the screen or off, and I cannot recall ever having seen him laugh. It is true that he could be charming when he wished. On the other hand, he could be extremely temperamental."

Lasky also remembered, "Valentino is a legend as the most perfect lover the screen has ever known, but he was not the most popular star on the lot, even during his comparatively short reign. Diffident and reserved, he was always on his dignity and not inclined to mix with studio personnel."

The Valentino mystique permeated into the roots of American society. The sideburns and plastered-down hair he wore in *Blood and Sand* were emulated by millions of young men all over America, while women organized worshipful cults. He created an atmosphere of *otherworldliness*, which affected youths who were then resurging from the horrors of the recent world war. "And with reason," Zukor recalled, "for there was much of *it* about him. The actor was convinced that a supernatural power watched over him."

George Ullman, Rudolph's companion and manager, recalled that it was not generally known that he was a mystic and a "spiritist" who believed in the guidance of a spirit, a long-dead Indian guiding him under the name of "Black Feather."

In an interview with Harry T. Brundidge, Ullman said, "I discovered that 'Black Feather,' the spirit of an Indian, was Rudy's 'guide' and that 'Jenny,' who was supposed to be the spirit of the mother of June Mathis, noted scenario writer and close friend of Rudy and Natacha, was his adviser. Rudy and Natacha would do absolutely nothing of importance without first consulting 'Black

Feather' and 'Jenny.' This was done by going to the home of a Hollywood medium, or mystic—not a paid professional, by the way—who would go into a trance with a pencil gripped in her hand. Then, the messages would begin to come. Questions were asked and answered and advice given. I have seen as many as sixty pages of typewritten paper filled at one sitting—and the woman who did the writing never looked at the paper. I will say, in all frankness, that many of the things predicted by this supposed psychic force actually came to pass, and most of the advice was good."

A lobby card showing Rudolph Valentino and Gloria Swanson in *Beyond the Rocks* (1922).

Rudolph had sheer animal magnetism greater than any other actor, and the first films he made for Zukor and Lasky elevated him to a pinnacle of public adoration before he even knew the basics of screen acting. It mattered little, because women did not attend his films to see him act—they came to swoon.

Lasky and Zukor wanted to build him up in earthy plots, the type used so successfully to enhance the glamour of Gloria Swanson. In fact, the idea of pairing Swanson and Valentino seemed ideal to the producers.

Gloria Swanson, the great star of the later classic *Sunset Boulevard*, entered films as an "extra" and quickly found success. Young women identified with her portrayals of ordinary girls rising through poverty to achieve the "American dream." They were among the studio's most valuable stars, and it seemed like a good idea to pair them in a film. They chose to use a lurid Elinor Glyn novel, *Beyond the Rocks*.

Author Elinor Glyn visiting Rudolph Valentino on the set of *Beyond the Rocks* (1922).

Gloria Swanson recalled in her autobiography, *Swanson on Swanson*, "I had met Rudolph Valentino right after the studio had made me a star. The second time I sent to the stable to get my new horse, he was there. He smiled and called me Mrs. Somborn, and I recognized him as the good-looking Italian in *Eyes of Youth*, the Clara Kimball Young picture. After that, we frequently rode together in the Hollywood hills on Sunday mornings, not as a regular thing, but more often than not. Each of us knew the other would be there if one of us felt like having company."

Rudolph Valentino and Gloria Swanson in a scene from the flashback sequence from *Beyond the Rocks* (1922).

She also remembered: "Everyone wanted *Beyond the Rocks* to be every luscious thing Hollywood could serve up in a single picture: the sultry glamour of Gloria Swanson, the steamy Latin magic of Rudolph Valentino, a rapturous love story by Elinor Glyn, and the tango as it was meant to be danced, by the master himself. In the story, I played a poor but aristocratic English girl who is married off to an elderly millionaire, only to meet the love of her life on her honeymoon."

Rudolph Valentino and Gloria Swanson in a publicity photo from *Beyond the Rocks* (1922).

In the story, Rudolph played a handsome English lord who saves the girl from falling down a mountain in the Alps. In Paris, they meet again and realize their love, but consider the honorable thing to do is part forever. Unable to forget her, Rudolph pursues her on a trip across the English Channel until her husband learns about their passionate love affair. Inexplicably but conveniently, he goes on a trip to Arabia, and then he inexplicably but conveniently dies during a bandit attack. Rudolph takes advantage of this opportunity and smolders intense passion as Gloria parades around in a fantastic beaded gown. The euphoria of their passion causes the lovers to mysteriously drift into a mutual vision of an earlier era, giving each of them the opportunity to wear lavish period costumes. Once done, they mysteriously drift back to the present to overwhelm audiences with their embraces. The whole concoction smacked of sensationalism, but audiences loved it. Elinor Glyn personally adapted her story into the screenplay.

Glyn wrote moderately successful romance novels before scoring a sensation with *Three Weeks*. In 1907, the ribald romance was considered scandalous. Like *Lady Chatterley's Lover*, critics vilified it while the book became a worldwide smash hit, in spite of having been initially banned in the United States and Great Britain. After Hollywood later made a softened film version of the sensational *Three Weeks*, Glyn found that she was elevated on a pedestal in the film community, and milked the uncertain position for all it was worth. She concocted the frou-frou story of *Beyond the Rocks* especially for Valentino and Swanson.

A form of censorship was gripping Hollywood during 1922, the result of a string of scandals that ruined more than one career. President Harding's Postmaster General, Will H. Hays, was drafted by the studios to head up the Hays Office, assuring the American public that decency would be managed with rigid standards. Their dictums influenced how *Beyond the Rocks* was filmed. "One of the first stipulations of the office was that kisses should run no longer than ten feet of film," Gloria recalled in her autobiography. "So we shot each kiss twice, once for the version to be released in America, and once for the European version. Poor Rudy could hardly get his nostrils flaring before the American version was over. Only Europeans and South Americans could see Swanson and Valentino engage in any honest-to-goodness torrid kisses. American fevers were now controlled by a stopwatch."

Rudolph insisted on taking extra pains in the creation of the foreign language film versions of his motion pictures. Not only were the love scenes played more heatedly than in the American version, but he also made a point of speaking any dialogue that was shown in a close-up in the language of the country for which the negative was being produced. For example, in the Spanish-language version, he spoke his lines in close-ups in the Spanish language, giving those audience members adept at lip reading the opportunity to understand what was being said. Many scenes in silent films were often given subtitles that mimicked the actor's words. In the case of *Beyond the Rocks* and other films, these titles were heavily censored scripts, jarringly different from what was clearly visible on the moving lips of the actors. Rudolph wisely adapted his unheard speech to fit the language lip readers would use. How this technique went over when illegal, bootlegged dupes of his films made their way from Barcelona to Bangkok has not been recorded.

The film's title came from a scene where Gloria tipped over in a rowboat "beyond the rocks" and the English lord Rudolph plays has to rescue her and return her unconscious and dripping wet to the shore. *Beyond the Rocks* is not one of the finest films in which either star appeared, but it was a skillfully made, commercial product that was extremely popular in its time. For many years, the film was considered lost, but in 2004, one surviving print resurfaced to please an entirely new generation.

The *New York Times* said of the film: "Gloria Swanson can wear clothes. So can Rudolph Valentino. And the talents of each are given full play in the Elinor Glyn story, *Beyond the Rocks*, as it has been screened and brought to the Rivoli this week. Also, there is something humanly appealing in the self-sacrifice of an unhealthy and physically unattractive man well passed middle age, who realizes that his young wife is in love with a romantic youth, and eliminates himself so that she may be happy. But if this situation is reached through a series of incredible incidents, and if the leading characters do little else but wear clothes, and if, also, much of the action takes place on apparently artificial mountains and before what seems to be painted back drops, can the result be called an interesting photoplay? Not by those who want a little character and a little truth in their entertainment, anyhow."

The reviewer went on to report, "If you sit through the photoplay, however, you will be rewarded, for after it comes the latest Buster Keaton comedy, *The Paleface*. It is not as funny as *The Boat*, but it is funny enough. It restored to life one reviewer who had been reduced to a state of somniferous weariness by *Sherlock Holmes* and *Beyond the Rocks*."

After the release of this film, Rudolph began work on *The Young Rajah* in April 1922, and when released, the film did not receive critical acclaim. His fans filled theaters to see him in spite of the weaknesses of the vehicle. The studio renegotiated his contract, upping him to $7,000 a week.

He discussed the generous offer with his second wife, Winifred Hudnut. Winifred had exotic aspirations and a talent for design. To more closely fit her self-conceived, exotic image, she had changed her name to Natacha Rambova. She took charge of his career, and told him to balk at the Lasky offer. Unfortunately, he took her advice. He also felt, at Natacha's urging, that the roles he was being given were not befitting a star of his stature. Natacha's nerves begat a show of Rudolf's nerves, and the result nearly cost him his career.

One day, while Natacha had him on edge, Zukor was privileged to see an exhibition of Rudolph's temper. The producer was visiting a set one morning and found the star arguing with an assistant director. His face was pale with fury, and his whole body shook. It was obvious to Zukor that the star was nearly in a state of hysteria. He made no idle threats. Fully fed up with the drivel the studio was forcing him to film, Rudolph left the studio and refused to return. The producers were forced to secure a legal injunction on September 14, 1922, to prevent him from appearing on the screen for any other film producer.

Headlines in the *New York Times* proclaimed on October 1, 1922, "Famous Players Win Valentino Injunction." Rudolph contended that he sought other employment because Famous Players broke the contract first by refusing to give him proper treatment when he was making *Blood and Sand*, and also charged that he was humiliated when his employers ordered his wife off his set and sent her packing to New York only two days after their marriage. He further cited that they compelled her to ride in an ordinary berth, where she was subject to annoyances from pesky, prying reporters, instead of giving her a private compartment in keeping with her self-induced renown. Famous Players insisted they had kept their agreement fully. The injunction remained in effect. It appeared that Rudolph's film career had skidded to a standstill.

Rudolph Valentino in a scene from the film *The Young Rajah* (1922).

Rudolph countered by going on a lucrative personal appearance dancing tour, and earned all the money he needed without the film business. He even devised a non-theatrical film appearance by appearing in a documentary film, *Rudolph Valentino and His 88 American Beauties*, an appearance that got him back onto movie screens and circumvented the injunction barring him from acting in films. Selznick Pictures released the film in early 1923.

He found other innovative ways to keep before the public. On December 22, 1922, Rudolph took part in an early radio broadcast, "*The Truth About Myself.*" On May 14, 1922, he recorded two songs at the Brunswick Studios in New York. *The Kashmiri Song* was recorded in English, and *El Relicario* was recorded in Spanish. Both musical renditions revealed a soft, tenor voice with a pleasant tone. He published a book of poetry on May 29, 1923. *Day Dreams* was full of mystical phrases and odd verses, and sales were tremendous.

Paramount caved in and welcomed him back on July 18, 1923, with a new contract, but insisted as part of the agreement on barring Natacha from the set of his next films. Rudolph reluctantly agreed, and work resumed on *Monsieur Beaucaire* (1924) and *A Sainted Devil* (1924) in quick succession, recapturing his magical charms as well as the studio could muster. Natacha remained sidelined as a seemingly invisible, but nonetheless constant adviser.

She prodded him to inch toward independence from Paramount, not from her artistic direction of his life and work. Rudolph again followed her well-intentioned but misguided advice.

Another film producing company, Ritz-Carlton, announced their acquisition of Rudolph Valentino for a series of films with multi-page color layouts in *Moving Picture World*. With this agreement, no injunction barring Natacha from influencing the creative process was in effect. He and Natacha set out on a European buying spree for costumes and antiques for a proposed film to be called *The Hooded Falcon*. The production never got off the ground. Alarmed at the wildly excessive expenses, Ritz-Carlton slashed the budget for the proposed film, and then put it temporarily aside. Instead, Rudolph was rushed through a low-budget melodrama, *Cobra*. He was right back in the thick of the same kind of mediocre, improbably stories that caused him to initially break with Paramount. Natacha again urged him to inch toward independence, from Ritz-Carlton, not from her artistic direction of his life and work.

United Artist offered him an enticing contract paying $520,000 a year and 42% of the profits from three pictures to be made each year. He signed that contract in 1925, not knowing he had only one year left to live. *The Eagle* (1925) was a well-made film, and presented him in a romantic adventure that pleased his fans. He was back on track with quality work and quality distribution. The inferiority of Natacha's advice seemed obvious to everyone, including Rudolph.

A divorce from Natacha was inevitable, and in 1925, when he traveled to London in November for the premier of *The Eagle*, Natacha filed for a divorce in Paris. It was granted on January 18, 1926.

According to an article in the *Zanesville Signal,* Natacha Rambova said, "I don't feel the slightest sadness when I think that we never, at any time or under any conditions, will be together again. I have only a sense of completion, for our karma is worked out, our problem is solved—whatever it was—and our time together is over. That is why we separated." Natacha Rambova was dangerously close to becoming Winifred Hudnut again. With no star to which she could attach her stylistic whims, she soon disappeared into obscurity.

Rudolph continued in the costume picture genre with a sequel to his most-renowned early film, *The Sheik*. In *The Son of the Sheik*, he played two roles, the young, burnoose-draped son and his aged, burnoose-draped father from the original film. His work in both roles was exceptional.

Irving Sindler, a property man on *The Son of the Sheik*, believed his strenuous work on this film may have cost Rudolph his life. He watched the actor change from a blithe, happy youth to a weary man, his heavily shadowed eyes showing every indication of some serious illness. Rudolph did not have the physical resistance to throw off the strain of his last location trip to the bitter wastes of the Arizona desert. Irving kept a diary during the filming of *The Son of the Sheik*. Here are several entries:

"Monday night: Oh, boy what heat. It rose right up and smacked you in the face. Twenty miles of trek by auto and horse across the desert. Nothing but heat, sand, and flies. Well, we'll get Mr. Valentino's lovely, beautiful desert scenes. This can't last forever.

Tuesday: Miss Vilma Banky put her spoon in a bowl of something that looked like blackberry jam, and when the flies flew away, it was the sugar bowl. Montagu Love is sick, but carrying on. He says it's the brackish water.

Thursday: The thermometer in Mr. Valentino's tent went to 123 degrees at 11 o'clock. We worked in the sun, toiling up the side of a big sand dune. Our assistant director intended to take a shower this afternoon, but news spread that somebody had killed a sidewinder in the shower room. At midnight it is still too hot to sleep. Sheets are like fire.

Friday: We got up at four o'clock. Had two hours' sleep. At sunrise Mr. Valentino's white helmet looked solid black. Flies all over it. They get in your eyes and mouth. Evening. A little cooler, but still over 100 degrees.

Saturday: We climb the sand dune again, sometimes on hands and knees. Mr. Valentino deserves much applause. He does his work without complaint. His horse fell in the sand twice today. It was galloping. He never complained."

After completing *The Son of the Sheik*, Rudolph took a short rest with a vacation to New York City while waiting for the premier. He traveled there by train, and soon after he arrived, he invited Adolph Zukor to lunch. Zukor remembered the conversation in his autobiography. "I only wanted to tell you that I'm sorry about the trouble I made—my strike against the studio and all that," Rudolph apologized. "I was wrong, and now I want to get it off my conscience by saying so."

Zukor shrugged and replied, "It's water over the dam. In this business, if we can't disagree, sometimes violently, and then forget about it, we'll never get anywhere. You're young. Many good years ahead of you."

Rudolph loved artistic things, and went on to speak to the

producer of his ambition to direct pictures. Zukor thought the young man was a victim of a very odd sort of fame that was thrust upon him too rapidly. He did not have the basic instincts necessary to handle phenomenal fame like Mary Pickford handled hers. They parted after the lunch.

George Ullman recalled a member of the New York Board of Education questioning Rudolph about his physical condition:

"Do you smoke?" the interviewer asked.

"Yes, from 40 to 50 cigarettes a day."

"Do you drink?"

"Yes—frequently."

"What about your eating?"

"I eat everything I please."

"What is the secret of your health?"

"I do what I want to do when I want to do it."

The next day, Rudolph fell ill, stricken with severe stomach pains. Doctors determined that he was suffering from an acute gastric ulcer and a ruptured appendix. He was rushed to New York City's Polytechnic Hospital.

For one week, he fought death as doctors attempted to arrest the peritonitis then taking a vice-like grip on his body. The effect on the public was equally gripping. Flowers came from all over the world in such quantities that a special staff had to be organized to handle the profuse shipments of bouquets. Newspaper headlines carried daily descriptions of his condition, and as he worsened, a macabre deathwatch ensued. Speculation about his chance for recovery heated.

On waking from an operation, he asked the doctor, "Am I a 'pink powder puff?'" He was referring to a scurrilous campaign waged against him in an American newspaper in which a writer inferred that his personal habits were effeminate.

On Monday, August 23, 1926, he took a turn for the worst. Father Joseph H. Congedo, a native of Castellaneta, administered the last rites of the Roman Catholic Church. At 12:10 that night, Rudolph died.

In an article in the *Athens Messenger,* reporters revealed that in the week of his illness, Rudolph wasted until he died. His features were far from the handsome figure that was seen on the screen. Morticians worked most of the night before and on the day of

August 24, 1926, to remove from his stilled form the effects of the illness and suffering he endured.

The star's brother, Albert Gugliemi, on his way from Italy to tend to the disposition of Rudolph's body, vigorously denied mounting rumors surrounding allegations of wild partying the night before he entered the hospital. He and his attorney, Michael Romano, remained focused on taking charge of the actor's estate and collecting the $200,000 that Joseph M. Schenck, head of the United Artists Film Corporation, said was due to be paid from a life insurance policy. Schenck also said to Albert's disappointment that Rudolph had spent nearly every cent of the one million dollars he made the previous year from his contract and from his percentage of the gross receipts from his pictures.

The ensuing hysteria reached undreamed-of proportions. Rudolph's body was laid in state at Campbell's Funeral Home at Broadway and 66th Streets, and the public was allowed to view it. A crowd of 30,000 people immediately gathered. Rioting began, the worst in the city's history, as police attempted to order the lines into a controllable mass. Store windows were smashed while dozens of mounted policemen repeatedly charged into the crowds. Some women rubbed soap on the pavement to make the horses slip, causing pandemonium on top of the rioting.

On the day of the funeral, more than 100,000 people, mainly women, lined the streets around the church where the rites were held. As the funeral procession left the church, the throngs became ominously silent except for the weeping of many women.

Immediately after his death, a songwriter published sheet music about his demise entitled, *There's a New Star in Heaven*. Reissues of his films flooded the market. His earlier films in which he had played minor roles were re-edited to put in all existing, unused footage, and re-released with his name above the title, creating the false impression that he had been the star. His two previously recorded songs were reprinted and widely circulated. It did not matter to the public. They could not get enough of Rudolph Valentino memorabilia. Seeing his old films only added to the mystique haunting his near-mythic persona. The man was gone. Only the myth survived. And the myth was myrrh to the lonely, palpitating hearts watching his shadows in the darkness of movie theaters.

His body was transported by train from the east coast to the Church of the Good Shepherd in Hollywood. There, a second funeral was staged like an eerie reprise, and then the body was finally entombed at Hollywood Memorial Park in a vacant crypt hastily borrowed from June Mathis.

As late as 1934, eight years after his death, Rudolph's heirs were still collecting money from his pictures. They scraped up every last dollar they could find. In October of 1934, the administrator of his estate informed Probate Judge Walton J. Wood in Hollywood that *The Son of the Sheik* and *The Eagle* had earned $6,993.75 in royalties as part of their 43 1/2-percent due on all pictures that the former screen idol made during his lifetime. The heirs sued Art Cinema Corporation for the royalties due, and based on the submitted evidence, the court concurred.

In April 2004, Jan van den Brink from the Amsterdam Film Museum stunned the world with the news that the only existing print of *Beyond the Rocks* had been discovered basically complete and undamaged in the estate of a film collector from Harlem. About two minutes of the film were partially damaged at the edges, but the images were in good condition, and restoration work was in progress for a 2005 release.

"Because the collector was worried they would be stolen, he took the different reels and hid them in different warehouses," the historian told Dutch television.

The rediscovery of *Beyond the Rocks* was like an explosion, and Rudolph's sudden reappearance on movie screens around the world was like a phoenix rising from ashes. As he had done in the beginning, he again flashed brilliantly, and then disappeared as quickly as he had arrived.

To this day, interest in the man and the myths surrounding him continues to grow. To the uninitiated, the image and name of Rudolph Valentino is that of an icon of silent films. People know his name even if they have never seen his films. Few know about the real man behind the myth, Rodolfo Alfonzo Raffaelo Pierre Filibert Guglielmi di Valentina d'Antonguolla, the lost and nearly friendless gardener from Italy who led a lonely, sad life, made more mysterious by a tragic and untimely death.

Silent Filmography of
Rudolph Valentino

My Official Wife (1914)
The Quest of Life (1916)
The Foolish Virgin (1916)
Seventeen (1916)
Patria (1917)
Alimony (1917)
A Society Sensation (1918)
All Night (1918)
The Married Virgin (1918)
Out of Luck (1919)
The Homebreaker (1919)
A Delicious Little Devil (1919)
Virtuous Sinners (1919)
The Big Little Person (1919)
A Rogue's Romance (1919)
Nobody Home (1919)
The Eyes of Youth (1919)
An Adventuress (1920)
Passion's Playground (1920)
The Cheater (1920)
Once to Every Woman (1920)
The Wonderful Chance (1920)
Stolen Moments (1920)
The Four Horsemen of the Apocalypse (1921)
Uncharted Seas (1921)
The Conquering Power (1921)
Camille (1921)
The Sheik (1921)
Moran of the Lady Letty (1922)
Beyond the Rocks (1922)
Blood and Sand (1922)
The Young Rajah (1922)
Rudolph Valentino and His 88 American Beauties
Monsieur Beaucaire (1924)
A Sainted Devil (1924)

Cobra (1925)
The Eagle (1925)
The Son of the Sheik (1926)

Chapter 14
Crane Wilbur

Crane Wilbur was a prolific writer and director of at least sixty-seven motion pictures from the silent era into the sound era, but it was as an actor that he found lasting recognition, particularly playing opposite Pearl White in the iconoclastic serial, *The Perils of Pauline*. He brought to the first motion pictures merry eyes, a great, thick crop of wavy, black hair, and an athlete's interest in swimming and horseback riding. Twelve years of stage experience prepared him before he ventured into the then new art of silent motion pictures. He was one of the first to explore the techniques required to communicate through the wordless shadows of the movies.

He was born Irwin Wilbur on November 17, 1889, in Athens, New York. His father was a shipbuilder, who tragically died by his own hand while his son was a young man.

In an article in the October 1915 *Motion Picture Magazine*, Crane recalled, "My life hasn't been a path of roses, nor always the straight and narrow road. It has been mostly uphill, rocky climbing, with many a slip and stumble, a few falls and several scars to tell the tale."

He went on to add, "I have become what I am and have gained what I have by hard work. My preparatory school was the Academy of Experience, and I was finished in the College of Hard Knocks! I come of a theatrical family—was born at a rehearsal on a one-night stand; so, you see, I had to be an actor—I couldn't help it."

Throughout his boyhood, he had but one ambition: to be an actor on the stage. He also wanted to write plays, and his first effort in that line was at the age of twelve with a play called *Diamond Dick's Revenge*.

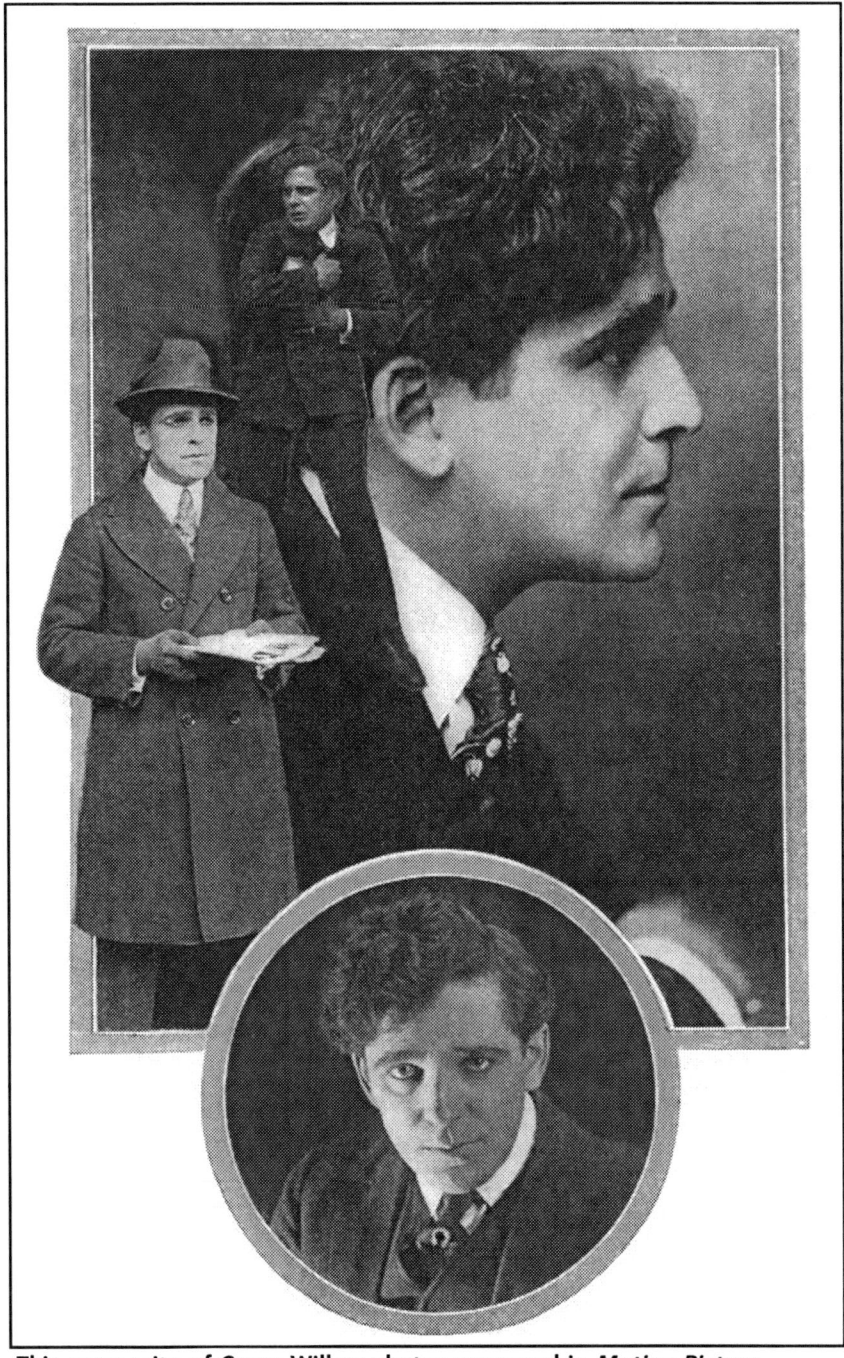

This composite of Crane Wilbur photos appeared in *Motion Picture Magazine*, October 1915.

Crane remembered, "We produced it in the hayloft of a barn belonging to the father of the villain of the play. He was a little, fat German boy, the villain, and he now runs the village barbershop at home. The play was first performed at a matinee performance in the hayloft theater, and it was a failure. Everything went well until my death scene in the third act. Just then the villain's father drove up with a load of hay, started to pitch it up into the loft, and then covered up half of our audience."

He left school at the early age of thirteen, and went to work as a butcher in a meat market. Other odd jobs followed, as a bootblack, newspaper carrier, grocer, in a knitting-mill, and as a bookkeeper for $3.50 a week.

With the help of his uncle, Tyrone Power, Sr., his big chance came at the age of sixteen, shortly after he got fired from the mill.

"My first leading part—my very first?" Crane asked an interviewer from *Motion Picture Stories*, in 1912. He smiled broadly, as he recollected, "It was with Henry Irving. I led a mule across the stage. My first speaking part was in *Robespierre*. The line was, 'Qui, qui, monsieur!' I forgot it, and I got fired. They re-engaged me, though, and after that, I went to Australia and played Little Billie in *Trilby*."

He went to New York and applied for a position with Mrs. Fiske's company, an acting troupe then presenting the play, *Mary of Magdala*, at the old Manhattan Theater. His pay was fifty cents a night.

Crane later reminisced, ". . . and that very night I went on and played a leading part—I led a mule across the stage in a market scene. For this I received fifty cents per night. In the last act, I had to rush on with the mob and run down a flight of steps supposed to be cut in solid rock. I tripped on the top step and fell all the way to the bottom. When the curtain fell, Mrs. Fiske asked me if I couldn't do that fall every performance; she said it just fitted the scene. Could I do it! Why, I would have fallen off the top of the theater if she gave the word."

He quickly became noted as an up-and-coming playwright. According to an article in the *Williamsport Gazette and Bulletin*, Crane's 1909 play, *Joe Hortiz and Fritz*, was a beautifully sentimental comedy with music. A reviewer called Crane a "brilliant young writer," and noted he had composed the songs as well as the four-act book. "It is clean, clever, and bright, and holds the interest of the audience from the rise of the curtain until its final fall on the last act," the reviewer added.

An opportunity soon came to work in motion pictures, and Crane found the roles greatly to his liking. "When I first worked before the camera, I liked it so that I wanted to make good with all my heart. I was wild to please every one—the public, my director and my employers. No effort was too tiring, no risk, no enthusiasm too great."

His first appearance in a movie was in 1910 in *The Girl from Arizona*. Years later, he remembered the experience: "When my first picture was finished I haunted the picture theaters, trying to see it, and when I finally did see it, oh, what a disappointment! It isn't always pleasant to see yourself as others see you. But it was a great lesson, that first picture. I did many things in that first one that I did not do in the second. It has always been most pleasant work to me, out in the open most of the time, playing manly, vigorous roles, living a hundred different lives before the camera."

Crane became typed as a figure fit for heroic parts in films, and he found there was a great deal of satisfaction in portraying men with noble ambitions, men known for making great sacrifices, men loving beautiful women, and men protecting women from designing villains. In the earliest days of filmmaking, directing actors was not usually more than pointing to a spot on the ground and telling the men and women what to do. The thoughts an actor should have that motivated his or her actions were rarely discussed. Crane had the ability to withdraw into a make-believe frame of mind, which gave him the chance to feel every inch of the character he was supposed to be. He took the roles seriously, and made every effort to bring realism to his performances. The public took notice, but often believed in error that he was really the character he portrayed.

"I treasure the good opinion of the hundreds of thousands who watch me nightly on the screen in thousands of theaters throughout the world," he thought back years later. "It is their opinion that counts; it is they who have made me. Often they misjudge, for they do not know; they do not realize that sometimes a poor story or bad photography will mar a player's work. But as a whole they are charitable, kind and more than appreciative, as the many hundreds of letters I receive every week go to show. One little girl in California writes me that she is blind and has never seen me on the screen, but that her sister has told her all about my pictures until she feels that she can really see me. She *does* see me—through the eyes of the heart—and I only hope I have pleased the rest as well as I have that little blind girl."

In seventeen films made between 1910 and 1913, Crane established himself as a realistic performer who brought youth, good looks, and strength to his characterizations.

Crane Wilbur and Pearl White in a tense moment from the serial, *The Perils of Pauline* (1914).

In April 1910, the American Pathé studio formed and began producing films in a remodeled cash register factory at Bound Brook, New Jersey. Paul Panzer was one of its first players. Pearl White, a performer from vaudeville who had some movie experience with the Powers Picture Play Company, joined the fledgling studio. Crane connected up with these players and became part of their stock company.

When the company planned to make a serial, *The Perils of Pauline*, in 1914, Crane wanted the lead male role that would pair him with Pearl White. He tested for and won the coveted role of Harry in the proposed serial. His riding and swimming abilities, as well as his stage background, convinced Louis Gasnier, a director for Pathé, to pick him for the leading role opposite Pearl White. Pathé broke ground for their new studio in New Jersey, and production began.

Serials had already taken a feverish hold with the public. In 1912, Edward A. McManus and Gardner Wood were trying to increase the circulation of a popular publication, *The Ladies World*. Their editorial department dreamed up a continuing feature built around a mythical heroine known as Mary. The inspired notion to tie-in with a monthly motion picture version of a published story was arranged with the Edison studios. Mary Fuller, a prominent star of films for six years, was hired to impersonate the heroine. On July 26, 1912, the first chapter, *The Escape from Bondage*, was released. Each installment was independent and complete, and though release dates were not in exact unison with the printed versions, the promotion between film and newspaper was a great success.

At that same time, the city of Chicago boasted seven newspapers, and competition was fierce. The *Chicago Tribune* recruited Colonel Selig to put the power of his Selig-Polyscope Company into production of a genuine serial story to be written for the newspaper by Harold MacGrath. Gilson Willets of the Selig staff was hired to translate the stories into silent motion pictures. The unique feature of their brainstorm was to be the simultaneous release in print and on film of a closely-knit series. They took the name of the popular actress, Kathlyn Williams, a member of the Selig stock company, for their fictional heroine. On December 29, 1913, *The Adventures* of Kathlyn burst upon the world simultaneously each week in print in the *Chicago Tribune* and on the screen by the Selig Company. The pictures enjoyed a startlingly popular, worldwide success, and resulted in a thousand new subscribers for the *Chicago Tribune*.

The *Chicago Examiner* drafted their Sunday color supplement editor, Morrill Goddard, to engage the Edison Company in a similar co-production, and on January 13, 1914, Edison released the first chapter of *Dolly of the Dailies*. Each weekly chapter was also syndicated in print in their newspapers around the country, bringing both the star, Mary Fuller, and the story plots directly to the homes of tens of thousands of readers.

The *Chicago Herald* immediately followed in April 1914 with their tie-in with the Universal Film Manufacturing Company, releasing the first installment of *Lucile Love*, starring Francis Ford and Grace Cunard. As with their competitors, the motion picture releases were syndicated in print in the newspaper at the same time.

Not to be outdone, the Eclectic Film Company announced on April 11, 1914, that Pearl White would star in the title role as Pauline in *The Perils of Pauline*, with Crane Wilbur and Paul Panzer rounding out the cast. The stories were to be presented in the Hearst newspapers, as they valiantly dug into the raging newspaper war.

Screenwriter George W. Seitz fashioned the scenarios for each weekly episode based on the newspaper stories. He chose not to provide logical cliffhanger endings to each episode of the comparatively unpolished plots, but contained each episode as a complete story within itself.

During the three years the serial appeared, Crane made $75,000, a tremendous sum for an actor in that day. He recalled the daredevil Pearl White as "a good friend . . . she feared nothing. She was absolutely calm. Her greatest passion was to drive a car and to find the cheapest gasoline. She was very, very careful about spending money. There was never any romance between Pearl and me. But, if we had a new property man, for example, she would come to me and say, 'Crane, I like him. Will you introduce him to me?' Nothing ever unpleasant, nor unnatural, nor unreal happened. But whenever she liked a boy, she would come to me. We were friends in that way."

The choice of Pearl White for the heroine of the serial was fortunate. There were more accomplished actresses around and greater beauties, but she had that indefinable, extra quality that stood her out from others. She seemed to greatly enjoy the hair-raising action in the weekly films, and conveyed this joy to audiences with a healthy, open-air, big sister fashion. She had a laughing face dotted with deep dimples, and a plucky demeanor that suggested she needed little protection and was quite capable of taking care of herself and her boyfriend. Her blonde good looks and bouncing personality matched her off-screen self perfectly. She shook hands vigorously while being lovely to look at. Crane's dark masculinity contrasted well against her blonde femininity. More than anything else, it was her energy and charisma that overcame the rough edges of *The Perils of Pauline* screenplays. She always appeared to be having fun despite the mind-boggling horrors taking place around her.

Stuntwomen were used for many of the most difficult moments in these episodes, but Pearl White did some of them herself. There were anxious moments during some of the stunts that were initially planned to be relatively safe.

In one episode, a scene in a Chinese restaurant called for the Chinese actors to break into a riot. Eager to please the director, the untrained actors turned the attack from mock violence into the real thing. The director lost control of the mob, and in the violent melee, Pearl's cape and much of her gown was ripped off. Police had to be called to restore the chaos to order. In another scene with the same, inexperienced actors, Pearl was to be used as a battering ram, carried by the Chinese men unconscious as they rushed headlong toward a wall. Giving themselves over to the moment and forgetting that they were supposed to fake the bluntness of the contact of her head with the wall, they slammed her head full force into the plaster and injured the actress. It took several hours for Pearl to recover. Later, the same actors displayed martial arts skills greater than her ability to fight. They actually beat her in a fight scene. Through it all, the cameraman cranked, the real violence was recorded, and the finished footage only added sparks to the supposedly fictional melodrama. It was no wonder that audiences around the world were aghast at the dreadfulness of the activities they saw her endure.

Crane suffered other mishaps during the series' production. While filming on a yacht off the coast of Florida, a catastrophe occurred as Pearl and Crane were acting an escape scene. The producers failed to check the water before dashing their actors into the raging waves. Pearl and Crane found themselves floundering in the middle of a swarming pack of sharks, which lunged toward the actors intending to attack. They fought the beasts off, and were pulled from the water into a small boat just moments before the predators could reach them with their open jaws. Crane remembered with horror feeling the touch of the shark's rubbery skin against his flesh, as they tore his costume while he scrambled into the small boat.

The Perils of Pauline was filmed in and around New York City with some scenes taken in Florida. The series consisted of twenty unrelated episodes. Each film in the series was bound to the others only by the basic plot structure of the series.

The story follows Pauline, played by Pearl White, a vivacious and trusting girl with a profound love of adventure. She stands to gain an inheritance, a treasure coveted by the fund's administrator, Koerner, played by Paul Panzer. Koerner pretends to be her friend while secretly planning to kill her so he can gain the money for himself. To keep up the guise of friendship, he arranges various horrible threats by way of a parade of gypsies, cutthroats, and gangsters. Through it all, Pauline remains innocent of any suspicion surrounding Koerner. Crane Wilbur plays Harry Marvin, her boyfriend. He appears totally without any means to convince her beyond a doubt that Koerner is responsible for her repeated misfortunes. Pauline is kidnapped by gypsies, and in another episode, captured by Indians and forced to race down a hill while boulders roll after her. Koerner plots to sink her in a doomed submarine, sends her skyward in a runaway balloon, and in another attempt on her life, plans her doom in a sabotaged airplane. All attempts on her life are ultimately thwarted, and Koerner is frustrated to the point of exasperation. Harry shows up at the last minute to save her throughout each horrid ordeal.

All acts of treachery are solved in the final episode when Pauline barely survives a sinking boat and a bombardment by missiles. She sends her dog swimming to shore with a note for help. Koerner drowns in a fight with a sea captain, and Pauline ends the series by renouncing her adventurous ways, planning to settle down and marry Harry Marvin.

There was a variance in the quality of each weekly episode. In a review in the *Moving Picture World,* a critic closely examined the sixth episode of the series. "We cannot truthfully say that this Pauline series is holding up very well. It started off finely, but is poor this week. This number carries the action on without getting it, in any true sense, along any. Rough incidents, in which the players are or seem to be in great peril, are not real action; they are film users and need to be a bit better done than in this two-reel offering to be thrilling. The photography is poor."

A few weeks later, the *New York Dramatic Mirror* reviewed the twelfth episode: "Near the opening of this picture, several ingeniously arranged dissolves show a peril that Pauline avoided in the previous installment. While she reads a newspaper account of the escape of lions at the wedding, which fate and Harry prevented her attending, the scene changed into the actual enactment of the startling events described in the paper. Of course, dissolves of this nature are not original with the Pathé director, but those used here seem particularly appropriate and well contrived."

The review went on to say, "The twelfth chapter of Pauline lacks the thrills of some of its predecessors, although there is a fair amount of melodrama introducing the usual characters, supplemented by a band of gypsies. Owen engages the leader of the band to kidnap Pauline and hold her prisoner in a sequestered camp. The plan works smoothly up to the point where the jealousy of a gypsy woman in love with the leader is aroused. As usual, Harry is scouring the country in search of his sweetheart. He meets the jealous woman, is advised of the whereabouts of Pauline, and downs her captor in a rough fight."

After the success of *The Perils of Pauline,* The Lubin Company of Philadelphia nabbed Crane for six months to appear in another serial, *The Road O'Strife.* Thomas H. Ince then engaged him, but after six weeks without making a film, Crane and Ince mutually agreed that David Horsley of the Nestor Company would buy out his contract. With Nestor, Crane wrote and directed many scenarios and played leading roles in dozens of them.

David Horsley and the Mutual Company proudly promoted Crane Wilbur when they ran this announcement in *Moving Picture News,* September 25, 1915.

In late 1915, while war was on the public's mind, more outstanding reviews were earned for his attention-getting work. Crane was the author and star of a three-part feature produced by David Horsely. *The Blood of Our Brothers* was a powerful argument against war and its horrors. The story follows a young farmer, who is suddenly called to arms. Having a horror for shedding blood, he refuses, only to meet with cries of cowardice from all sides. When returning to his home, he finds the dead bodies of his wife, child, and parents, victims of the enemy's hand. From then on, the young man forgets his hate for warfare, and breathes vengeance on those responsible for the destruction of his family.

In 1916, Crane scored a personal hit with a five-reel Mutual Masterpiece film, *Vengeance Is Mine*, a thrilling story about the abolishment of capital punishment.

Vitagraph then hired him for his next assignment, *The Heart of Maryland* (1921), and on completion of the film, Crane broke from film work altogether.

For several years, he dropped out of Hollywood, and returned to the stage, his first love. He wrote a modernization of *The Bat*, an old play by Mary Roberts Rinehart and Avery Hopwood. There just was no work for him as an actor in films, so he took to the road. In 1924, Crane was touring in his own play, *The Monster*, a mystery story that made his other shocking play, *The Bat*, look like a bedtime story. He was notable for his 1926 success on Broadway in *The Bride of the Lamb* with Alice Brady, and later in 1930 in *On the Spot* with Anna May Wong.

Crane returned to Hollywood in 1929 to resume his acting, writing, and directing career with many fictional and documentary films. He had a reputation as a prolific writer, but was struggling to find work in Oakland, California. He had arrived back in Hollywood to market his stage successes and write additional dialog for film studios. The Great Depression, along with the tumultuous changes taking place within the film industry as it converted from silent pictures to sound pictures, had severely limited opportunities for him. Crane was multi-talented, and having proven himself capable as an actor, writer, and director, his many-sided ability became his greatest asset.

In 1930, Crane was busy with several projects at once. The financial woes of the Great Depression were affecting people in all walks of life. He was living off royalties still rolling in from his successful plays, including many productions of *The Monster*. Except for his iron-gray hair, he still looked like he did when he was a hero of *The Perils of Pauline*. Pearl White was by then married to a Egyptian millionaire, and Crane spent his days in his office in Culver City, jotting down sentences on a pad of yellow paper as thoughts randomly came to him for various projects-in-the-works.

He appeared as an actor in three 1934 sound films: *Name the Woman, High School Girl,* and *Tomorrow's Children,* and he directed the last two.

In 1935, he again acted in a film, *Public Opinion*, and the following year, wrote and acted in *Captain Calamity*. In 1936, he wrote, directed, and played an uncredited role in *Yellow Cargo*.

Throughout his life, Crane's imagination opened doors for new opportunities. In 1938, while on the set of the Warner Bros. film *Marked Woman*, a picture starring Bette Davis, Crane stood quietly beside the cables strung loosely across the floor, his face partially hidden behind the blazing lamps, and watched Jane Bryan in a scene with Bette. After the director called a temporary halt to the action, Bette walked into the off-stage area to converse with him. She told him the story of the film-in-progress. Immediately, Crane thought of an idea for another film. He told her about it, and planned to call it *Girls on Probation*.

"The real title, as it occurs to me, is that girls on probation are the 'marked women' of tomorrow," he told Bette. "You see, *Marked Woman* is such a startling piece that it cries for another which will show how marked women come into being. Women such as you and the other girls portray in this piece—victims of circumstances." The genesis of a new idea for his next film was conceived on the set that day. Within a short while, *Girls on Probation* was filmed by Warner Bros., and starred Jane Bryan and Ronald Reagan.

As an actor, he played his last onscreen part in the serial *Jungle Queen* (1945). His work as a writer and director continued for the next twenty years. Outstanding successes, many of which are still shown today, include the horror film, *House of Wax* (1953). In 1959, Allied Artists made a contemporary film of Crane's old play,

The Bat, starring Vincent Price and Agnes Moorehead. Crane's modernization of the play by Mary Roberts Rinehart and Avery Hopwood had been an enormous success for many years, grossing upwards of $9,000,000. (Rinehart's play was filmed previously in 1915, 1926 and 1930.) The story of eerie happenings in a creepy mansion rented for the summer by a writer of mystery novels had been perennially exciting for audiences, and kept him comfortably funded with royalties for years. Crane directed the new motion picture. Other films followed, including *Solomon and Sheba* (1959) and *Mysterious Island* (1961).

Crane suffered a stroke, and then passed away on October 18, 1973, in Toluca Lake, California.

Although much of his early film work has been sadly lost, as long as film exists, Crane will continue to be seen with his merry eyes, his great crop of wavy, black hair, and his heroically masculine personality as he valiantly rescues Pearl White in the ever-popular episodes of *The Perils of Pauline*.

Silent Filmography of
Crane Wilbur

The Girl from Arizona (1910)
Tommy Gets His Sister Married (1910)
The Hoodoo (1910)
A Summer Flirtation (1910)
Jimmy's Misfortune (1912)
Texan Twins (1912)
A Nation's Peril (1912)
On the Brink of the Chasm (1912)
Anona's Baptism (1912)
Gee! My Pants! (1912)
Pals (1912)
The Compact (1912)
The Receiving Teller (1912)
The Artist's Trick (1913)
The Infernal Pig (1913)
The Moonshiner's Last Stand (1913)
$1,000 Reward (1913)
The Perils of Pauline (1914)
The Corsair (1914)
The Road O' Strife (1915)
Vengeance is Mine! (1916)
A Law Unto Himself (1916)
The Love Liar (1916)
The Conscience of John David (1916)
The Wasted Years (1916)
The Painted Lie (1917)
The Single Code (1917)
The Eye of Envy (1917)
The Blood of His Fathers (1917)
The Finger of Justice (1918)
Breezy Jim (1919)
Devil McCare (1919)
Stripped for a Million (1919)
Unto the End (1919)
Something Different (1920)
The Heart of Maryland (1921)

Bibliography

JOHN BARRYMORE

Zukor, Adolph. *The Public is Never Wrong.* New York: G. P. Putnam's Sons, 1953.

Barrymore, Ethel. *Memories.* New York: Harper & Brothers, 1955.

"Barrymore in New Picture—Raffles." *The New York Times*, February 19, 1918.

Barrymore, John. *Confessions of an Actor.* Indianapolis: The Bobbs-Merrill Company, 1926.

Barrymore, Lionel. *We Barrymores.* New York: Appleton-Century-Crofts, Inc., 1951.

"Barrymore Strand Star—On the Quiet." *The New York Times*, April 26, 1918.

Brundidge, Harry T. *Twinkle, Twinkle, Movie Star!* New York: Garland Publishing, Inc. 1977.

Carlisle, Helen. "The Path of Glory-Is Hard Work and the Strain Attendant Upon Fame Killing our Screen Stars?" *Motion Picture Magazine*, January, 1927.

Franklin, Joe. *Classics of the Silent Screen.* New York: Cadillac Publishing Co., Inc., 1959.

Gish, Lillian. *The Movies Mr. Griffith and Me.* New Jersey: Prentice-Hall, Inc., 1969.

Griffith, Richard. *The Film Til Now.* Great Britain: Fletcher & Sons, Ltd., 1967.

Hall, Mordaunt. "The Sea Beast." *The New York Times*, January 18, 1926.

Kotsilibas-Davis, James. *The Barrymores The Royal Family in*

Hollywood. New York: Crown Publishers, Inc., 1981.
"On the Quiet." *Picture-Play Magazine.* New York: Street and Smith Corporation, September 1918.
"The Screen." *The New York Times*, February 3, 1919.
"The Sea Beast." *Variety*, January 18, 1926.

LIONEL BARRYMORE

Barrymore, Ethel. *Memories.* New York: Harper & Brothers, 1955.
Barrymore, Lionel. *We Barrymores.* New York: Appleton-Century-Crofts, Inc., 1951.
"Bennett Presents Lionel Barrymore in Jim, the Penman, English Melodrama." *Moving Picture World.* New York: Chalmers Publishing Company. December 25, 1920.
Gish, Lillian. *The Movies Mr. Griffith and Me.* New Jersey: Prentice-Hall, Inc., 1969.
Griffith, Richard. *The Film Til Now.* Great Britain: Fletcher & Sons, Ltd., 1967.
"Here's to the Under-Dog B A Talk With Lionel Barrymore." *The Pictures Magazine.* Chicago: The Pictures Magazine Corporation. February 1917.
Kotsilibas-Davis, James. *The Barrymores The Royal Family in Hollywood.* New York: Crown Publishers, Inc., 1981.
Ramsaye, Terry. *A Million and One Nights.* New York: Simon and Schuster, 1926.
Stedman, Raymond William. *The Serials.* Oklahoma: The University of Oklahoma Press, 1971.
"The Copperhead." *Variety.* February 13, 1920.
"The Drama—How Mummies are Made Men." *The New York Daily Tribune*, September 5, 1902.
"The Screen—The Copperhead." *The New York Times*, February 9, 1920.

RICHARD BARTHELMESS

Balyeat, Peggy. "Barthelmess—the Unwilling Vamp." *Pantomime*, March 18, 1922.
Barthelmess, Richard. "The True Story of My Life" in *Movie Weekly*, April 11, 1925.

Gish, Lillian. *The Movies Mr. Griffith and Me.* New Jersey: Prentice-Hall, Inc., 1969.
Fletcher, Adele Whitely. "The Idealistic Builder." *Motion Picture Magazine*, October 1922.
Griffith, Richard. *The Film Til Now.* Great Britain: Fletcher & Sons, Ltd., 1967.
Hall, Gladys. "Frenzy Says Dick." *Movie Mirror.* New York: Movie Mirror Publishing Company, February 1934.
Hall, Gladys. "I Have Said Good-bye to Youth." *Modern Screen*, January 1935.
Hall, Mordaunt. "The Screen—The Patent Leather Kid." *The New York Times*, August 16, 1927.
Hall, Mordaunt. "The Screen—Weary River." *The New York Times,* January 25, 1929.
Mook, Samuel Richard. "The Stars Hit Back." *Picture Play*, January 1930.
Ramsaye, Terry. *A Million and One Nights.* New York: Simon and Schuster, 1926.
"Richard Barthelmess, 68, Dies." *The New York Times*, Sunday, August 18, 1963.
"The Luck of Richard Barthelmess." *Pictures and Picturegoer*, April 1923.
"The Patent Leather Kid, *Variety,* August 17, 1927.
"The Screen—Scarlet Days." New York: *New York Times*, November 10, 1919.
Vantol, Jan. "A Lot of Bunk about Stardom." *Hollywood Magazine*, July 1931.

JOHN BUNNY

Agnew, Frances. *Motion Picture Acting.* New York: Reliance Newspaper Syndicate, 1913.
"A Tireless Actress—Clara Kimball Young." *Motion Picture Stories*, January 18, 1913.
Hayes, Helen. *On Reflection.* New York: M. Evans and Company, Inc., 1968.
Pratt, George C. *Spellbound in the Darkness.* New York: New York Graphic Society Ltd., 1966.
Ramsaye, Terry. *A Million and One Nights.* New York: Simon

and Schuster, 1926.
Slide, Anthony. "John Bunny." *The Silent Picture*. New York: Arno Press, 1977.
Smith, Albert E. *Two Reels and a Crank*. New York: Doubleday & Company, Inc., 1952.
Talmadge, Margaret L. *The Talmadge Sisters*. Philadelphia and London: J. B. Lippincott Company, 1924.
Talmadge, Norma. "Close-Ups." *Saturday Evening Post*, March 12, 1926.
"The John Bunny Show." *Variety*, March, 19, 1915.
Wagenknecht, Edward. *The Movies in the Age of Innocence*. New York: Ballantine Books, 1962.

FRANCIS X. BUSHMAN

"Ben-Hur." *The New York Times*. January 6, 1926.
Blum, Daniel. *A Pictorial History of the Silent Screen*. New York: G. P. Putnam's Sons, 1953.
Brownlow, Kevin. *The Parade's Gone By*. New York: Ballentine Books, Inc., 1968.
"Bushman, Film Star, Lover, Dies." *The Dallas Times Herald*, August 23, 1966.
"Fall Fatal to Francis X. Bushman." *The Dallas Morning News*, August 24, 1966.
"Francis X. Bushman, Actor, Dies at 83." *The New York Times*, August 24, 1966.
"Francis X. Bushman." *Photoplay*, August 1927.
"Francis X. Bushman to Play The Palace." *Publicity Release Solters, O'Rourke & Sabinson*, July 11, 1966.
"Forty-two Cameras Used on Scenes for Ben-Hur." *The New York Times*, November 1, 1925.
Hall, Mordaunt. "Ten Best Films of 1925 Helped by Late Influx." *The New York Times*, December 31, 1925.
Maturi, Richard J. and Mary Buckingham Maturi. *Francis X. Bushman A Biography and Filmography*. Jefferson, NC.: McFarland & Company, Inc., 1998.
Maturi, Richard J. and Mary Buckingham Maturi. *Beverly Bayne, Queen of the Movies*. Jefferson, NC.: McFarland & Company, Inc., 2001.

"Niblo Talks About Work in Filming Ben-Hur." *The New York Times*, January 3, 1926.

"On the Set with Francis X." *Newsweek*, May 8, 1961.

Ramsaye, Terry. *A Million and One Nights*. New York: Simon and Schuster, 1926.

Swanson, Gloria. *Swanson on Swanson*. New York: Random House, 1980.

LON CHANEY

Brundidge, Harry T. *Twinkle, Twinkle, Movie Star!* New York: Garland Publishing, Inc. 1977.

Franklin, Joe. *Classics of the Silent Screen*. New York: Cadillac Publishing Co., Inc., 1959.

Griffith, Richard. *The Film Til Now*. Great Britain: Fletcher & Sons, Ltd., 1967.

Hall, Mordaunt. "Ten Best Films of 1925 Helped by Late Influx." *The New York Times*, December 31, 1925.

Hall, Mordaunt. "The Screen: The Clown's Revenge—He Who Gets Slapped." *The New York Times*, November 10, 1924.

"Hell Morgan's Girl. *Variety*, March 2, 1917.

Mantle, Burns. "The Shadow Stage—The Penalty." *Photoplay Magazine*, February 1921.

"Mr. Chaney Studies Human Nature." *The New York Times*, August 23, 1927.

Miller, Virgil E. *Splinters from Hollywood Tripods*. New York: Exposition Press, Inc., 1964.

Ralson, Esther. *Some Day We'll Laugh*. New Jersey: Scarecrow Press, 1985.

Ramsaye, Terry. *A Million and One Nights*. New York: Simon and Schuster, 1926.

"Riddle Gawne." *Variety*, August 22, 1918.

Sherwood, Robert E. "The Phantom Jinx." *Photoplay Magazine*, January 1926.

"The Miracle Man. *Variety*, August 29, 1919.

"The Screen: The Hideous Bell-Ringer." *The New York Times*, September 3, 1923.

"The Screen—The Miracle Man." *The New York Times*, August 27, 1919.

"The Shadow Stage—The Road to Mandalay." *Photoplay Magazine*, September 1926.
"The Shadow Stage—The Unholy Three." *Photoplay Magazine*, July 1925.
"The Shadow Stage—The Unknown." *Photoplay Magazine*, August 1927.
"Treasure Island." *Variety*, April 16, 1920.
"What Price Film Fame?" *Picture Show*, June 11, 1927.
Wagenknecht, Edward. *Fifty Great American Silent Films*. New York: Dover Publications, Inc., 1980.
Waterbury, Ruth. "The True Life Story of Lon Chaney." *Photoplay*. New York: Photoplay Publishing Company, December 1927.

JACKIE COOGAN

Blum, Daniel. *A Pictorial History of the Silent Screen*. New York: Alfred A. Knopf, 1989.
Chaplin, Charles. *My Autobiography*. New York: Simon and Schuster, 1964.
"Circus Days." *The New York Times*, August 2, 1923.
"Circus Days." *Variety*, August 9, 1923.
Franklin, Joe and William K. Everson. *Classics of the Silent Screen*. New York: Citadel Press, 1971.
"Goodbye Kid." *Photoplay*, December 1926.
Griffith, Richard. *The Movie Stars*. New York: Doubleday and Company, Inc., 1970.
Harris, Genevieve. "Circus Days." *Chicago Evening Post*, August 9, 1923.
"Metro Gets Jackie Coogan." *The New York Times*, January 12, 1923.
Ramsaye, Terry. *A Million and One Nights*. New York: Simon and Schuster, Inc., 1926.
Reel, Rob. "Circus Days." *Chicago Evening American*, August 9, 1923.
Tinee, Mae. "Circus Days." *Chicago Daily Tribune*, August 8, 1923.
Wood, Polly. "Circus Days." *Herald and Examiner*, August 8, 1923.

Zierold, Norman J. *The Child Stars*. New York: Coward-McCann, Inc., 1965.

WILLIAM S. HART

Fennin, George N. with William K. Everson. *The Western from Silents to the Seventies*. New York: Grossman Publishers, 1973.

Franklin, Joe and William K. Everson. *Classics of the Silent Screen*. New York: Citadel Press, 1971.

Griffith, Richard. *The Film Til Now*. Great Britain: Fletcher & sons, Ltd., 1967.

Hart, William Surrey. *My Life East and West*. New York: Houghton Mifflin Company, 1929.

Pratt, George C. *Spellbound in Darkness*. New York: New York Graphic Society Ltd., 1966.

Ramsaye, Terry. *A Million and One Nights*. New York: Simon and Schuster, 1926.

Slide, Anthony. "The Stage Career of William S. Hart 1898 to 1912." *The Silent Picture*. New York: Arno Press, 1977.

"The Testing Block." *Moving Picture World*, December 18, 1920.

"The Testing Block-Review." *Moving Picture World*, December 18, 1920.

"William S. Hart, 75, Film Veteran, Dies." New York: Associated Press, June 24, 1946.

"William S. Hart Wears Famous Sombrero in Testing Block, Latest Paramount." *Moving Picture World*, December 25, 1920.

Zukor, Adolph. *The Public is Never Wrong*. New York: G. P. Putnam's Sons, 1953.

Tom Mix

Franklin, Joe and William K. Everson. *Classics of the Silent Screen*. New York: Citadel Press, 1971.

Griffith, Richard. *The Film Til Now*. Great Britain: Fletcher & sons, Ltd., 1967.

Hart, William Surrey. *My Life East and West*. New York: Houghton Mifflin Company, 1929.

Macgowan, Kenneth. *Behind the Screen*. New York: Delacorte Press, 1965.

Mix, Olive Stokes with Eric Heath. *The Fabulous Tom Mix*. New

York: Prentice-Hall, Inc., 1957.
Mix, Paul E. *The Life and Legend of Tom Mix.* New York: A. S. Barnes and Company, 1972.
Ramsaye, Terry. *A Million and One Nights.* New York: Simon and Schuster, 1926.
"Riders of the Purple Sage." *The New York Times*, April 15, 1925.
"Riders of the Purple Sage." *Variety*, April 15, 1925.
"Soft Boiled is New Mix Picture for Fox." *Moving Picture World*, July 21, 1923.

ANTONIO MORENO
"Alice, Rex & Tony." *Photoplay*, November 1925.
"Antonio Moreno." By DeWitt Bodeen in *Films in Review*, June-July, 1967.
"Antonio Moreno." *The Clearfield Progress*, August 26, 1920.
"Antonio Moreno of the Vitagraph Players." By Violet Virginia in *Motion Picture Magazine*, December 1914.
"Antonio Moreno, Silent-Film Star." *The New York Times*, February 16, 1967.
Katchmer, George A. *Eighty Silent Film Stars.* Jefferson, N.C.: McFarland & Company, Inc., 1991.
Lahue, Kalton C. *Bound and Gagged.* New York: A. S. Barnes and Company, 1968.
"Maré Nostrum." *The New York Times*, February 16, 1926.
"Maré Nostrum." *Variety*, February 17, 1926.
"Public Pleased by Vitagraph's Move to Return Antonio Moreno to Feature Films." *Moving Picture World*. New York: Chalmers Publishing Company. December 25, 1920.
"The Naulahka." *Variety*, March 22, 1918.
"The Unretouched Portraiture." *The Motion Pictures Magazine*, February 1921.
Quirk, James R. "Review of the Year." *Photoplay*, December 1920.

JACK PICKFORD
Arvidson, Linda. *When the Movies Were Young.* New York: Dover Publications, Inc., 1969.

Barry, Iris. *D. W. Griffith American Film Master*. New York: Doubleday & Company, Inc., 1965.
Brownlow, Kevin. *The Parade's Gone By*. New York: Ballentine Books, Inc., 1968.
Eyman, Scott. *Mary Pickford America's Sweetheart*. New York: Donald I. Fine, Inc., 1990.
"Fight Over Mary, Picture Show Star." *The New York Times*, October 15, 1911.
Gish, Lillian. *The Movies Mr. Griffith and Me*. New Jersey: Prentice-Hall, Inc., 1969.
Henderson, Robert M. *D. W. Griffith His Life and Work*. New York: Oxford University Press, 1972.
"His Majesty Bunker Bean. *Variety*, April 12, 1918.
"Huck and Tom." *Variety*, March 8, 1918.
Klepper, Robert K. *Silent Films 1877-1996*. North Carolina: McFarland & Company, 1999.
"Paris Authorities Investigate Death of Olive Thomas." *The New York Times*, September 11, 1920.
Talmadge, Margaret L. *The Talmadge Sisters*. Philadelphia: J. B. Lippincott Company, 1924.
"The Spirit of '17." *Variety*, January 25, 1918.
"Tom Sawyer in Movies." *The New York Times*, December 3, 1917.
"Tom Sawyer." *Variety*, December 14, 1917.
"Sandy." *Variety*, July 26, 1918.
"What Money Can't Buy." *Variety*, August 10, 1917.
Whitfield, Eileen. *Pickford The Woman Who Made Hollywood*. Kentucky: The University Press of Kentucky, 1997.

WALLACE REID
"Big Reception for Human Wreckage." *Moving Picture World*, July 1923.
"Boston Welcomes Mrs. Reid Warmly." *Moving Picture World*, August 18, 1923.
"Col. Selig's Stories of Movie Life—Wallace Reid." *Screenland*. Chicago: Screenland Publishing Company, April 1923.
DeMille, Cecil B. *The Autobiography of Cecil B. DeMille*. New Jersey: Prentice-Hall, Inc., 1959.

"Editorial in Praise of Human Wreckage." *Moving Picture World*, July 21, 1923.

Griffith, Richard. *The Film Til Now*. Great Britain: Fletcher & Sons, Ltd., 1967.

Hays, Will H. *The Memoirs of Will H. Hays*. New York: Doubleday and Company, Inc., 1955.

"Human Wreckage Has Notable Opening." *Moving Picture World*, July 21, 1923.

"Human Wreckage." *Moving Picture World*, August 11, 1923.

"Human Wreckage." *The New York Times*, August 10, 1923.

"Human Wreckage." *Variety*, August 9, 1923.

"Kisses According to Cecil B. DeMille." By Hazel Simpson Naylor in *Motion Picture Magazine*. New York: Brewster Publications, Inc., June 1921.

Koszarski, Richard. *An Evening's Entertainment: The Age of the Silent Feature Picture 1915-1928*. Berkeley: University of California Press, 1990.

Lasky, Jesse L. *I Blow My Own Horn*. New York: Doubleday & Company, Inc., 1957.

Magill, Frank N. "The Affairs of Anatol." *Magill's Survey of Cinema Volume 1*. New Jersey: Salem Press, 1982.

"Many Stars Attend Human Wreckage." *Moving Picture World*, July 1923.

Smith, Albert E. *Two Reels and a Crank*. New York: Doubleday & Company, Inc., 1952.

Stern, Seymour. Griffith: *The Birth of a Nation Part 1*. New York: Film Culture, 1965.

Swanson, Gloria. *Swanson on Swanson*. New York: Random House, 1980.

"The Screen—The Affairs of Anatol." *The New York Times*, September 12, 1921.

Uselton, Roi A. "Opera Singers on the Screen-Geraldine Farrar." *Films in Review*. New York: April 1967.

"Wallace Reid Dies in Fight on Drugs." *The New York Times*, January 19, 1923.

"Wally, the Genial." By Maude S. Cheatham in *Motion Picture Magazine*. New York: Brewster Publications, Inc., October 1920.

"What Price Film Fame?" *Picture Show*, June 11, 1927.

Rudolph Valentino

"A Delicious Little Devil." *Variety*, April 25, 1919.

"Body of Rudolph Valentino Rests Today." *The Athens Messenger*, August 24, 1926.

Brundidge, Harry T. *Twinkle, Twinkle, Movie Star!* New York: Garland Publishing, Inc. 1977.

"Eyes of Youth." *Variety*, November 7, 1919.

"Famous Players Win Valentino Injunction." *The New York Times*, October 1, 1922.

Gish, Lillian. *The Movies Mr. Griffith and Me*. New Jersey: Prentice-Hall, Inc., 1969.

Koszarski, Richard. *An Evening's Entertainment The Age of the Silent Feature Picture, 1915-1928*. California: University of California Press, 1990.

Lasky, Jesse L. *I Blow My Own Horn*. New York: Doubleday & Company, Inc., 1957.

"Metro Inaugurates Poster Contest to Exploit Ibanez' The Four Horsemen." *Moving Picture World*, December 25, 1920.

"Rudolph Valentino Films Are Still Being Shown." *The Edwardsville Intelligencer*, October 13, 1934.

Smith, Albert E. *Two Reels and a Crank*. New York: Doubleday & Company, Inc., 1952.

Swanson, Gloria. *Swanson on Swanson*. New York: Random House, 1980.

"Beyond the Rocks." *The New York Times*, May 8, 1922.

"The Amazing Love Theory of Mrs. Valentino." By Winifred Van Duzer in *The Zanesville Signal*, January 10, 1926.

"The Career of Rudolph Valentino." By Theodore Huff in *Films in Review*. New York: National Board of Review of Motion Pictures, Inc., April 1952.

"The Path of Glory-Is Hard Work and the Strain Attendant Upon Fame Killing our Screen Stars?" By Helen Carlisle in *Motion Picture*, January 1927.

"The Young Rajah." *Moving Picture World*, July 21, 1923.

"The Young Rajah." *The New York Times*, November 6, 1922.

"The Young Rajah." *Variety*, November 10, 1922.

"Valentino Earned and Spent Millions." *The Havre Daily News Promoter*, August 24, 1926.

"Valentino, the Immortal." By Evans J. Casso in *Italian-American Digest*, Fall, 1985.

"Valentino Silent Film Print Found." *Associated Press*, February 20, 2004.

"Virtuous Sinners. *Variety*, May 16, 1919.

Wagenknecht, Edward. *Fifty Great American Silent Films*. New York: Dover Publications, Inc., 1980.

"What Price Film Fame?" *Picture Show*, June 11, 1927.

Zukor, Adolph. *The Public Is Never Wrong*. New York: G. P. Putnam's Sons, 1953.

CRANE WILBUR

"Bat, The." *Great Bend Daily Tribune*, November 8, 1959.

"Behind the Scenes in Hollywood." By Dorothy Herzog in *The Sheboygan Press*, April 30, 1930.

"Blood of Our Brothers, The." *The Lancaster Daily Eagle*, November 29, 1915.

"Chats With th" Players—Mr. Crane Wilbur, of the Pathé Frères Company." *Motion Picture Story*. New York: Harry E. Wolff, Publisher, Inc., 1914.

"Crane Wilbur, Mutual Star." *The Newark Advocate*, November 18, 1916.

"Feature Films of the Week: The Perils of Pauline." *The New York Dramatic Mirror*, August 26, 1914.

Franklin, Joe. *Classics of the Silent Screen*. New York: Cadillac Publishing Company, 1959.

"Girls on Probation." *The Bismark Tribune*, November 29, 1938.

Griffith, Richard. *The Movie Stars*. New York: Doubleday and Company, Inc., 1970.

"Independent Specials." *The Moving Picture World*. June 13, 1914.

"Joe Hortiz and Fritz." *The Williamsport Gazette and Bulletin*, December 29, 1909.

Lahue, Kalton C. *Ladies in Distress*. New York: A. S. Barnes and Co., 1971.

"Monster, The." *The Chronicle Telegram*, February 19, 1924.

"Mutual Program Ad." *Moving Picture News*, September 25, 1915.

Index

45 Minutes from Broadway 122
A Boy of Revolution 224
Academy of Motion Picture Arts and Sciences 64
Acker, Jean 275
Adams, Maude 76, 200
Addams Family, The 150
Adventures of Kathlyn, The 179, 301
Affairs of Anatol, The 253, 254, 256, 257, 259; photos 257
Age of Innocence, The 98
Aguilas Frente Al Sol 210
Alden, Mary 226
Alexander, Colonel Robert 60
Allen, Winifred 55
Allied Artists 308
Allin, Grace 177
American Mutoscope and Biograph Company (*see Biograph*)
Ames, Robert 45
An American Citizen 15
Anderson, G. M. 91, 93, 158
Arbuckle, Roscoe "Fatty" 82 143, 258
Are You a Mason? 15
Art Cinema Corporation 293
Artcraft 55
Arthur, Julia 157
Ayres, Agnes, 254, 272; photo 257
Back to the Primitive 179
Bad Man, The 209
Baker, Richard Roster 94
Banky, Vilma 290
Bara, Theda 55
Barbin, Beatrice 269
Barrier, The 158

Barrymore Lionel photos 41
Barrymore, Ethel 8, 14, 15, 20, 31, 37, 46
Barrymore, John 3, 5, birth 8; childhood 10; first stage roles 10-11; newspaper cartoonist 12; San Francisco earthquake 13-14; stage star 14-15; silent films 15; in *Hamlet* 19, 24; in *The Sea Beast* 20-23; first sound film 24; death 25; 38, 43, 66, 205; photos 9, 16, 19, 21, 31
Barrymore, Lionel 7, 8, 15, birth 27; school 28; stage debut 30; first film 34; in *The Copperhead* play 39-40; divorce 44; directing films 45-46; death 46; 202; photos 31, 35, 41
Barrymore, Maurice 8, 27, photos 28, 29
Bartelemys, Alfred 50
Barthelmess, Richard birth 50; at college 51-52; first stage roles 52; first film 53-54; making *Way Down East* 57; first marriage 59; Inspiration Pictures 59; making *The Patent Leather Kid* 60-63; Academy Awards 63-64; marriage to Jessica Sargent, 67; on Broadway 69; sound films 64-65; in World War Two 69; retirement and death 70; 274; photos 51, 58, 61, 62
Barthelmess, Stewart 70
Bat, The 307, 309
Batman 111
Bayne, Beverly Pearl 52, 94, marriage 95; divorce from Francis X. Bushman 98; photo 96
Beach, Rex, 237
Beau Brummel 24
Belasco, David 44, 219
Bells, The (play) 157
Belmore, Lionel 37
Beloved Rogue, The 24

Ben-Hur (novel) 98; (silent film) 98-106; (play) 153, 158; (sound film) 112; photos 103, 104
Benson Murder Case The 209
Bernhardt, Sarah 15, 29, 200
Bernstein, Arthur L. 149
Beyond the Rocks 281, 283; making of film 284; 285, 293; photos 282
Big City, The 133
Big Diamond Robbery, The 184
Bikini Party in a Haunted House 109
Billy 50
Biograph 33, 34, 36, 201, 220-226, 246, 248, 322
Birth of a Nation, The 247, 249
Bishops Carriage, The 93
Bitzer, Billy 34
Blackbird, The 131-132
Blackwell, Carlyle 272
Blood and Sand 279
Blood of Our Brothers, The 307
Blue, Monte 98
Boat, The 285
Boomerang Bill 44
Booth, Edwin 20
Boots 56
Bosworth, Hobart 227
Bow, Clara 209
Bowers, John 99
Boy of Flanders, A 147
Brabin, Charles 100, 101
Bradley, Mary Hay 70
Brady, Alice 307
Brady, Diamond Jim 13
Brady, William 74
Brand of Cowardice The 38
Brenon, Herbert 53, 54, 55
Bride of the Lamb The 307
Brink, Jan van den 293
Broken Blossoms 56, 68
Bronco Billy (*see* Anderson, G. M.)
Browning, Tod 129, 131-133
Brundidge, Harry T. 122, 123, 279
Brunswick Studios 288
Bryan, Jane 308
Buffalo Bill Cody 175
Bugle Call, The 148
Bunny in Funnyland 84, 85
Bunny, George 73
Bunny, John 3, 5, birth 73; marriage 73; first stage work 73; personal appearances 81; first film 77; death 85; 244, 272; photo 74, 79, 83
Bunny's Dilemma 82
Burke, Billie 52
Bushman, Francis X 52, birth 91; first marriage 91; on Broadway 93; Essanay films 94; marriage to Beverly Bayne 95; scandal 95; Metro films 95; divorce from Bayne 98; making of *Ben-Hur* 99; fight with Louis B. Mayer 108; sound films 109; death 112; 272; photo 92, 96, 103, 104, 110
Bushman, Francis X. Jr., photo 110
Bushman, John Henry 91
Bushman, Mary Josephine 91
Buttons 148
Cabin in the Cotton 65
Cain, Hall 158
Cain, James M. 69
Call of the Circus, The 109
Camille 277
Capra, Frank 46
Captain Calamity 308
Captain from Castile 210
Captain Kidd, Jr. 230
Carmen 12, 249, 250
Carrington, Margaret 19, 24, 25
Carter, Mrs. Lesie 200
Cat Creeps, The 209
Chaney, Caroline 119
Chaney, Creighton 122
Chaney, George 119
Chaney, John 119
Chaney, Lon 3, 37, birth 118; youth 120; stage roles 121; first films 122; marriage and divorce from Cleva Creighton 122; first films 122; sound film 133; death 134; 144; photos 119, 125, 126, 130
Chaplin, Charlie 140, 143, 181, 252.
Chatterton, Ruth 45
Chatterton, Tom 162
Cheat, The 251
Child Wife, The 218
Christian, The 157
Circus Days 144, advertisement 145; premier 146-147
Clansmen, The 247, 249
Clark, Marguerite 55
Classical Cinematograph Corporation 99
Claw, The 44
Cobra 288

Cody, Lew 37
Cohen, George M. 55
Cohen, Jeanne 278
Collier, Constance 38, 200
Columbia Pictures 80
Confession 45
Conklin, Chester 131
Coogan, Jack 140, 143, 144, 147, death 149
Coogan, Jackie 99, 128, birth 140; film debut 140; discovered by Chaplin 143; feature films 147-148; marriage to Bette Grable 149; meeting Pope Pius XI 148; the Coogan Law 150; in *The Addams Family* 150; death 150; photos 141, 142, 145, 146, 150
Coogan, John Leslie, Jr. (*see Coogan, Jackie*)
Cooper, James Fenimore 244
Copperhead, The (play) 39, (film) 40
Cornwall, Anne 40
Cortez, Ricardo 129
Costello, Dolores 21, 22, 23, 272
Costello, Helene 272
Costello, Maurice 21, 272
Crane, Ward 131
Crawford, Joan 132
Creature from the Black Lagoon, The 210
Creighton, Cleva 122, 122
Cripple Creek Barroom 178
Crisman, Pat 180
Crisp, Donald 226
Cruse, James 227
Cummings Stock Company 216
Cunard, Grace 302
Curtis, Allen 122
Curtis, Benjamin 197, 199
D'Antonguolla, Rodolfo Alfonza Raffaelo Pierre Filibert Guglielmi (*see Rudolph Valentino*)
Daddy 144
Daniels, Bebe 254
Danziger, Daisy Canfield 205
Daring Hearts 97
Davenport, Dorothy 244, 245, 261
Davenport, Fanny 245
Davenport, Harry 245
Davis, Bette 308
Davis, Owen 232
Dawn Patrol, The 65
Day, Mabel 121
Day's Pleasure, A 143

Day Dreams 288
De Grasse, Joseph 123
De Mille, William 251
Deaf and Blind Institute of Colorado 118
Delicious Little Devil, The 274
DeMille, Cecil 219, 249, 250, 251, 253, 254, 255, 260; photo 256
Dempster, Carol 274
Desmond, William 99
Devil Stone, The 250
Devil's Garden, The 42
Devil's Garden, The 43
Diamond Dick's Revenge 296
Dick Tracy 109
Dickens, Charles 81
Dickey, Will 178, 179
Dictator, The 15
Dillon, Edward 226
Doe, Doctor 233-234
Dog of Flanders, A 147
Dolliver, Lillian 140
Dolly of the Dailies 302
Don Juan 24
Dope 226
Double Speed 253
Dr. Cupid 76
Dr. Jekyll and Mr. Hyde 18
Dracula 134
Dresser, Louise 129
Drew, Georgianna 9, 27; photos 28, 31
Drew, John 14, 27; photo 28
Drew, Mrs. John 9, 27; photos 28, 30
Drew, Sidney 27, 50, 272
Drifter, The 184
DuBarry 200
Duffy, Olive Elaine (*see Olive Thomas*)
Eagle, The 288, 293
Éclair Film Company 228
Eclectic Film Company 302
Edison Company 2, 17, 44, 92, 178, 179, 301, 302
Edison, Thomas 2, 3
Edmund Burke 219
Edward VII 38
Edwin, Walter 200
El Cuerpo Del Delito 209
El Gato 209
El Hombre Malo 209
El Relicario 288

El Senor Y La Cleopatra 210
Erlanger, Abraham 98, 99
Escape from Bondage, The 301
Essanay Film Manufacturing Company 93, 94, 95, 140, 322
Eternal City, The 44
Eternal Love 24
Eternal Sin, The 55
Excuse My Dust 253
Exploits of Elaine, The 202
Eyes of Youth 275, 282
Eyton, Bessie 181
Eyton, Charles 259
Fabian 109
Face in the Fog, A 44
Fairbanks, Douglas 205
Famous Players-Lasky Film Company 14, 15, 18, 249, 286
Fanchon the Cricket 227
Farnum, Dustin 158, 272
Farrar, Geraldine 249, 250
Fatal Wedding, The 217
Fawcett, George 91
FBO Pictures 237
Fenwick, Irene 44
Fields, Lew 74
Fires of Fate 32
First National 42, 43, 59, 61, 70, 108, 127, 144, 147, 206, 260, 322
Fiske, Minnie Maddern 298
Five Kisses (see *The Affairs of Anatol*)
Flag, The 109
Flauduene, Josephine 91
Floor Above, The 226
Flynn, Emmett J. 271
For Her Brother's Sake 224
For the Son of the House 226
Ford, Francis 302
Ford, John, 210
Forde, Victoria 180
Forrest, Allan 99
Four Horsemen of the Apocalypse, The 275, 278
Four Hours to Kill 68-69
Fox Film Company 180, 181, 210
Fox, William 180
Fra Diavolo 121
Frazer, Robert 99
Freckles 227

Fred Ott's Sneeze 2
Free and Easy 46
Friends 34
Frohman, Charles 32, 75
Frohman, Daniel 12
Frost, George 171
Frou Frou 226
Fuller, Mary 301, 302
Gang War 237
Gangsters of New York, The 226
Garbo, Greta 208
Garland, Judy 109
Gasnier, Louis 301
General Crack 24
Ghost in the Invisible Bikini, The 109
Gibbons, Cedric 104
Gibson, Hoot 272
Gilbert and Sullivan 121, 122
Gilbert, John 129
Gilbert, John 37
Gillespie, A. Arnold 104
Girl and the Ranger, The 242
Girl from Arizona, The 299
Girl of the Golden West, The 52
Girl Who Stayed at Home, The 56
Girl Who Wouldn't Work, The 44
Girls on Probation 308
Gish, Dorothy 24, 55, 56, 226, 227, 247, 274, 275
Gish, Lillian 7, 24, 33, 36, 55, 56, 57, 58, 201, 216, 226, 247, 274, 275
Gish, Mary 216
Glass, Bonnie 270
Glyn, Elinor 208, 209, 253, 254, 281, 283, 284, 285; photo 281
God's Outlaw 97
Goddard, Morrill 302
Going Some 93
Gold Is Not All 223
Golden Chance, The 251
Goldwyn Company 44, 99, 102
Goldwyn, Samuel 205, 273, 278
Gone With the Wind 46
Good Catch, A 94
Goose Woman, The 237
Gordon, Robert 229
Grable, Betty 149
Grasse, Joseph De 123
Grauman, Sid 104

Great Adventure, The 42
Great Leap, The 226
Great Train Robbery, The 2, 92, 178, 322
Greatest Question, The 274
Green, Alfred E. 236
Greenstreet, Sydney 76
Grey, Zane 183
Griffith, D. W. 7, 15, 17, 33, 34, 35, 36, 56, 57, 59, 201, 202, 220, 221, 222, 223, 225, 226, 227, 246, 247, 248, 274, 275, 278
Griffith, Linda Arvidson 220
Guglielmi, Alberto 269, 292
Guglielmi, Giovanni 269
Haines, William 132
Hamilton, Neil 209
Hamlet 18, 24
Happy Jack, a Hero 224
Harbert, Hugh 118
Hardy, Oliver 272
Harlow, Jean, 46
Harris, Caroline 50
Harron, Bobby 226, 275
Hart, Mary 169
Hart, William Surrey 3, 99, in *Ben-Hur* play 98; birth 152; 158, 123, childhood and first stage role 154-158; in vaudeville 158; first films 162; marriage and divorce 168; birth of son 168; final film appearance and voice recording 169; retirement 169-170; death 170-171; photos 153, 160, 163, 164
Hart, William Surrey, Jr. 168, 171
Hastings, Hazel Bennet 123
Hawks, Howard 69
Hawley, Wanda 254, photo 257
Hay, Mary 59, 67
Hayakawa, Sessue 251
Hayes, Helen 74, 75, 80
Hays, Will 258, 259, 258, 260, 284
He Who Gets Slapped 129
Heart of Maryland, The 307
Hearts Courageous 158
Hedda Gabler 53
Hell Morgan's Girl 123
Hello Frisco 147
Henry V 38
Henry, Patrick 170
Her Marriage Vow 98
Here Comes the Bride 18

Heston, Charlton 112
High School Girl 308
His Father's Son 244
His Friend's Wife 94
His Hour of Manhood 162
His Majesty Bunker Bean 231
Hit the Trail Holiday 56
Hitchcock, Alfred 210
Hitchcock, Rex (*see Rex Ingram*)
Hold Up, The 158
Holmes, Sherlock 285
Holt, Jack 278
Home Sweet Home 226
Hooded Falcon, The 288
Hope Chest, The 56
Hopkins, Arthur 43
Hopper, Hedda 272
Hopwood, Avery 309
Horsely, David 305, 307
Horton, Clara 228, photo 229
House of Hate, The 202, advertisement 203
House of Wax 308
Houston, Walter 20, 209
How Could You, Jean? 230
Huck and Tom 228, 231; photo 229
Huckleberry Finn 149
Hudnut, Winifred (*see Natacha Rambova*)
Huff, Louise 227, 232
Hughes, Rupert 60
Hulette, Gladys 55
Human Life, A 217
Human Wreckage 261
Hunchback of Notre Dame, The 128
Huntsville 111
Idol Dancer, The 57
If I Were King 12
IMP (see Independent Motion Picture Company)
In a Hempen Bag 220
In Convict's Stripes 219
In Old California 223
In the Latin Quarter 202
Ince, Thomas H. 161, 162, 225, 305
Incorrigible Dukane, The 15
Independent Motion Picture Company 179, 224, 225, 322
Ingraham, Beatrice 200
Ingram, Rex 207, 208, 273, 275, 277, 278
Inspiration Pictures 59

Intolerance 36, 226, 227
Invisible Hand, The 204, photo 204
Iron Test, The 202
Irving, Henry 298
It 209
Jackson, Helen Hunt 223
Jannings, Emil 64
Jean and the Calico Doll 80
Jest, The 14, 39
Jim, the Penman 42, 43
Joan the Woman 249, 250
Joe Hortiz and Fritz 298
Johanna Enlists 230
John Rance, Gentleman 202
Johnny Get Your Hair Cut 148
Johnson, Arthur 221
Johnson, Effie 222
Jolson, Al 271
Jones, Robert Edmond
Judith of Bethulia 36
Jungle Queen 308
Justice 15, 18, 24
Kashmiri Song, The 288
Keaton, Buster 285
Kennedy, Emma 118
Kennedy, Madge 55
Kenyon, Doris 70
Kerrigan, J. Warren 123
Kerry, Norman 271, 274
Kid, The (Biograph film) 220; (Chaplin film) 143, 144
Kimball, Alonzo 93
Kipling, Rudyard 202
Kirkwood, James 261
Klaw, Mark 98
Klein, George 93
Kolb and Dill 122
Konti, Isadore 93
La Rocque, Rod 278
La Tosca, 30
Lackaye, Wilton 200
Lady and the Mouse 36
Lady Chatterley's Lover 284
Lady in Ermine, The 109
Lady of Quality Street, A 157
Laemmle, Carl 122
Landis, Frederick 40
Lasky, Jesse 242, 249, 250, 251, 252, 253, 255, 259,
 260, 278, 279, 280, 286
Last Flight, The 67
Laugh, Clown, Laugh (play) 44, (film) 133
Lawrence, Norma 272
Leah, the Forsaken 11
Learning to Love 207
Leonard, Marion 201
Life's Whirlpool 37
Lincoln, Abraham 40
Lincoln, Elmo 247
Linda 261
Little Lord Fauntleroy 236
Little Minister, The 200
Little Red Schoolhouse, The 216
Little Robinson Crusoe 147
Little Shepherd of Kingdom Come, The 233
Little Tycoon, The 122
Lloyd, Frank 128
London After Midnight 132
Lone Star 46
Long Live the King 147
Look Your Best 205
Lost and Found 205
Lost Bridegroom, The 17
Love Among the Roses 223
Love Flower, The 57
Love, Bessie 261
Love, Montagu 64, 290
Love's Pilgrimage 158
Lowe, Edmund 99
Lubin Company 305
Lucile Love 302
Lugosi, Bela 134
Lyon, Ben 99
Lytell, Bert 44
M'Liss 232
Macbeth 43, 44
MacDonald, J. Wilson 242
MacGrath, Harold 301
Mackaill, Dorothy 129
MacPherson, Jeanie 251
Madame X 45
Magda 10
Maigne, Charles 41
Main Street to Broadway 46
Majestic Film Company 225, 246
Man from Mexico 15
Man in the Iron Mask, The (play) 157; photo 153

Man or Devil 44
Man Who Talked Too Much, The 69
Mansfield, Richard 121
Mare Nostrum 207-208; advertisement 208
Maria Rosa 249, 250
Marked Woman 308
Married Virgin, The 272
Marsh, Mae 226, 247
Mary of Magdala 298
Mascot Pictures 186
Masked Model, The 271
Master Mind, The 43
Master Thief, The 97
Mathis, June 99, 275, 278, 279, 293
Mayer, Louis B. 100, 101, 106, 108, 109
Maylie, Rose 127
Mayor of 44th Street, The 69
McManus, Edward A. 301
Meighan, Thomas 124-126, 278
Merry Monarch, The 271
Merry Widow, The 44
Message, The 220
Metro Company 37, 39, 95, 97, 102, 147, 278
MGM 44, 45, 98, 99, 104, 105, 106, 107, 109, 131, 148, 150, 206, 109, 322
Metro-Goldwyn-Mayer (*see MGM*)
Midsummer Masquerade 108
Midsummer Night's Dream, A 75, 76
Mikado 121
Mile-A-Minute Kindall 232
Miller Brothers' 101 Real Wild West Ranch 177
Miller, Colonel Joe 161, 177
Miller, Marilyn 236
Miracle Man, The 123, 124, 125, 126; photos 125, 126
Miracle Rider, The 186
Miracle, The 45
Mix, Amos 174
Mix, Edward 174
Mix, Elizabeth 174
Mix, Harry 174
Mix, Ruth, 184, 185, 186, 187
Mix, Thomas Hezikia (*see Tom Mix*)
Mix, Tom 3, 174; Spanish-American war 176; first marriage 177; Boer War 177; marriage Olive Stokes 177; first film 178; divorce Olive Stokes 180; marriage Victoria Forde 180; sound films 184; circus 184-185; marriage Mabel Ward 184; death 187; photos 175, 182
Moby Dick 20
Mockery 243
Modern Marriage 97-98
Modjeska, Madame 29
Moffet, Adeline 199
Mohawks Way, A 261
Mong, William V. 178
Monsieur Beaucaire 279, 288
Monster, The 307, 308
Moonshine 158
Moore, Colleen 205
Moore, Owen 221, 224, 225, 226
Moorehead, Agnes 309
Moran, Lee 122
Moreno, Ana 197
Moreno, Antonio 99, birth 197; photo 198; youth in America 199; first plays 200; in serials 202-205; marriage to Daisy Danzinger 205; first sound films 209; Spanish-language films 210; stroke 210; photos 204, 206, 207
Morgan, Charlotte 199
Morrison, Jimmy, photo 83
Moths 226
Motte, Marguerite de la 44
Mountain Rat, The 226
Mr. Wu 132
Mrs. Wiggs of the Cabbage Patch 52
Mulhall Wild West Show 177
Mulhall, Lucille 177
Mummy and the Humming Bird, The 32
Murray, Johnny 64, 65
Murray, Mae 274
Musketeers of Pig Alley, The 201
Mutual 226, 246, 306, 307
Mutual Masterpiece 307
Muybridge, Eadweard 3
My American Wife 205
My Boy 144
My Official Wife 273
Myers, Carmel 273
Mysterious Island 309
Najezda 29, 30
Name the Woman 308
Naulahka, The 202
Nazimova, Alla 53, 54, 277
Negri, Pola 206
Nestor Film Company 305, 322

New York Motion Picture Company 161
Next Corner, The 129
Niblo, Fred 101, 105, 106
Nobles, Dolly 244
Nobles, Milton 244
Noose, The 50, 64
Normand, Mabel photo 83
Notorious 210
Novak, Eve 167
Novak, Jane 168, 169
Novarro, Ramon 99, 100, 105, 106, 201; photos 103-104
O'Day, Molly photos 62, 63
Oland, Warner 202
Olcott, Chauncey 219
Old Clothes 148
Old Dutch 74, 75
Oliver Twist 127, 144
On the Quiet 16, 18
On the Spot 307
Once to Every Woman 275
One Wonderful Night sheet music 96
Only Angels Have Wings 69
Only Son, The 50
Ott, Fred 2, 3
Our Mutual Girl 201
Out of Luck 274
Outlawed 184
Owen, Catherine Dale 45
Oxon, Sir John 157
Paleface, The 285
Panthea 50
Panzer, Paul 301, 302, 204
Paramount 149, 205, 206, 209, 230, 231, 232, 251, 252, 258, 274, 279, 288
Passing Show, The 271
Patent Leather Kid, The 50, 59; making of 63
Pathé 202, 301
Pathfinder, The 244
Payne, John Howard 226
Peck's Bad Boy 144
Penalty, The 127
Pennington, Ann 55
Pennington's Choice 95
Perils of Pauline, The 202, 296, 300, 301, 302, 304, 305; photo 300
Perils of Thunder Mountain, The 203
Perrine, Kitty Jewel 177

Peter Ibbetson 14, 38, 39
Petrova, Mme. 50
Petrova, Olga 55
Phantom of the Opera, The 129
Phantom Planet, The 109
Philbin, Mary 129
Phillips, Dorothy 123
Phillips, Dorothy 94, 275
Phillips, Mary 69
Phillips, Norma 201
Phoenix, The 244
Piccolo Midgets, The 85
Pickford, Charlotte 215, 216, 217, 218, 220, 221, 222, 225, 226, 234, 236, 237; photo 224
Pickford, Gwynne 226
Pickford, Jack 3, birth 215; stage debut 216; one-night stands 218; first films 220-223; 225; scandal 233-234; marriage Olive Thomas 235-236; marriage Marilyn Miller 236; Volstead Act scandal 236-237; marriage Mary Mulhern 237; death 237; photos 219, 229, 232
Pickford, Lottie 3, 34, 215, 216, 217, 218, 220, 225, 226, 232, 233, 236; photos 219, 224
Pickford, Mary 179, 181, 201, 215- 222, 224-226, 228, 230, 232, 236, 237, 251, 252 291; photo 219, 224
Pickwick Papers, The 81, 82
Piker, The 44
Poor Rich Man 97
Poor Little Peppina 227
Pope Pius XI 148
Porter, Gene Stratton 227
Postman Always Rings Twice, The 69
Powell, Frank 220
Power, Tyrone 210
Power, Tyrone Sr. 200, 298
Powers Picture Play Company 228, 301
Pranks 220
Price, Vincent 309
Protest, The advertisement 306
Public Opinion 308
Quarter Before Two, A 225
Queen Elizabeth 15
Queen of the Moulin Rouge, The 93
Quirk, James R. 204
Quitter, The 38
Raffles, the Amateur Cracksman 18
Rag Man, The 148

INDEX

Ralson, Esther 127, 128
Rambova, Natacha 279, 286, 288, 289
Ramee, Louise de la 147
Ramona 223
Ranch Life in the Great Southwest 178
Range Rider, The 178, 179
Rankin, Doris 32, 42, 44
Rankin, McKee 10, 11, 30, 31
Reagan, Ronald 308
Redemption 18
Reid, Bertha 242
Reid, Florence 244
Reid, Hal 216, 242-244
Reid, Wallace 3, 205, 216; birth 242; in vaudeville 242; at *Motor Magazine* 244; marriage 245; birth of son 245; first films 246; in *The Birth of a Nation* 247-249; drug scandal 259; death 260; 278; photos 243, 245, 248, 256, 257
Reinhardt, Max 44
Reliance Film Company 201, 226, 246
Rex the Wonder Horse 209
Rex-Universal Studios 200
Rich Mr. Hoggenheimer, The 122
Richard III 18, 24, 43
Riddle Gawne 123
Riders of the Purple Sage 183, 184
Right to Happiness, The 200
Rinehart, Mary Roberts 147, 309
Ritz-Carlton Pictures 288, 299
Rivals, The 30
Road O' Strife, The 305
Road to Mandalay, The 131
Road to Ruin 261
Roaring Road, The 253
Roberts, Theodore 227
Robertson, Clifford 127
Robespierre 298
Robinson, Gertrude 221
Rockett, Al 61
Rogers, Saul 258
Rogers, Will 37, 177
Rogue Song, The 45
Rogue's Romance, A 274
Romance of Elaine, The 36, 202
Romano, Michael 292
Romeo and Juliet (film) 52, 95; (play) photo 153
Rooney, Mickey 109
Ross, Thomas 50

Rosson, Dick 244
Rotters, The 250
Rowland, Richard A. 61
Rudolph Valentino and His 88 American Beauties 288
Russell, Annie 75, 76
Russell, Lillian 37
Russell, Gordon 166
Ruy Blas 226
Sag Harbor 31
Said Pasha 121
Sainted Devil, A 279, 288
Sam B. Dill Circus 184
Sand, George 227
Sandy 233
Santa 210
Sapho 226
Saratoga 46
Sargent, Jessica Sargent 67
Sawyer, Joan 271
Scallen, Clara 73
Scammon, Leon P. 210
Scarlet Days 56, 274
Schenck, Joseph 147, 292
Schnitzler, Arthur 254
Schubert Brothers 53
Searchers, The 210
Seastrom, Victor 129
Seidel, Adolph 105
Seitz, George 202, 302
Selig Polyscope Company 93, 178, 179, 180, 181, 243, 301, 302
Selig, Colonel William N. 93, 180, 301
Sells-Floto Circus 184
Selznick Pictures 288
Selznick, Lewis J. 258
Semon, Larry 131
Shakespeare, William 43, 95
Shearer, Norma 129
Sheik, The 269, 278, 279, 289; photo 278
Sherlock Holmes 24
Short, Antrim photo 229
Show of Shows, The 24
Siegman, George 226
Silent Man, The 168
Silver King, The 216
Sindler, Irving 289
Sistrom, William 123
Skinner's Baby 140

Slaves of Gold 242
Smiling All the Way 97
Smith, Albert 76, 77, 81, 85, 201, 204, 205, 244, 272
Smith, Charlotte (*see* Charlotte Pickford)
Smith, Lottie (*see* Lottie Pickford)
Smith, Frederick James 204
Smith, Gladys (*see* Mary Pickford)
Smith, Jack (*see* Jack Pickford)
Smith, John 215
Santell, Alfred 61, 63
Snow White 55
So Near, Yet So Far 201
Society Sensation, A 273
Soft Boiled 181; advertisement 182
Solomon and Sheba 309
Son of the Sheik, The 269, 289, 290, 293
Sothern, E. H. 12, 200
Spanish Dancer, The 206
Spanish Main, The 210
Spencer, Anatol De Witt 253
Spirit of '77, The 230
Spoilers, The 69
Spoor, George K. 93
Squaw Man, The (play) 158, 159
Stark, Pauline 205, photo 207
Steadman, Myrtle 178
Stella Maris 230
Still Voice, The 32
Stokes, Olive 176-178, 183
Stone, Lewis, 37
Story, Edith 202
Stowe, Leslie 121
Strongheart 202
Suburban, The 158
Sucker Money 261
Sunnyside 140
Sunset Boulevard 280
Svengali 66
Swanson, Gloria 95, 205, 253, 254, 259, 280-285; photos 257, 282, 283
Swanson, Gloria, Jr. 254
Sweet, Blanche 202, 226, 247
Talbott, Hayden, 271
Talmadge, Constance 78, 202, 207, 209, 227
Talmadge, Margaret 78, 80
Talmadge, Norma 78, 79, 85, 202, 272
Tampico 210

Taps 44
Taylor, Estelle 133
Taylor, William Desmond 228, 230, 231, 232
Tearle, Conway 129
Tell it to the Marines 132
Tempest, The 23
Temptress, The 208
Tenth Woman, The 98
Terry, Alice 207
Test of Honor, The 18
Testing Block, The 163, 164, 165, 167; photos 163-164
Thaïs 200
Thalberg, Irving 101, 104, 150
There's a New Star in Heaven 292
Thirty Days 260
Thomas, Augustus 41
Thomas, Bernard Krug 234
Thomas, Olive 234, 235, 236, 237
Thompson, Fred 80
Thoroughbreds Don't Cry 109
Three Weeks 254, 284
Through the Back Door 236
Thunder 133
Tibbett, Lawrence 45
Tipton, Charlie 178
To Save Her Soul 220
Toby Tyler, or Ten Weeks with a Circus 144
Tol'able David 59, 68
Tom Mix Circus, The 184-185
Tom Mix Radio Show, The 186, 187
Tom Sawyer 149, 228, photo 229
Tomorrow's Children 308
Tourneur, Maurice 125
Tower of Lies, The 130
Trail of the Lonesome Pine (play) 159, 161
Treasure Island 125
Triangle Studios 234
Trilby 298
Trotsky, Leon 273
Trouble 144
Troublesome Secretaries photo 83
Truth About Myself, The 288
Tucker, George Loane 123
Tumbleweeds 169
Turner, Florence 272
Twain, Mark, 29
Twisted Trails 181

Two Daughters of Eve 201
Two Women 200
Ullman, George 279, 291
Unholy Three, The (silent film) 129, 131 (sound film) 133
United Artist's Film Corporation 181, 292,
Universal Film Manufacturing Company 108, 123, 128, 131, 161, 184,224, 244, 245, 246, 276, 302
Universal-Joker 122
Unknown, The 132
Upheaval, The 38
Valantina, Rudolpho Di (*see Rudolph Valentino*)
Valentino, Rudolph 3, 56, 206; birth 269; military school 270; in America 270; marriage Jean Acker 275; making *Beyond the Rocks* 283-284; on radio and records 288; divorce from Natacha Rambova 289; illness 291; death and funeral 292; photo 271, 276, 277, 280, 281, 282, 283, 287
Valez, Lupe 133
Vallee, Rudy 25
Valley of the Giants, The 252
Veiled Mystery, The 204
Vengeance is Mine 307
Venus of Venice 209
Violin Maker of Cremona, The 220
Virginian, The (play) 158, 159
Virtuous Sinners 274
Vitagraph Company 3, 22, 76-78, 80-82, 84, 85, 92, 93, 97, 201, 202, 204, 205, 207, 244, 246, 247, 272, 273, 275, 307
Voice of the Million, The 201
Voyage to the Bottom of the Sea 111
Wagon Tracks 168
Wallace, General Lew 98, 99, 108
Walsh, George 100, photo 103
Walthall, Henry B. 202, 226, 247
Wanted, a Child 220
War Brides 53, 54, 55
Ward, Fannie 251
Ward, Mabel 184
Ware, Helen 199, 200
Warner Bros. 64, 98, 206, 308
Warner, Jack 20
Warrens of Virginia, The 219
Way Down East 56, 57, 59, 64, 68, 74
Webb, Clifton 270

Webster, Henry McRae 94
West of Zanzibar 133
West, Charles 221
West, Dorothy 222
Westbrook, Bertha (see *Bertha Reid*)
Westbrook, Mary G. 210
Westover, Winifred 168, 171
What Money Can't Buy 227
Wheel of Chance 64
When a Man Loves 23
Where East Is East 133
While the City Sleeps 133
White, Pearl 36, 202, 205, 296, 301, 302, 303, 304; photo 300
Widerman Wild West Show 178
Wilbur, Crane 3, 296; first films 299; making *The Perils of Pauline* 302-304; sound films 309; death 309; photos 297, 300, 306
Wilbur, Irvin (see *Crane Wilbur*)
Wildfire 37
Willets, Gilson 301
Williams, Clara 162
Williams, Kathlyn 179, 301, 302
Wister, Owen 159
Woman Condemned 261
Woman God Forgot, The 250
Wong, Anna May 307
Wood, Gardner 301
Wood, Sam 129
Wood, Walton J. 293
Woods, A. H. 44
World's Champion, The 255
Wyler, William 105
Yellow Cargo 308
Yellow Streak, The 38
You Can't Take it With You 46
Young Rajah, The 206, 286; photo 287
Young, Clara Kimball 81, 82, 84, 275, 282; photo 79
Zanetti, Enrique de Cruzat 197, 199
Zanuck, Darryl F. 109
Ziegfeld Follies 236
Ziegfeld, Florenz 59, 234
Zukor, Adolph 14, 15, 17, 18, 168, 170, 226, 258, 260, 279, 280, 286, 290, 291

Silent Stars Speak!
New CD

Thrill to actual voices of the world's greatest stars on *Silent Movie Stars Speak*, a compilation of rare recordings of 21 of the greatest stars of the silent film era. You'll hear these fascinating, lost interviews:

- BLANCHE SWEET RECALLING WORKING ON BIOGRAPH FILMS WITH D. W. GRIFFITH
- LILLIAN GISH REMINISCING ABOUT HER FIRST FILM WITH HER SISTER, DOROTHY GISH.
- HAROLD LLOYD REMEMBERING HOW HE PROGRESSED FROM HIS EARLY BEGINNINGS.
- STAN LAUREL THINKING BACK TO BOYHOOD TOURS AND WORKING WITH OLIVER HARDY.
- BUSTER KEATON REVEALING HOW HE BECAME "THE GREAT STONEFACE" IN FILMS.
- JOHN AND LIONEL BARRYMORE TELLING HOW THEY ROSE FROM OBSCURITY TO FAME.
- BRONCO BILLY'S THRILLING RECOUNT OF MAKING *THE GREAT TRAIN ROBBERY*.

You will also witness first-hand performances given on wax cylinder records, 78 rpm records, film, or on live radio broadcasts Ramon Novarro, Mary Pickford, Jackie Coogan, Charlie Chaplin, Laurette Taylor, Sarah Bernhardt, Douglas Fairbanks, Gloria Swanson, John Gilbert, and Greta Garbo. In the finale, William S. Hart is heard in the heartrending speech he gave in a Prologue for the 1930s re-release of his film, *Tumbleweeds*.

Each recording has been digitally re-mastered to improve clarity. They vary in quality, and on some tracks there is slight surface noise that cannot be removed without damaging the recording, but on each, the voices of the great stars come through loudly and clearly.

New CD in factory shrink-wrap. $12.95 + postage
Postage $4.95 on Priority Mail inside the USA only.
$12.00 Global Priority mail outside the USA.
$10.00 Air Mail for Italy only.

BearManor Media · PO Box 71426 · Albany, GA 31708
e-mail: books@benohmart.com
Telephone: 229.436.4265 · Toll Free: 1.800.566.1251 · Fax: 814.690.1559
Or online at: www.bearmanormedia.com

Silent Movie Stars Speak

The Lost Recordings of Hollywood's Greatest Stars

ETHEL BARRYMORE	DOUGLAS FAIRBANKS	STAN LAUREL
LIONEL BARRYMORE	GRETA GARBO	HAROLD LLOYD
JOHN BARRYMORE	JOHN GILBERT	RAMON NOVARRO
SARAH BERNHARDT	LILLIAN GISH	MARY PICKFORD
BRONCO BILLY	D.W. GRIFFITH	GLORIA SWANSON
CHARLIE CHAPLIN	WILLIAM S. HART	BLANCHE SWEET
JACKIE COOGAN	BUSTER KEATON	LAURETTE TAYLOR

Track 1	2:00	RAMON NOVARRO
Track 2	0.59	BLANCHE SWEET
Track 3	6:47	HAROLD LLOYD
Track 4	5:52	MARY PICKFORD
Track 5	4:56	STAN LAUREL
Track 6	2:55	JACKIE COOGAN (WITH HIS FATHER)
Track 7	5:19	BUSTER KEATON
Track 8	2:47	CHARLIE CHAPLIN
Track 9	0:54	ETHEL BARRYMORE
Track 10	1:36	LIONEL BARRYMORE
Track 11	2:00	JOHN BARRYMORE
Track 12	3:29	LAURETTE TAYLOR
Track 13	0:58	BRONCO BILLY ANDERSON
Track 14	4:03	SARAH BERNHARDT
Track 15	2:23	D. W. GRIFFITH (WITH WALTER HOUSTON)
Track 16	2:23	LILLIAN GISH
Track 17	2:08	DOUGLAS FAIRBANKS
Track 18	3:30	GLORIA SWANSON
Track 19	4:02	JOHN GILBERT
Track 20	3:59	GRETA GARBO
Track 21	7:28	WILLIAM S. HART

Printed in the United States
142463LV00004B/11/A